Praise for "Alone Together"
on YouTube:

Chris Arnell
Less of a documentary, more like a template for living.

Don Black
Wow, what a journey! Thanks for the life thoughts!

Ray Essiambre
You are a great storyteller. I often wondered what I would do
with so many days by myself. Now I know....

Michael Drago
"I'm not sure if you could ever be alone, not when your head is
full of people, not while the conversation continues." Bravo!

Jesse Jagoda
This gives me pause to think, I too can do this!

Erwin Melzer
I am still smiling at your wonderful sense of humor.
I truly felt as if I was sailing with you.

Ibrahim
Thank you, Christian. This reminded me about my own life
and how I want to finish living it.

Philip Rawsthorne
Very thoughtful commentary. The loneliness and the excitement of
a voyage so many of us want to take but few actually do.

TVMaine
One of the best narrators I have ever heard. Well done.

Alain Pascal Routhier
I love your recounting of your journey…
for never being alone with all the people in your head!

Shaun Street
Thanks for sharing, mate. I appreciated seeing a regular guy do
something so grand. Onya!

CHRISTIAN WILLIAMS

ALONE TOGETHER

SAILING SOLO
TO HAWAI'I
AND BEYOND

East Wind Press
A division of East Wind Productions, Inc.

Copyright © 2016 by Christian Williams
Second Edition

Printed in the United States of America

ISBN-13: 978-0997253108
ISBN-10: 099725310X

Inquiries:
Olmstead Williams Communications, Inc.
10940 Wilshire Blvd., Suite 1210
Los Angeles, CA 90024
310-824-9000

alonetogether@olmsteadwilliams.com

For Jeffrey Cadwalader Williams
Combat infantryman, Vietnam, 1967-68

"Don't listen to me, I'm supposed to be accompanying you."

Thelonious Monk
Jazz pianist and composer

CHAPTER I

INVITATION

I HAVE IN MIND to sail alone to Hawai'i on a 32-foot sloop. Sounds exciting, don't you think? What a yachting adventure, chasing the flying fish down the trade winds to the island paradise of Kaua'i. From Southern California the Hawaiian Islands are 2,700 miles away, about the distance from New York to Los Angeles. It ought to take three weeks or so, maybe four weeks coming back against the wind. If you're wondering why anybody in his right mind would want to set off alone, I know what you mean. I like people as much as anybody, and have certainly never been alone for long before. There won't be anybody to share the adventure with, and having nobody to talk to sounds like the definition of loneliness. On the other hand, it's a small boat with a cabin the size of a walk-in closet, and alone means not getting on anybody's nerves or endangering anybody but yourself, which has a noble sound to it, in a sort of theoretical way. Don't you agree? Bear with me a minute here.

Most of us are never alone. By alone, I mean no cell phone, no radio, no television, no police sirens in the distance, no ships in sight, no jets overhead, no chance of a knock on the door by an attractive UPS person in shorts, in other words, none of the usual signs that confirm the existence of other people alive on the planet. More alone, when you think about it, than a prisoner in solitary confinement, who at least sees his guards for an hour a day. More alone than jilted on Valentine's Day, when no matter how abandoned you might feel the phone still rings with all the wrong people. More alone than driving your motorcycle to the edge of the Sahara and turning off the headlamp to be stunned by the moonless silent dark that falls like a blanket there. In that case, come to think of it, I was with someone, and what she said after five minutes was, "OK, can we get out of here now?" Nobody chooses to be alone for very long.

They do say that by being alone you might learn something about yourself you didn't know. But why would anybody want that? Most of us are trying to keep the lid on, not have the real you pop up suddenly in the mirror like a jack-in-box. For all I know, a long solo voyage may not be evening vespers in a wine-country monastery. I'm not a monk, and I don't know any. So even though I've been preparing for this expedition for more than a year, I have no idea what it will be like to be alone.

That's why I want you to come with me.

You wouldn't be in any danger, I think I know what I'm doing on a boat by now. I've been sailing since I was a kid and once added up more than 15,000 nautical miles out of sight of land. But in all that experience there was only one long weekend singlehanded, in which, because I couldn't convince anybody else to come along, I set off solo from Annapolis, Md., for St. Michaels, Md., 25 miles across the Chesapeake Bay. I left at night under spinnaker and was run down from behind by a 50-knot thunderhead which knocked the boat flat on its side. The next day it rained, and the day after that it took 14 hours to sail home against a very light breeze and 100 degrees of humidity. I learned nothing at all about myself except not to fall asleep with a spinnaker up, and was late for work Monday morning. I do remember that there was nobody to talk to, and I would have liked it better if there were.

Why have I always wanted to do this? Oh, I can tell you that. To sail a boat across water using only the wind is like a miracle, every time. The wind is free and gives its gift not just to you but to the waves and the sky, the clouds and the birds, who all move with it, day and night. Sometimes the wind is soft and warm, sometimes it stands on its hind legs and the universe cowers, but always the wind is the senior god and always the ocean obeys. If you come, the wind will teach us everything it knows. I promise to add what I can.

I can't guarantee a deck chair and a Pym's Cup every tea time, because our yacht is small. Not that small, mind you, plenty big enough for the job. We have comfortable bunks, a stove on gimbals to keep it level, 75 gallons of water and food for 60 days. We'll go where most people never will, as far from land as it is possible to be on earth. We'll come back knowing when to shake out a reef as a night squall bustles away to leeward, doze to our personal alarm clock under the Milky Way, and know security as the hard feel of a folded rigging knife in your pocket, there because you might need it and needed because you like to know it's there. I can promise that, but not much else, because I've never done this before, either.

The boat is sound and I'm ready. For a year I worked to teach myself every system aboard, obtain every necessary spare, and think through every potential catastrophe. I recorded the preparations long before I knew why I was doing them. Reading the entries now, on the eve of departure, they seem ancient, like Noah's packing list before the flood, when all the old man had was a voice in his ear that told him to prepare for something big. In fact, I hadn't set out to buy a sailboat at all.

{PREPARATION}
The Boat

IT WAS SUPPOSED TO be a Grand Banks 36, a classic motor trawler yacht. On a sea trial in San Diego, on the flying bridge of this stately vessel plowing at seven knots under the hum of twin Lehman 120 diesels, I imagined myself a tugboat captain in Rotterdam in 1943, perhaps being sent out to rescue a torpedoed tanker and then coming home to Sophia Loren, as in the movie of Jan De Hartog's novel "The Key." I reflected on the great cruising range afforded by 400 gallons of diesel under the deck, and how that would get me, if not to Rotterdam, at least to Catalina Island a couple of hundred times. Observing all the room on board, I imagined how easily I could entertain a dozen people in Gucci loafers, and how good that might be for business. But then I recalled that I am not in business and never have been, that most everybody who fell in love with Sophia Loren (in the movie *only*) drowned in flaming bunker oil as Nazis watched through periscopes, and that deep down inside I don't love motorboats and never have and that although older now am not really exactly dead, and never learned to play golf, which seems to go so seamlessly with the bar stools of a mahogany-planked Grand Banks.

Then the broker called to say that the owner was backing out of the sale after a full survey and check deposit. *What! I'll sue!* Well, the broker explained, I was certainly within my rights, but in his experience it was somewhat difficult to force anybody to sell you his boat. He was sympathetic, as befits someone who had shown the boat 27 times and now would never receive a commission. I expressed as much outrage as I could muster, but was already smiling before I hung up. Whew! I was astonished to discover how much I did not want to become the owner of a Grand Banks 36. It was as if a large weight the size of all the obsolete navigation equipment in my garage had been lifted from my shoulders. I didn't know why this was such a strange feeling. It was like being turned down for a date by someone asked out of duty: chivalry accomplished, and a boomerang ducked. Or maybe it was because I have a hunch that a Grand Banks motorboat rolls like a drunken pirate in a quartering sea.

The sailboat was moored at a floating dock and the tide was very low, so you looked down at it. I shielded my eyes from the afternoon sun with my checkbook. I wasn't sure what it was, but it looked like a Bruce King design from the mid-1980s. Maybe an Ericson yacht. Probably an Ericson 32-III, the "III" denoting a third iteration of a popular family cruiser-racer. Sailboat design is a compromise of speed, comfort and affordability. Pick any two. From the quarter view astern, the Bruce King lines were remarkably lovely—the reverse transom almost perfect, the cockpit rational, the sheer lovely and natural, the cabin house proportional. And the mast tapered beautifully. Of all the masts on that dock, it was the only one that didn't look like a vent pipe on an oil rig. Speed, comfort, affordability: King was famous for the first two, but in 1985, when this yacht was built, it was expensive. Time had lowered the price, and I realized I was looking at all three.

So now I am the owner not of a luxury tugboat but of a 27-year-old Ericson sloop. Naturally there is a list of improvements and upgrades, but each one is quite inexpensive and won't take very long to do, unless each one turns out to be very expensive and to take 10 times longer to accomplish than any intelligent person would have ever

CHAPTER 2

DEPARTURE

How marvelous! Now I won't be talking to myself, not that I would have been. I prefer a sort of stoical approach, taking what comes as it may. An even keel in life, if you will, as well as when crossing oceans in the wake of the heroes who first showed the way. Man of few words, is the goal. And between us, not every voyager has achieved the Yankee taciturn that will be my aim. Joshua Slocum, the father of singlehanding, ran on talking a good deal, at least for a Nova Scotia man. Odysseus himself did a lot of complaining about storms and sirens and his own crew, and was subject to bursting into tears from time to time, which I myself plan not to do. Even Ishmael of "Moby Dick" had a tendency to chat and reveal the personal hypos which got such an upper hand of him, he said, that it required a strong moral principle not to step into the street and start methodically knocking people's hats off, which is when he knew it was high time to get to sea. We will keep to the facts, as befits a more moderate sensibility. You will not be sorry you came. There may be a bit of autobiography, but nothing to come between us. Good shipmates, with never a venture toward the awkward sentiment or unasked detail, is what we'll be.

I'm glad we're finally away. Here in the channel that connects the artificial harbor of Marina del Rey to the Pacific Ocean I can stow the mainsail cover and prepare to raise sail. The safety harness which I swore to use is down below at the moment, but plenty of time for that. Our 21-horsepower auxiliary diesel is pushing us at 5 knots past the heavy smell of the guano-covered breakwater, with its gawking pelicans and unemployed sea lions. Hold your nose. Say, there's a breeze already, so let's get on with it. I'll explain all this later, right now I need to do it and feel the breeze in my face.

Finally.

Main up. Genoa set. Trim and cleat. The luff won't tension, why is that? Ah, forgot to let off the vang. Engine kill. Lift pump off. Gear in reverse, to stop the shaft spinning. The compass course to Hawai'i is 237 degrees magnetic, let's see where that points us. Why, we're going to pass north of the Island of Catalina! Good old Catalina, 26 miles across the sea, just as the song says. Twenty-six miles in a leaky old boat, but that's not us. We are prepared, sound of mind and body, and have headed off for Catalina a hundred times, so why should 2,600 miles be much different than 26?

It's good to move around the boat, feel her heel and prance under the gray marine layer, see the first sluice of cold water wash down the windward deck to carry away the footprints of land, a scrap of twine, a lost label from a can of beans. From up here on the bow, relaxing against the forestay and looking astern, the shore slips quietly away. Note the time. That needs to go into the log book right away. What shall we say? Something literary, like "The cleansing of the past has begun." How about, "This time and day, the cleansing of both past and future thus began?" Or, "This time and day, the unclean past begat the beginning of a clean and shiny future"—no, too Biblical, and sounds like an ad for a car wash. The logbook is at the navigation station below, which I have stocked with no fewer than 24 pencils. Nothing, not even a shortage of pencils, left to chance. However, it occurs that I forgot to bring a sharpener. Well, we can do that with sandpaper. First problem solved.

1221 hours, Day 1: Departed breakwater under main and 135 genoa, course 220m, wind SW 12, speed 5. Forgot pencil sharpener.

Let's turn our thoughts within and see what's there, at this epochal moment.

Hmmm. Nothing. Just an afternoon sail on a course to Hawai'i. No trumpets. Lines to be coiled, gear to be stowed. You expect more in the way of grandeur, or craziness, or excitement or drama. But this is good, don't you think? A rather professional start-off, stripped of amateur emotions or second thoughts or untimely reconsiderations. The anchor is still rigged on the foredeck, just in case the engine failed in the channel. That can come off now, because in a few hours the Pacific Ocean will be a thousand feet deep, and tomorrow half a mile deep, and since we carry only 300 feet of anchor line there is no reason at all to have an anchor at the ready. Just go up to the bow, de-rig and stow it.

We'll put on the safety harness at some point, but right now we're hardly three miles offshore and the anchor's clanking. That is not only esthetically incorrect but annoying. Digging out the harness is an unfamiliar act in these close waters and might be taken as an action caused by nervous anticipation, or an over-interpretation of the situation, or a slavish following of rules, or even an excuse to delay getting my feet wet on the bow. We don't make excuses on this boat. No one is looking over our shoulder with a notebook, judging. We are the captain of our fate, and come to think of it as captain we'd better alter course 30 degrees so we don't run smack into this gigantic oil tanker taking on cargo off Redondo Beach.

The harness will wait. It's up onto the cabin top, then, and scamper to the bow. Done it a thousand times, just now happen to be alone. The wind up here does seem unnaturally cool, the way it flows down the collar and across your chest as if to cause a constriction there. A sense that in the departure, we forgot something. A pencil sharpener and, what else?

A wave top bursts across the hull, wetting both legs. The afternoon breeze is stronger than usual. In our wake the harbor breakwater is shrinking as if to disappear. There were so many things to do, but I think I did them all. The list seemed to grow larger as departure approached, so that in the final moments it filled the world. I focused on what was important, which was to stop the thinking and the planning and begin the doing. I almost had to will myself away, because the natural compulsion to rehearse the plan threatened to stop the plan in its tracks.

I hardly remember the farewells already. My four-year-old granddaughter on the dock, waving goodbye with her tiny hand.

One daughter and one son, hiding concerns which are theirs, not mine, and knowing that restraint from interfering worry was the best parting gift possible. Tracy, my wife, drove me to West Marine to pick up one last item, a reading lamp, and we hurried back to the docks for the agreed-upon noon departure. Only after a quick hug before she took the last dock line from my hand did I see the shiny wellings under her eyes. But I was busy backing out of the slip, other voices were calling, my back was turned and there were paddle-boarders crossing ahead.

Now I know what I had forgotten. In my hurry I had neglected to meet her eyes. I took the line from her hand but never said the word goodbye. Too late now. All right, the anchor can wait.

In the main saloon I unpacked the orange safety harness that I had promised her to wear whenever on deck. It takes a moment to put on, tends to tangle, and is attached to a six-foot tether with a heavy carabineer. In place it feels like a costume, or a stage prop. But I have sworn to use it day and night, fair winds and foul, so Tracy would have a husband who came back.

The harness is put on in the safety of the cabin. You then reach up to the cockpit and attach the tether there, before climbing up. The tether reaches everything in the cockpit. To go forward, double the tether and clip onto the jacklines which run to the bow. Fall overboard and the tether keeps you with the boat. Solo sailors who go over the side unhooked are not heard from again.

I've practiced for hours with the safety harness on, but it is still an impediment. It tangles and restrains and requires thinking ahead. As I crawl over the cabin house toward the anchor at the bow the boat lurches off a wave, throwing me heavily into the stays and then back again to the lifelines. A splash of cold water fills my ear. I notice my hand on the lifeline grips hard, and the sea boots feel clumsy. We're off Point Vincente, where pretty, jagged cliffs glow gold in the lowering sun of the San Pedro Channel.

I feel nothing in the way of exaltation or even challenge. Just another afternoon practice sail in full offshore kit.

I was surprised at the tears in her eyes, it isn't like her. And now, with the wind strengthening and the north point of Catalina Island passing off the port bow, I wish I had said something more, at least taken time for our eyes to meet. But what's to say, after a year's preparation in which the topic of survival alone at sea never came up at all.

"I'm thinking about sailing to Hawai'i."

"When will you leave?" she said.

That was eight months ago, and I was really only thinking about it, testing the notion, wondering if the idea was possible or stupid or crazy.

Whoever it is we are is known first by someone else.

The harness hangs over my shoulders as I move carefully forward to kneel over the anchor in the spray at the bow. Access isn't good, and the heavy plow has little clearance between the forestay and the pulpit. Wrestling the anchor out of its roller my back twinges, a sea pitches us both off balance, and I sit heavily with the anchor in my lap and chain wrapped around my legs. Awkward and clumsy. I know how to do this stuff, and I'm good at it. But we're five hours out and the bow is wet and my hands are already cold.

"When will you leave?"

Now. This moment. Here.

On my unending lists I never thought to write: Remember to tell her you love her.

Have a look around, let's talk about the wind. It's cool, about 62 degrees Fahrenheit, and blowing 20 knots. The wind made these waves, which are about two feet tall and covered with whitecaps. This is chop, and chop makes spray as the boat cuts through it. Wind waves roll directly downwind, making every wave a weathervane. Ocean swells are caused by the wind, too, but they were born on the other side of the horizon. We'll meet swells in the open Pacific. We get all this information at a glance, as much as expensive modern instrumentation would show: wind speed, direction, angle, wave height, sea state and temperature.

The wind tells us how much sail to put up, and right now it's saying we have too much. *Thelonious* is heeled over too far, sheets of spray are showering the bow. We're sailing close to the wind to pass Catalina, so it's time to reduce sail and carry on. The movement of the boat is sharp and the bursting wave tops make it loud down below. Don't forget to hold on, always. One hand for you, one hand for the ship. It wouldn't do to break a rib the first night.

Thirty miles down.

{PREPARATION}

Ready

TOMORROW I DEPART MARINA Del Rey for Hanalei Bay, Kaua'i, Hawai'i. I'm sailing solo and looking for a passage of 22–25 days—or better, of course. The distance is 2,300 nautical miles, or 2,700 statute miles.

Thanks to all who have advised on the preparation of *Thelonious* for this voyage. Should things work out as on paper, my family will meet me there for a week and then I will head back to California, riding the gyre north and hoping to dodge the doldrums of the North Pacific High.

Despite a good deal of time offshore over the years, I've never attempted these distances alone, so you know as much about how it may go as I do.

So far, these are the unexpected lessons:

—There are innumerable systems and elements of systems on board, and learning them all and obtaining spares has been the bulk of the preparatory work. It is not especially rewarding. The more you learn, the more problem scenarios you recognize, so the more you prepare. It can be a mental rope burn. Eventually you have to say, enough already.

—A modern yacht is a Frankenstein of electronic appendages: satellite phone and weather downloads, tracking, GPS, emergency locators, chart plotter, AIS, MP3 player, NMEA sentences, TED talks and a snake basket of incompatible connection wires. The monster you create is you, in your own image. It's a monster you can rail against only to the mirror.

—If the diesel won't start or the alternator fails I may have to turn back. I'm not even bringing the sextant (forgot how to use it, anyhow). Like it or not, I'm a GPS person now, connected to satellites as if by marionette strings. Success depends on batteries, from AAA to Group 27s. It is all good or all bad, but we are who we are and it is what it is.

—Like many, I have read all the books of the singlehanders. You may notice that in every account of these heroes—the ones who ventured off alone on leaky boats when no one had done it before—that they always have a few words to say about the challenges not of the sea but of the last weeks: of the preparation, the advice, the worrying kin, the innumerable decisions, the nagging breakdown of formerly reliable gear, the endless new recognitions of stuff you need and ought to have and shouldn't go without, the count-down, the slowing of days, the sheer magnitude of the number of little things that need doing and can only be done by you. Well, I finally understand what they meant.

So tomorrow, off we go. I have too many books and not enough light air sails. I have 15 oranges. Should you have 20? Wouldn't 12 be really enough? I have stud lumber for shoring up a collision with a shipping container; duct tape if I break my arm; 60-days food in cans or pouch; garlic and onions, pasta and propane, a laptop that will disintegrate with one splash of water and a bucket that I remember being, so many times in the past, the best source of a cheer-up when dipped in the ocean and dumped over one's head naked with the sun at local noon overhead. Oh, and a good deal of Jack Daniels. But say, shouldn't I have more antibiotics? What about macrobiotics? What about probiotics? What about idiotics, got plenty of them. And a picavet, so I can fly my camera on a kite. I should have tested the picavet. Didn't have time. Never seemed to be wind enough. Ergo, you're right, completely screwed, picavet-wise.

The Pacific is vast and its size is daunting. Halfway to Hawai'i I will be as far from land as you can get on our globe. And from where I hope to end up, the island of Kaua'i, it is still a thousand miles more to Midway Island.

Well, this isn't a war and nobody's shooting at me, so what is there to worry about? I'll tell you what it is: that once dependent upon laptops and sat phones and GPS, it is entirely possible that the very gizmos that make what was hard easy will simply quit working. And then what does the prudent mariner do, a thousand miles offshore?

I'll check in if and when I know the answer.

CAPSIZED

1 735 HOURS, DAY 1. *Stowed anchor. Reef #1 in mainsail. Ate half an oatmeal cookie. No appetite.*

Does it concern you to heel over like this? It shouldn't. We tilt 10 or 15 degrees to leeward in response to the pressure of the wind, but seldom any further. Beneath the hull is 4,000 pounds of lead in a fin-shaped keel to counterbalance and sustain us. Even if the mast were to lay flat in the water, as does not ordinarily happen, we would promptly bob back up. Even if we were turned upside-down by the irresistible curl of a rogue wave, we would immediately return to normal, although probably stripped of mast, boom and sails.

But perhaps you're right, we do seem to be taking a battering from these chilly seas. It comes from heading into them, which is necessary to clear Catalina Island. They've had time to build up on their march south from Point Conception, urged on by offshore winds and the cold California current, and are perfectly in keeping with our location and progress. It's warmer belowdecks. I keep the old-fashioned oil lamp lit, not so much for light as to take the damp off and add a few degrees. The scent of burning kerosene is subtle but comforting, and oil makes a more cheery glow than our modern LEDS, whose light-emitting diodes are cold.

I find it homey down here, even though it feels and sounds somewhat like a Cadillac going too fast over ruts. Lie down and test that comfortable bunk. No, not the uphill one, because—well, you see what happens. You fall out. But in the bunk on the downhill side, the leeward one, it's pretty hard to fall out. It's even hard to get out. Comfortable, wouldn't you say? Like being rocked in a cradle, some think. The effects on the anatomy are useful to contemplate. In the rhythmic application and release of gravity, organs take on a new individuality. That is the stomach, rising and falling. That is the pancreas, waving hello. In the sigmoid colon, a lump of breakfast signals the stage of its current process. Too, the unweighted brain registers its condition, and then notes the heaviness immediately returning.

We will soon accommodate to resting like this, enjoying the supine view of salt water against the portlight overhead, the crash of waves against the hull near our ear, the clank of unsecured gear in hidden lockers, the swinging lamp, the low-frequency splashy hum of sea water released from attached flow to abandon us into the gurgling wake astern. And now, in our cradle, note the beads of sweat across the forehead and the brief negative intrathoracic pressure pulse commonly presaging emesis. I need some air, fast.

The cockpit is the place to be just now, harness on and braced solid. The trick is not to oppose the motion but, once wedged in place, relax and move with it. Never mind the sounds. When sailing close to the wind like this, occasionally a breaking sea strikes the side of the boat rather sharply, imitating an explosion. But it isn't. It just means we are clawing into the wind instead of running off before it, as we shall be eventually. Close-hauled like this, it tends to be wet. In Sir Francis Chichester's first long voyage alone, the singlehanded transatlantic race of 1960, he sailed into the wind for 40 days and nights. He thought the sounds of waves bursting against him were rather like "bombs exploding in the '39 war." I have "Alone Across the Atlantic" aboard, for consolation if ever the charm of the moment fades. His example is so robust that it always sets me back on course immediately. By the way, here in the cockpit, if you duck as soon as you hear the explosion, usually a hundred pounds of water will go right over your head. Good to know at night, when you don't see it coming.

But, yes, this is pretty uncomfortable and unnecessarily wet. I will put in another reef. That should ease our progress and reduce the heel.

It's good to have something to do, and now we're riding better. Even for experienced sailors, small nausea is common during the first hours, or days, or weeks of a passage. Charles Darwin, as a young botanist, was sick in his bunk almost the entire five years of his circumnavigation aboard the Beagle in 1832. But he did excellent work that changed the world. Have a cracker?

Well then, as I was saying, these first discomforts are nothing to be concerned about. Recall that you are in good hands, since I have been doing this a long time. Trained early and trained well, as they say. Why, I believe my very first memory of the yachting life was in Sewaren, New Jersey, on the banks of the Arthur Kill downriver from New York Harbor. I was about the age of six. I make this estimation on the recollection that the amber water, with its pretty sheen of light bunker oil, came up to my knees, and yet was pretty close to my eyes. And I recall holding mother's hand, which would be an unlikely circumstance at a more advanced age. So, six.

My father, a young surgeon with a small practice as yet, had come back from World War II with an interest in boats prompted by Atlantic coastal anti-submarine patrols and deployment to the South Pacific on the hospital ship *Sanctuary*. He had bought for $20 a red canvas kayak and put a sail on it, making a rudimentary lateen rig out of our household clothesline poles and by fastening leeboards on the kayak sides. This was his maiden voyage, and I watched his sail grow smaller in the warm evening breeze as he ventured away toward distant Staten Island. And then the sail abruptly disappeared and he was gone.

Mother's hand tightened upon mine. I was studying the killies swimming around my toes at that point, and looked up to ask where he had gone. All she said was, "Oh, no" in a tone I had never heard before. Dead? I wondered. The word as yet meant little to me, but as far as I could see, it applied. She denied it, but kept her grip on my hand. That wasn't unusual, people were always holding on to you in those days. I returned to trying to trap killies with my toes.

After a long time father appeared walking on the shallow river bottom, dragging a collapsed mass of swamped kayak and sails. I had never seen him all wet, shirt and trousers clinging, and it seemed to take a long time for him to get everything drained out and put back on the top of the car, during which mother was very quiet.

"Capsized," he explained, with an arm around my back. "I need to figure out how to sail a boat, and then you can go with me."

That seemed encouraging.

Some years later, in between seeing patients in our living room with mother dressed up as a nurse, he built a Penguin-class dinghy in the cellar, from a kit. At age nine I became increasingly impatient with his step-by-step self-education in boating, during which he seemed to think it took more than an instant to comprehend that a cross-wise boat seat was to always be called a thwart, that the sail fitted to the mast with something called a bolt rope, and that the pintle lock should be engaged on the transom so the rudder didn't come out of the gudgeons. He comprehended it all in slow motion, as if reading from a book, whereas it was all completely obvious to me.

That summer he learned to sail on warm Barnegat Bay. I stood knee-deep, waiting for him to get it, while all around me boys on sailboats split the whitecaps in clouds of spray, hiked out while sipping Cokes and not bothering to look at me as they sped by, I, who could only gape back with ineffectual insolence as crabs nibbled my feet and father practiced caution.

The next summer I begged with every argument I could think up to be allowed to go off sailing solo, unfettered from the parents who cluttered the 11-foot boat, my own boat, and to be unleashed to find my own course and destiny.

"How much do you suppose you weigh, now?" father said one day.

"Eighty-nine, almost 90."

He didn't think it was enough. Dinghies don't have lead keels, they are maintained upright by the weight of the crew hiked out over the side in the acrobatic and athletic postures I had studied and so wished to emulate, even in this interim time before the invention of girls.

But one afternoon he looked me up and down, nodded, and watched as I leaped eagerly aboard the little dinghy. You get on a boat like that with a smooth bending of the knees, so as not to tip over. You don't stand on the pointy front, that would tip you into the water straightaway. Rather keep low, be balanced, haul up the white cotton sail with practiced tugs of the halyard. Let the boom run free, otherwise the wind might catch you unaware and mayhem be the result. I knew all that as well as I knew my Yankees cap. I was 10, and the wind could shake the sail but not me. Hands off and cast me free. One person on a sailing dinghy has lots to do, but I knew how to do it: hiking stick to steer by in my right hand, the rope to the sail in my left, Yankees cap on backwards, and the world calling, come!

"Take this," father said, handing me his new rigging knife, which he had read ought to be in every helmsman's pocket. And as he pushed me off, "Don't cleat down the main sheet."

But I hardly looked back. Already the wind filled the graceful curve of cotton above me, already the bow wave rippled, and weighted only by my streamlined pre-teen frame we leaped forward faster than ever I recalled with two heavy adults aboard, out away from the pier toward open water.

As we heeled I climbed onto the windward rail to steady and flatten her. But my hands were full with tiller and sheet, and the rail seemed far away. With a quick turn I fastened the mainsail to its cleat, which everyone always did. Now I was free to climb in one elegant motion onto the windward rail itself, providing the necessary counterbalance to the wind while continuing to expertly control the tiller by its long hiking stick. We sped!

Whenever father sat on the rail, the boat came quickly back to level. When I did, nothing seemed to happen. I remembered the hiking strap for my feet, so I stuck them under it and, thus restrained, cantilevered my 89 pounds far out over the water. A new puff heeled us further, but I knew what to do. Simply ease the sail out to relieve the pressure of the wind. However, the line that controlled the sail, I found, was now cleated far below beyond my feet, on the centerline of the boat. When I tried to reach down there, my weight came off the rail and we tipped even more. So I hiked further out, straining in perfect form. But against the increasing pressure of wind on the sail it seemed to have no effect at all.

A quick glance over my shoulder showed the rapidly receding pier where father stood with binoculars to his eyes. I saw mother, one step behind, grasp his waist suddenly with both hands. Others were watching, too. Someone was emphatically waving his arms, a gesture that contained no information at all.

Water now began to pour over the undecked leeward rail and into the boat. I leaned further out, but to no avail. Our wonderful forward motion, the lap of the bow wave and the hiss of the passing bay, diminished. Still more water poured in. The horizon began to rise in a way I had not seen before. I felt my feet submerge, and then my legs, and then, for the first time in life, I was alone in the universe as time stopped and the dinghy and I, still half-sailing, slowly sank in the warm bay waters until I found myself floating beside it in a flotsam of oars, lines and my own hat.

It was a long time before they swam out to get me, and a long pull by a gang of strangers before the capsized dinghy was back to shallow water, bailed out, and the cotton sail laid to dry in the low sun. I stood on the sidelines, fully aware of the hidden smiles.

No one said anything to me until I climbed into the back seat of the car in my wet shorts.

"Can I have my new rigging knife?" father said gently, by way of assuaging the misery that must have been showing on my face.

"I lost it."

"Oh, he's crying," mother said. "I told you not to let him go sailing alone!"

UNDERWAY

DAY *1, MIDNIGHT. COURSE 220°m, speed 2-4 knots under #1 reefed main.*

We are undeniably underway. The night is black under a thick marine layer, the low stratus that oppresses the California coast in this season. Both the air and the sea are 64 degrees, which doesn't sound cold, but in the cockpit of a boat it will do. After a few hours sitting on a hard bench the marrow seems to gel despite full foul weather gear, harness and rubber boots. Two minutes of exertion, however, causes perspiration to pour and steam to rise under the chin. The wind is dying, so we should shake out the single reef in the mainsail. But it can wait. Everything can wait. No one is judging, there are no witnesses to this damp paralysis of will accompanied by a mild case of something or other in the stomach.

The weather report is for wind increasing to 25 knots at San Nicholas Island, which lies off the starboard beam. If we took the reef out, we'd just have to put it back in, and that's why we remain in full kit, ready for anything or nothing. When it's dark like this, sailing through gloom, we're a ship in a bottle with no sense of what might be approaching outside the glass. It's clear that we're definitely slowing down, our romping seven knots down to half that. But a wall of heavy air might come any moment as a line of white across the sea, and so we wait, alert and stiff. Not concerned, or chilled, or even particularly tired. Just—something.

I know what it is. It's the first of the nevers. Never been this far offshore alone before. Well, that's why we came. For the nevers.

CHAPTER 4

The GPS says San Nicholas is 10 miles away. I thought those dim lights were ships, at first. Maybe they are. They appear and disappear behind the invisible waves, which gives the appearance of erratic blinking. Don't look at them so much. If they're a ship aiming to run us down, we'll see the red and green of running lights soon enough. It would be a good idea to relax a little, rather than sitting with every muscle drawn like a bowstring. That's my advice.

By the ship's clock it has been five minutes since we checked the time. Therefore, let's agree not to look at the clock again for 15 minutes. No, that was not 15 minutes that was nine minutes.

According to the chart, San Nicholas Island is a military facility and no civilian approach is permitted within three miles. Well, that's why we're 10 miles away. The GPS is extremely accurate, but the lights look closer every time. Perhaps we have incorrectly entered our position on the chart, and suddenly black helicopters will appear to lower men in black masks on black ropes as we sit frozen and determined not to look at the clock.

Now the wind has died completely. The boat just sits here, rolling in the confused sea. I just sit here, too, inert, and why is that? Come to think of it, there was not much sleep last night and the day has been rather full of details and last-minute tasks. The imagination is better at preparation than dealing with the moment. We have anticipated storms, broken bones and dreadful psychiatric states, but not the mundane reality of three o'clock in the morning halfway between happy Catalina and hidden San Nicholas Island, windless in slop and paralyzed by readiness. A cramp rises in the leg, do you feel that? Stand up and shake it off.

The one thing that doesn't seem wise, this first night, is to go below where it's warm and dry. Sleep for the singlehander is better done in daytime, when ships can see you even if you don't see them. Besides, we're not tired, and even if tired we would just ignore it. Discipline is what we have practiced for and planned on: strength of character and a heart of oak, untrumpeted because that would be unseemly. One does not venture alone offshore without such self-confidence. If adventure is choice, success is will.

Dawn is a few hours off, however, so we can go below for a

cookie, and to change the scenery from the open cockpit with its tricking lights and thoughts like wild horses. Theoretically, we could stay below for 20 minutes before being cut in half by a speeding containership, because that's how long it would take such a ship to reach us from an empty horizon.

Funny how a cookie has no appeal. And I never get seasick. The ship's clock is broken, it doesn't even move.

0330 hours. AIS shows no ships in sight. Speed 2 knots in gentle seas. Warm below and quiet.

CHAPTER 5

MORNING

D AY 2, 0700 HOURS. *Overslept.*
Blinding light, the cabin illuminated suddenly as if by the billion-candlepower searchlight of a containership about to slice us in two. Up in a panic, rubbing my eyes, tripping over my boots, bracing for the impact. But the view from the companionway is only gray morning and an empty horizon.

It's 7 o'clock. My god, I fell asleep. I've been unconscious three and a half hours, violating all my own rules. The miracle is that *Thelonious* has quietly jogged on without us, still on course 220 magnetic. Big Pacific swells lift her easily, peacefully. I have no idea what happened. I remember jotting something in the log book and pulling off my foulies. Maybe testing the lee bunk. Maybe lying down, just for a moment, to see how it felt.

I feel like a passenger, and it's embarrassing. Oh well, let's have a yawn and a stretch and put on the coffee. In the locker behind the stove is a paper cone filter and a big bottom-heavy cup. With the cup on the unused left burner of the gimbaled stove, the right burner is available to boil water in the teapot. It's fast and keeps spills to a minimum.

In the cockpit, sipping coffee, you can see what a mess we made of last night. I remember a sort of whipping sound periodically from the rigging, and now I know what it was. It was the radar reflector, suspended from the spreaders to enhance our appearance on commercial shipping radar. It's gone. Only the halyard remains, tangled in knots around the starboard shrouds. The night reef I put in the mainsail is the lumpiest one I have ever made, and bound with a heavy dock line because I forgot where I put the gaskets that keep it neatly in place. The deck is still dirty from the land, a reminder of our very recent departure. The very emptiness of the horizon sends a shudder. We had no lookout for nearly four hours, and a sleep so sound it wiped memory clean. Perhaps in a collision I would never have woken at all, and now still be sinking slowly toward the bottom of the sea, 600 fathoms down. I am a runner who trained hard for a marathon, and at Mile One decided to lie down for a rest. In the middle of the street. In the path of trucks.

It was ships that came up most often in daydreaming about this voyage. In my prior experience offshore they often appeared suddenly and as a surprise, growing urgently in size with bows cleaving the water. The open sea isn't a road with lanes for traffic. Commercial vessels come from every point on the compass, first as a dot on the horizon, then as a moving city skyline. They can parallel your course for hours, or, even if only approximately intercepting, loom larger with amazing speed.

The disparity in bulk between us is provocative. We are 32 feet long and 6 tons. A typical container ship is 1,000 feet long and carries 150,000 tons. Our average speed is 5 knots, and they go 20 knots under the propulsion of 100,000 horsepower. At that speed, a ship that appears out of the mist five miles away is on you in 15 minutes. They're easy to see from a yacht by day and they're lighted at night like a used car lot. We aren't. From the bridge of a freighter a small sailboat among the whitecaps makes little visual impression, even if a lookout happens to look. Sailboats don't show up well on radar, either. We're ground clutter, or mistaken for something else. If a big ship does see a small boat he is not likely to change course anyhow, because a ship can turn only in grand slow motion, and that would probably only serve to confuse the skipper of a boat trying to get out of the way. On the ocean, ships are the boss.

Many singlehanders whose end remains mysterious are thought to be victims of collision with a larger vessel. That's how Joshua Slocum, the most famous singlehander of all, is presumed to have died, disappeared without a trace off North Carolina after successfully circumnavigating the world. Until recently, all a yacht without radar could do was fly a metal reflector intended to increase its hull signature, and make sure to keep a lookout. Thousands of solo sailors crossed the oceans that way.

AIS, which stands for Automatic Identification System, changed everything. AIS makes use of a transponder to share the current location, speed and direction of travel among all vessels so equipped. Similar transponders show flight control radar every plane in the sky. Commercial ships were required to install powerful AIS equipment in 2002, and now most of them have it. Small sailboats have adopted a lower-powered version. Today, even an inexpensive VHF radio is able to receive AIS signals and plot the course of an approaching ship. *Thelonious* has a Vesper Watchmate, a New Zealand product with a six-inch screen that looks at a glance like radar. The Vesper AIS not only receives but continuously sends out our location and course to any ship in the area. It's set to blare an audio alarm if any vessel comes within three miles.

That should let us sleep sounder, right? Well, yes, if it works. And if the other vessel has AIS installed. And if electronic instrumentation, so predictably unreliable in the world of salt crystals, functions when you need it most. I've never been able to effectively test our installation, which I did myself in order to know how it works, and troubleshoot if it doesn't. Along the coast the Vesper once picked up a giant containership 23 miles away. But it also has failed to pick up smaller vessels, tugs and commercial fishermen, and I had to alter course to avoid them.

The screen scale on *Thelonious* is set at the 12-mile range. The circular depiction shows us in the middle and nobody else anywhere. Our course and speed and coordinates are constantly on display, a contribution to situational awareness I am already grateful for. But what I want to see is a ship on the horizon, and a ship on the AIS, both at once. And I want to see that confirming picture by day, by night, in heavy seas and in the middle of a rain squall. Does AIS work, every time? We'll see.

Never mind all that. The rational mind says there's nothing to worry about right now, so why not relax? Easier said than done. The coffee, usually an accelerator pedal for the day, tastes oddly wrong. I flick it over the side but miss like an amateur, leaving a brown trail over the leeward deck. A sip of water will have to do. A cookie? Nah, maybe later. Do you ever get seasick? Me neither.

What a mess the boat is, so let's do something about it. We can just untangle and coil up the radar reflector halyard, the reflector is history and we don't have a spare. No matter, they don't work anyhow. And I have located the sail gaskets, which in the excitement of departure I guess I crammed deep under some canned goods in the food locker. Weird thing to do, but that's where I found them.

Now let's raise the mainsail. First, let the main sheet run free so the boom swings over to leeward. By the way, the sheet is a rope. I know, "sheet" is confusing because you'd naturally assume it refers to the sails. But the sails are called sails. Sheets are the lines that control them—main sheet, genoa sheet, spinnaker sheet and so on.

We hoist the mainsail using the main halyard. Halyard is a derivation of "haul-yard", from the days when square sails hung from horizontal yardarms. A halyard raises or lowers a sail. Sails can be heavy, but a good thing about a smallish boat like *Thelonious* is that ours aren't very big. Our main is only 200 square feet, so one fellow can raise or trim it alone, even when the wind comes up. On bigger boats the job gets to be a handful even for a full crew.

Haul the mainsail halyard hand over hand until you can't any more, then take two turns clockwise around the main halyard winch, insert the crank handle, crank it tight and cleat the halyard down.

A furled sail is nothing but a pile of cloth. But look at ours now, standing tall, luffing and bouncing and shaking its blocks and lines. The wind passes carelessly all around it, as if it were an intruder in the realm of the sky. The mainsail endures the shaking as if confused, banging this way and that. The boat shudders under it, wallowing.

But watch this. Just pull the main sheet to draw the boom in and everything changes. The luffing stops. The mainsail assumes a wing-like camber and the air obeys, bending around it. The more I draw in the boom the firmer the mainsail becomes, assuming its true identity. The yacht heels, feeling the power. We accelerate immediately from two knots to four, all six tons of us, lead keel, water tankage, bins of food and crew, too.

A glance tells when the trim is right. A well-set sail is a body-part fulsome and perfected. The breeze is attracted, and attaches itself all around, seeking only to be close on either side. It flows over the chord, bending to the will of the concupiscent shape. It is that bending of the wind, and the resulting decrease of pressure on one side, that draws us forward according to the principle of Bernoulli, which states that pressures tend to equalize. Our voyage is itself the equalization of pressures, although I have no principle to explain why. I just know that it is impossible to look at a well-trimmed sail and not be moved. We are made to admire curves.

It's gray and cool, and now that we're going fast again we can sit here a while and be alone, if this is what it means to be alone.

Are you enjoying it?

For me, I don't know. It feels more like something has begun that I began and now can't stop. Like I'm along for the ride, but not really the driver.

Day 2, noon position 32°41'N, 119°32W. Sixty miles offshore. Wind 10, speed 3.

It does feel good to tidy up, coil the lines, scrub away the dock dirt and fiddle with the placement of the genoa sheet block. Time for a deep breath, maybe the first since departure. We're out of sight of land and no doubt last night was an anomaly, a mere case of first-day nerves, a reminder of our pre-voyage state, a state now rapidly washing away with every mile straight out to sea. What is there, really, to worry about?

Worry is other people, and none of them is here.

We can doze in the cockpit. The heart rate slows. The soreness in the lower back fades. The ship's clock jumps 10 minutes, then 10 minutes again. Over the gray cloud layer above, a spot of sun rises higher as the morning progresses with no prompting at all. The rhythm is easy and new. We don't have to do anything at all, the day carries us with it as the wind carries our boat. We can go on like this forever.

The human eye is very good at discerning distant movement against a stationary background. That must've been a trait of successful hominids on the savannah, who generously passed it on to us all. And now, to the north, where San Nicholas Island lies unseen, a speck of white appears on the horizon, and with it a small charge of adrenalin.

A spouting whale? The whale book predicts that a pear-shaped spout indicates a humpback whale, while a bushy V-shaped spout identifies a gray whale. A blue whale has a characteristic spout, too, but I'll have to look it up. California has lots of whales, and in these waters there are just as many as there were a hundred years ago, a pretty rare piece of good news. Come this way, why don't you, whales.

The whale identification book is at the navigation station, and when I return to the deck the white speck is much closer. Through the binoculars, it has a bow wave. The bow wave is pointing right at us, which seems unlikely. A compass has 360 degrees, so there are 359 other choices. This vessel, because that's obviously what it is, has chosen the only point on the entire compass that leads directly to us. We're 60 miles offshore and 200 miles from the Mexican border. Much of the drug trade off Southern California these days is by sea, commonly in motorboats called pangas that can travel far offshore to elude interdiction. Every cruising yacht decides whether to carry firearms for self-protection. I decided not to.

Now the bow wave looks like a wild head of white hair parted in the middle and there's no mistaking that we are the target. For armament, I do have a Very pistol that fires magnesium flares, but when Tom Hanks tried that in "Captain Phillips" the flare gun didn't shoot straight worth a damn. We also have winch handles, for hand-to-hand combat. They used to be heavy cranks of bronze right out of a Viking carry-on bag, good for close-quarters clubbing work. But bronze is expensive, and if dropped overboard, it sinks. So ours are plastic floating versions with the defensive capability of a spatula. Why, exactly, don't we have firearms? There were good arguments against, but just now I can't remember any of them.

The binoculars show white towers on the speeding vessel, so maybe it's just an aggressive tuna boat. Or maybe atomic war began last night and they're speeding over because we're the only ones left on the planet. Would that be better than drug dealers? No, I guess not. We could turn on the engine and try to escape at six knots, but what a laugh that would be. No choice but to sit here, sailing along, and wait to see what the devil brings.

The way binoculars work, or maybe it's actually the brain, you peer through them at a jiggly and indistinct picture, then lower them and let the mind put together the fragments of what you saw.

It didn't take long to piece together the puzzle of a white bow wave, a high tower and a big orange slashing chevron and to recognize a 110-foot United States Coast Guard Cutter approaching at 20 knots, deck gun manned and ready.

BOARDED

" Ah, Coast Guard cutter approaching at high speed, this is sailing vessel *Thelonious*, good day to you."

I was on the VFH radio at the navigation station, and the transmit light confirmed my transmission on hailing Channel 16. No response. On the AIS screen there was no blip or other indication that we aren't the only ship on the ocean. The cutter was still coming fast, as if possibly unaware of one little yacht in the way. After a moment more:

"Coast Guard, this is the yacht *Thelonious* dead ahead of you, range 2,000 yards. State your intentions."

That sounded firm, at least. The cutter swung broadside at a good distance, a handsome vessel showing its profile against the empty ocean.

"Good morning, prepare to be boarded for a courtesy inspection" a voice said with loud clarity out of the speakers of the radio.

So much for being alone. After 15 minutes the cutter disgorged an inflatable boat with a bridge of communications gear and four men in sidearms and combat boots. They closed the distance and came alongside, bouncing on the waves to match our speed as we rolled and plunged through the sloppy three-foot seas. It's not so easy to come alongside a sailing boat, offshore. Objects in the grip of waves rise and fall vertically, and even matching our gentle speed required the helmsman of the boat to gun his outboard motor as the chop knocked him off course.

The heavy-laden crew, more concerned with their roles than me, discussed boarding strategies. A wave top wetted them. With a roar of the engine the inflatable closed on *Thelonious*, but bounced off and away. They tried again, with the same result.

"Do you want me to heave to, gentlemen?"

That maneuver, easy enough, would stop the forward progress of the yacht, but in fact a little speed makes for a steady and more predictable course. No answer.

"Go for that ladder at the back," someone said. The inflatable spun and sped aggressively toward the stern.

"What's up?" I called out, loud.

"We're going to use that ladder back there."

Back there on our stern was indeed a boarding ladder, folded and secured. Rising next to it, however, was the delicate vane of the servo-pendulum self-steering mechanism, the device that makes solo crossing of oceans possible. Its push rods and bearings, submerged steering oar and lightweight honeycomb polycarbonate weathervane are intended to withstand gales, but not a troop of armed men.

What's more, boarding a yacht from the stern is a bad choice unless you like mounting a hobbyhorse in full swing.

"Stop!"

Still they sped toward the vane, skidding across the chop half in control and half out. One man grabbed our stern rail, only to have a wave wrench his hand away.

Every boat has a captain, ostentatious as the term may sound, and as legally irrelevant in the face of an armed boarding party. However, a captain at least has moral authority, and so the Coast Guard crew was informed in stern tones that boarding would not be permitted except in a safe and seamanlike way, and that way was to direct their vessel to the center of the yacht, where the mast is. And once there, to grasp the wires that hold up the mast, time the waves, and climb aboard.

That was how I met Lieutenant Daniel Trainor, accompanied by an enlisted man who had spent a lot of time in the weight room. Both wore blue jump suits, inflatable vests, helmets, sidearms and uncertain expressions, as if they had just stepped out of a hot air balloon into the Land of Oz.

The first question of their protocol was, "Do you have fire in the bilge?" After asking to have the question repeated twice, I declared that we did not.

Fire in the bilge, it seems, is a grave danger when boarding an unknown vessel. The bilge, as lowest point, collects explosive gases of spilled fuel or oils. In bilges, the bearings of machinery may become heated, electrical conduits breached by time or inadequate maintenance. Farm machinery in transport may leak fluids, chemical cargos weep unseen, even grease neglected by the kitchen staff can be a problem. It all runs into the bilge, so I was asked to open ours for inspection.

I removed a floor plate the size of a comic book.

"Where's the rest of it?" the burly seaman asked.

That's all the bilge we have, I explained as he peered into three inches of water sloshing under the floorboards.

After a while Lt. Trainor accepted my invitation for us all to sit down, since three people strap-hanging pretty much fills up the cabin of a small boat. Together we went over the list of safety items, the fire extinguishers, required placards, visual distress signals, personal floatation devices and the throwable cushions required of sailboats, to be tossed as a first response to any crew member who should fall overboard.

"Thanks for digging those out," Lt. Trainor said as his colleague checked the ownership and registration certification. "But they should always be kept on deck, so you can throw them."

I agreed, but felt obliged to point out that, being alone on board, there would be nobody to throw one to, and nobody to throw one to me. To that, he nodded thoughtfully. It's also why I don't wear a life jacket, I explained. A safety harness is much more important.

Safety harnesses, however, were not on the list of required equipment.

Half an hour was enough to inspect a 32-foot boat, with its 10-foot cabin, towards the end of which the boarders relaxed their guard and occasionally even smiled. They communicated with the cutter via radio. They entered items in a computer. Eventually, after a huddled conference, they explained that we would be cited for the offense of expired emergency flares, since among our 20 flares, Very pistol and smoke signals, none had been purchased within the past six months. When could I correct this oversight?

In—Hawai'i?

OK, Lt. Trainor said, but if inspected again between here and there I would be deemed uncompliant.

They departed over the deck at amidships, swinging more confidently now from the sturdy wire shrouds, to drop easily into the boat returned to take them off. On the near horizon the 110-foot cutter *Edisto*, out of District 11, waited like a mother duck for the return of its chicks.

In an hour the cutter was five miles away, with no bow wave at all visible through binoculars. Even at that distance the rakish white vessel seemed a hive of activity, rehearsing its mission to aggressively protect American shores. I didn't mind being a training exercise, and thought that probably the boarding team had never been on a small sailboat before, and now knew what to expect.

Anyhow, there's no complaining. The Coast Guard is the primary maritime law enforcement agency of the United States, authorized to make seizures and arrests and to use all necessary force to compel compliance while conducting boardings. They can also save your bacon.

After waving goodbye *Thelonious* seemed smaller than before, a miniature ship jogging west as *Edisto* steamed the other way. It was quiet again. You would think human voices would linger, like thoughts. That they might hang in the air a while to keep you company before diffusing gradually, like skywriting.

But they don't.

The cutter lingered on the eastern horizon. Then the thud-thud-thud of her bow gun arrived over the water, and through the binoculars she showed her bow wave, maneuvering as she fired. The warlike sounds continued for half an hour until the dull gray of the marine layer closed down and *Thelonious* was alone again, or perhaps alone for the first time.

SELF STEERING

EVERY SOLO VOYAGE BEGINS with a self-steering device. Who steers day and night? Not us. Our helmsman is a Sailomat-brand servo-pendulum mechanical steering vane. Such a contraption bolted to the stern is the unmistakable insignia of long-distance cruisers. It's a flag that says, "So Long."

Modern self-steerers have been around since 1960, when a small club of men dreamed up the idea of a singlehanded transatlantic race from England to New York, the wrong way against the winds of a cold and stormy ocean. I can still recite their names, they were such heroes to me: Francis Chichester, who won it aboard *Gipsy Moth III* with a time of 40 days; "Blondie" Hasler, sailing *Jester*, with its junk rig; Dr. David Lewis, aboard a 25-foot production Virtue; Valentine Howells on *Eire* and Jean Lacombe on tiny *Cap-Horn*. All but *Gipsy Moth* were much smaller than *Thelonious*. The race demanded some kind of automatic steering, since the sole occupant also had to sleep, eat and work the sails. Chichester designed his own device, which he named Miranda. Hasler developed a trim-tab mechanism that went on to become the standard self-steering unit of its time.

Today we have electric auto-steer systems that can keep a yacht on a GPS course in gale or calm. The motor and brains are invisible within the boat and the cost is about the same as a wind vane. So why don't we have one? Because motors need electric power. Power means more batteries. More batteries mean solar panels or a generator. Also, I can't fix an autopilot with a corrupted circuit board. A wind vane needs only the wind, and if it breaks, open the tool box.

CHAPTER 7

Sometimes the big decisions in our lives aren't apparent until after we've made them. So it was that I found myself last year pulling off the San Diego Freeway for an unplanned rest stop near Oceanside, California. I needed to think for a moment just what I was doing. I was on my way to see Stellan Knoos, PhD, inventor of the Sailomat. I intended to check it out, but for some reason had also brought a checkbook. What was the plan? It occurred to me that this might not be just a 40-year private chat with myself anymore, because vane steering is a commitment to long-distance sailing that could be inconvenient and embarrassing to pull back from. When you talk to yourself like that it's a good bet nobody will answer.

I got out of the car and looked to the Pacific for a sign. The coastline was long and cold, with multiple lines of breakers under a steel-gray sky. It didn't know I existed. Half an hour later I was driving up a winding road to the Knoos residence, high above pearly La Jolla.

Stellan is a Stanford-trained aerospace engineer, originally from Sweden and still with a passable resemblance to Thor Heyerdahl. He didn't invent the servo-pendulum, but in my comparison of competing brands I concluded that over 40 years of design and manufacture he had improved and simplified it. In the European manner of not rushing into business, we chatted in soft chairs about our lives and our wives and the Sailomat until I couldn't stand it anymore.

"I'll take one," I said. Now I knew the answer to the question of why I was there.

Unfortunately, Stellan had only one Sailomat unit in his shop, which he showed me. It was being packaged into boxes for shipment to a sailor in Brazil. Other units were arriving from Sweden soon, he promised offhandedly. We chatted some more about boats, installations and the aerospace industry, during which I put my hand on the Sailomat to Brazil.

Utilizing a model mounted on the wall, Stellan demonstrated how a servo-pendulum works. Once a boat is on course, the counterbalanced plastic vane is set vertically in the wind, so its edge parts the air evenly and doesn't tilt to either side. Any subsequent change of course will alter the wind angle on the vane, and push it over. The movement of the light and sensitive vane is not nearly powerful enough to steer a boat. But it is sufficient to twist an oar hanging like a pendulum in the passing water. The trailing oar offers little resistance to the great potential force of the ocean rushing by. But once twisted in the flow, it deflects instantly, just as a hand would if turned palm up outside the window of a speeding car. It is that powerful hydrodynamic force, harnessed by lines and blocks to a yacht's steering wheel, which turns the rudder and therefore the boat. The corrections are continuous and smooth. A human brain finds it all difficult to visualize. The human eye, observing a vane in action, doesn't readily understand it either. But a wind vane doesn't have a brain. It doesn't require a computer and fluxgate compass like its electronic brother. Once set, it just does what's necessary and automatically corrects its mistakes. If a wind vane ran for President, I'd vote for it.

As Stellan explained the similarities of aerodynamics and hydrodynamics, I lifted the Sailomat out of its box and onto my lap.

"Sorry, but that one is going to Brazil."

"No, sir, this one is going to Hawai'i."

Mrs. Knoos arrived just then, with grocery bags and a wonderful smile. As her husband disappeared into the kitchen to lend a hand I scribbled a check, and when he came back thrust it into his hand. Stellan hesitated. But the Brazilian was far away and I was blocking his way out of the kitchen. With a nod, the deal was done.

On the ride home, loaded with parts and installation diagrams, everything seemed changed. I had perhaps not known myself why exactly, for the past year, I had been refitting *Thelonious* to a standard beyond the necessary for family weekends at Catalina Island. I had certainly not told anybody about sailing off to Kaua'i alone. I had hardly admitted it to myself, much less to anybody else.

When I got home I informed Tracy that I had bought a Sailomat self-steering gear. Marriage is like a clock. The cogs may be hidden, but one glance at the hands tells all.

"What took so long?" she said without looking up. "You've been talking about it constantly for months."

{PREPARATION}
Vane Installation

SELF-STEERING VANES ARE hard to compare, since yacht hull and steering characteristics can be very different. So after much consideration of theory I went with what I thought looked best on the stern: a Sailomat 800.

Stellan Knoos has been selling his patented take on the servo-pendulum vane for 40 years, with many incremental improvements. Unlike the Monitor and other competing vanes, the unit is anodized aluminum rather than stainless steel, which makes it relatively light—about 40 pounds, all up. Yes, you hear warnings (from the Monitor people) that stainless fasteners are incompatible with aluminum, implying that such a design will quickly start to smoke, then corrode in a flash and immediately fall off the boat. However, I looked at my mast and boom, composed of anodized aluminum and stainless fittings, and they are still there.

Installing the Sailomat is easy. The assembly attaches to the transom with a three-point bracket from which it can be removed for storage. Dr. Knoos has steadily reduced the size of the bracket over the years, because there is not really much force on it and the oar is free to deviate. The unobtrusive bracket can remain on the stern while the rest of the Sailomat goes home to the garage.

On the boat the unit has two positions at rest: One in which the sheer pin of the pendulum oar is removed and the oar folded neatly vertical; or the extended oar can be lifted sideways out of the water so the apparatus forms a "V," for motoring.

Like many sailboats, *Thelonious* has an off-center boarding ladder built into the stern rail. The Sailomat can be mounted up to 18 inches off centerline with little effect on performance. Even with the unit mounted pretty much on center, as mine is, the boarding ladder remains fully functional.

I used 5mm Spectra for the all-important steering lines, and expensive Harken turning blocks. Friction in the system degrades performance, so the arrangement of steering lines from stern to steering wheel is worth some thought. My rig comes pretty close to the recommended angles. Owners of the Ericson 32-3 will be charmed to hear that the bolts for the blocks on the port cockpit side happen to penetrate right where an important interior bulkhead is, and that installing them requires removing an interior shelf and headliner and groping blind at arm's length with washer, lock washer and nut held with the fingertips. I feel I now know what it is like to artificially inseminate a cow who is not in a sexy mood.

It was good to discover that the Sailomat drum on the wheel cohabitates happily with my existing Raymarine SPX-5/P70 wheel pilot mechanism. The Raymarine clamps do interfere with the new drum. However, it is a simple matter to trim an inch off each plastic clamp using a Dremel saw.

I've had the Sailomat out sailing twice so far, and it seems to work pretty well. Familiarity is important, and I'm not quite there yet. If there's any wind, it's a no-brainer. As the breeze fades away, so does the performance of all pendulum steering vanes. They rely on the boat moving through the water to provide the force to deflect the oar and amplify the signal from the vane. Therefore, no boat speed, no mechanical steering. That's where the light-duty Raymarine electric wheel pilot comes in handy.

For about the same money, of course, you can choose a motor-driven, energy-hungry electric autopilot—with nothing at all hanging off the stern to give away your offshore plans.

CHAPTER 8

THE BILGE

1 *400 HOURS. WIND N at 18, sky gray, speed 5-6 knots. Ate half cookie, not much appetite. Forecast wind 25 knots later today west of San Nicholas Island.*

It's clear even before my eyes are open from a nap that conditions have changed. The tell-tale compass next to the bunk shows the same course, 220 magnetic for Hawai'i. What's different is the motion. We're heeled more, and the rumbling course of seawater against the hull two inches from my ear is louder and more urgent. Spray runs in rivulets across the transparent hatch directly above. I'm still in safety harness, foul weather gear bib and high black sea boots. It's hard even to sit up when the bunk is heaving like this. Grab the overhead rails, that's what they're for. Time the roll, rise with it, don't fight it. We must learn to accept superior force.

Superior force was the natural law of the ancients. Every sailor reads Homer, because the "Iliad" begins with a cloud of black-hulled ships off to adventure, and the "Odyssey" is about the long journey home. Their tradition shrugged off an afterlife and demanded every citizen grow into his destiny or be cut down by fate. Gods and men lived to the full, usually at the expense of somebody else. But despite the invention of metaphysics and democracy, brilliant, argumentative Greece was extinguished by an excess of overweening pride. From the famous stand against the Persians at Thermopylae to the suicide pact of Athens and Sparta, only about 80 years passed. The Greeks ruled the world, and lost it.

I doubt any singlehander ever set out without a dangerous cargo of pride. Pride is what casts off the lines, and it's no good claiming we're here for anybody but ourselves. The Greek gods were like them, petty and unpredictable. If Hercules was your hero, you could be as bold as he was, or as crazy, and share the glory or the blame. Without personal gods, we can only blame ourselves. The Greeks had better company.

How's the bilge doing at the moment?

I was surprised to see so much water in it during the Coast Guard inspection, and now there's even more. Might be a clog in the intake screen, which happens.

Let's make some tea, coffee is still too strong for me. We can add a peel of lemon from the cargo hammock full of fruit. We have enough fruit aboard for a class picnic, all swinging in its cargo net. Fifty pounds of fruit and half a pound of fruit flies.

Well, I can't find the tea. Maybe we forgot it. The kettle on the swinging stove steams the cabin with warm fog. Let's try some hot water with sugar and lemon. I read about a yachtsman who landed in China during the revolution of Mao Tse Tung and was interrogated by Red Guards. They were all starving and had no tea, so everyone sipped hot water. He found it quite a luxury.

What do you think? I agree, it tastes like hot water with sugar in it and it's making me turn green and sweat. Let's get some air. Stand at the ladder and clip into the fitting in the cockpit. That way we're secured even before we come on deck. We'll always do it the same way, sunshine or storm. Pride goeth before a fall overboard, and I plan to stick around.

Looks like it's blowing about 18 knots now. There are lots of whitecaps and wind waves, and we're heeling over too much. A leeward rail submerged in the water looks good in a photograph, but it actually slows the boat down, creating sideslip and unnecessary drag from the rudder. We need to put a reef in, so slack the main sheet. As soon as the mainsail starts luffing you can feel the boat get back on its feet. Uncleat the halyard and let the mainsail drop half way. Now double the tether around a deck jackline and swing up onto the cabin house.

Ah, the air's cool and clean up here and the whitecaps are

waving hello! At the base of the mast grab the reef clew and secure it over the horn. Scamper like a monkey back to the cockpit and crank the halyard tight again. The mainsail has been flapping like laundry, but winching tight the reef line pulls it into triangle shape again. Amazing, isn't it? We've just created a smaller version of our mainsail, and 40 square feet of unneeded Dacron now hangs powerless beneath the boom. We can furl that or just let it hang. It no longer drives the boat.

Haul in the reefed mainsail until it regains its familiar curve. Good, we now have an easier motion and a happier boat. We're still going more than 6 knots close-hauled into three-foot seas, just as *Thelonious* was designed to do. The rightness of a well-trimmed boat is so contagious it immediately transfers to the crew renewed confidence and clarity of intention. No talk necessary.

I need to go below and get to the bottom of this bilge-water thing.

The electric pump is on again, that's good. Actually, I heard it whine going on and off the whole time I was asleep. But is it pumping? Hard to tell, because the bilge is sloshing around so much. The water seems to go down, then the intake sucks air, and in a moment the level begins to rise again. I doubt there's any more water in the boat than before. The larger waves we have now are just sloshing the same amount of water around, causing the pump to go on and off. That's all it is, probably.

I know the pump works because I installed it myself. It's brand new and we also have a spare. It is powered by a 12-volt nervous system of wires strung through inaccessible places from the central panel to the top of the mast. On an older boat the system corrodes and degrades. I knew that if we were ever going offshore to serious water the electrical system would have to be renewed. And if I were going alone, it should be me who did the work, with my own hands, in order to understand every part of it.

My master class began more than a year ago, and although I have worked on boats all my life, the tangle of hidden wires meant starting over again.

{PREPARATION}
Panel Wiring

A YACHT DISTRIBUTION PANEL that is a bad hair day from the 1980s is easy to ignore if the boat electronics sort of work. When I installed a new stereo system, I just crimped and crammed the new wires in. Then a few months later came a new GPS. Soon I was wiring in a new wheel auto-pilot, and noticing that my own stereo connectors were already falling apart. With all the new electronics, the lid to the main instrument panel now closed like the door of a Japanese subway at rush hour. With AIS to install, there was no choice but to dive in and deal with the 12-volt spaghetti behind the wall.

The original Ericson DC panel is screwed closed, and the face of it has to be pulled out and turned against the resistance of three heavy battery cables mounted on the back. A hinged door works better. Since the existing lid was robust enough to hold 15 circuit breakers and the battery selector switch, I just cut two 3/4 x 3/4 wood stiles and fixed one at either end. Some hardware-store brass hinges now allow the door to open 110 degrees for easy access.

Inside the DC panel were a hundred wires leading invisibly to two fully-charged Group 27 deep-cycle batteries. They say 12 volts won't kill you unless you really deserve it, but just putting my hand in there took an act of will. I had watched enough episodes of a British bomb-squad drama called "Danger UXB" to know that cutting mystery wires with your eyes closed can lead to a distant explosion that turns every head in the pub. Blimey, another new guy just blew himself up. So the first goal was to discover what every single unlabeled wire was, did, was supposed to do, or was disconnected from. And they were all unlabeled.

By day's end I had identified the wiring remains of Loran, the obsolete navigation system; a stone-age transducer; a frozen paddlewheel that once measured speed; ancient coaxial cables; a refrigerator I don't have; an engine compartment blower fan I don't use; a shower bilge pump that isn't there and no fewer than three previous tape decks. My guide was an original factory wiring diagram copied so many times that the schematics seemed printed in fudge.

Just understanding the purpose of every wire took me all over the boat from engine panel to engine harness and battery compartment, through bilges, under the zippers of the headliner, inside the mast, under the steering pedestal and through the river to grandma's little house in the bow pulpit where the running lights live.

Sure, the wiring is color-coded. But I soon discovered that a wire's color, and even its gauge, can change unaccountably at any hidden butt connector. How good are you at telling orange from red or gray from white by flashlight? Who hooked up the tiny NMEA wires from the GPS this stupid way? Oh, it was me. Why did the factory pigtail the dozen original black negative wires down to three? Apparently so they'd all fit on a really small bus bar.

Took forever, but it's not a bad idea to really understand your own boat. You're probably the first person since launch who ever did.

For the benefit of other amateur electricians, the wiring plan of a 12-volt system is simplified by attaching many wires to common points called bus bars and terminal blocks (which are also called connector strips). One side of each circuit breaker joins a positive bus bar. The other side of each breaker leads through its electrical device and completes the circuit at a negative bus bar. By definition, a bus bar connects to positive or negative, and therefore so does any wire attached to it. A terminal block isn't connected to anything—it's just a convenient meeting place for wires that need to stop for a rest, change direction, or pick up friends. My panel was spaghetti because it had no connector strips and my negative bus bar was small, overloaded and floating unsecured in the tangle.

By now I sort of had a plan, thanks to hours with Nigel Calder's "Boat Owners Mechanical and Electrical Manual" and much advice from the Ericson Yachts Forum. But before cutting the first wire I needed a whole bunch of specific electrical components and some decent tools. My rusty electrical kit was junk—and the reason the crimps of my stereo wire connectors were failing after only six months.

My favorite tool turned out to be a #909 Channelock-brand crimper with long handles for reach and good snippers at the end. The money for an Ancor "autostrip" was well spent. Screwdrivers loomed important. A new set of every size imaginable helped, and I think I used them all because many specialized screw heads, especially those accessed upside-down across an abyss in which if dropped they will be lost forever, will only stick on the tip of a driver that fits perfectly.

I chose BSP Clear Seal ring terminals and butt connectors in sizes 18-22, 14-16 and 10-12. Maybe it's overkill, but they crimp well and the integral heat shrink with glue fits right every time. I learned the hard way to make sure that the stud size of terminal blocks and bus bars matches that of the ring terminals. I bought 50 feet of expensive tinned #10 wire (too much) and #14 wire (not enough); 20-stud Blue Sea bus and terminal bars; six feet of one-inch loom;

a store of nylon wire hangers and small stainless screws for them; several new circuit breakers and various heat shrink tubing. I did run out of the small ring terminals, but that's all right. Side trips for unanticipated parts are inevitable, and wasted time makes the sun go down early.

There came a time when every wire was pulled and crudely identified, every surface below decks was covered in specialty tools and many irreplaceable tiny set-screws had disappeared into crevices of the bilge. Locking up as night fell, I just stared down the companionway ladder at what I had done, wondering if I would ever get this jack-in-the-box back in its box.

While others went sailing, I worked. There were shiny new bus bars and connector strips to mount, so I cut pieces of half-inch marine plywood, painted them white to increase visibility, and screwed them to a batten against the bare hull inside the panel. That made mounting gear and wire hangers easy.

Finally I had the confidence to plunge in and start cutting away the original tangle. I discovered corroded terminals and cleaned them up with sandpaper. I cut out all the pigtails so that each ground could connect individually to the new bus bar. I don't know if it was necessary but, like a fifth can of beer, it seemed right at the time. I did notice that when I stripped the original untinned copper wire, it was black from corrosion. I replaced much of it with expensive tinned wire. Soon I had a large box full of unnecessary or redundant wire left behind by previous installers.

Now it was just a matter of joining every negative lead to the new 20-post bus bar, heat-shrinking on a ring connector and connecting it up. I labeled each one so I'd know what it was if the time ever came again. I learned quickly that in the minimal space of the panel, tying other wires out of the way was the key to sanity and progress. When the negative bus was filled, I installed two big new connector strips nearby—room for future expansion.

The use of connector strips may be obvious, but makes all the difference. You lead the boat's wires to the strips, then run jumper extensions to circuit breakers labeled "steaming light," "bow light," "wheel pilot" and so on. The use of jumpers allows the panel door to open fully, so a future human being can work on it without a dental mirror and a hara-kiri dagger within reach.

An adjacent space became the Realm of Very Small Wires. I was adding a new Watchmate 850 dedicated AIS, and with it an antenna splitter that required independent power. Those two gizmos, like the GPS, Bluetooth stereo and DSC VHF radio, are little Rapunzels who let down hair-sized sub 22-gauge NMEA 0183 wires that seem more like fuzz. The Raymarine wheel pilot has its own miniature communications world of 2000NG. It's now a real fairyland in that compartment. Why, you expect to see Tinkerbell fly in, land on one of those impossibly delicate wires, and start chattering away in NMEA sentences.

Such small wires aren't designed for standard ring connectors. Some say to double the wire over to make it thicker. Some say solder. Some say buy a specialty D-sub crimp die.

One workaround is Clear Seal 18-22 gauge heat shrink connectors. For some reason the barrel of this brand is smaller than the same-size nylon connectors in my kit. If you use the "insulated" jaw of the crimper, which neatly flattens the barrel around the stripped wire-end, no dice— they fail the tug test. But crimping with the "non-insulated" jaw, which makes a dimple in the barrel, creates a sound connection. Of course the dimple usually punctures the heat shrink. But at least they won't come apart, and the glue in the shrink helps reinforce the mechanical bond. Not saying it's right, but it worked for me.

The finished job came out pretty well and solved the tangle problem. Now every wire is protected with the appropriate fuse or breaker. The main bilge pump is wired to be automatic, if the level rises it just turns itself on.

LEAKING

1 *600 HOURS. SEACOCK INSPECTION.*
The electric bilge pump not only works, it works all the time. There's only one explanation for that.

We have a leak.

The backup for the 1500 gallon-per-hour automatic pump is a manual diaphragm pump. It operates from the cockpit and moves even more water, faster. I replaced the diaphragm and hoses in case we ever needed it. And now here we are, bent over and pumping. I can feel the weight of the water lifting through the hose. It takes 20 strokes before the hose sucks air and the bilge is empty. That will give the automatic pump a rest.

We should not be leaking. Leaking boats sink.

Let's get the floorboards up and see what's going on under there. Each of the four bilge compartments is covered by a teak panel secured by 12 screws. One panel also mounts the heavy cabin table on its aluminum pedestal. One is under the diesel engine, covered by a large removable case. We need to get them all off at once, which presents the problem of where to put them in the confines of the ever-moving saloon.

In half an hour each cover is off and the belly of the boat is open to the world, revealing its own shallow sea of lapping waves. The first thing to do is have a taste. It's salt water, all right, so we can eliminate leaking fresh water tanks. Check the AIS display. No ships. *Thelonious* sails on, steered automatically by the wind vane while we contemplate our interior ocean.

CHAPTER 9

The potential sources of a leak in a boat are seacocks, packing glands, keel bolts or a pierced hull.

I think we'd know if we had hit something and cracked the boat open. Hulls can fail if a construction or design flaw is revealed by the unremitting flexing of a yacht at sea. But a hole below the waterline can fill a boat pretty fast and tends to mean life jackets and distress signals. We aren't in life jackets yet, we're merely eliminating sources of unexpected water entry. Put it like that and it sounds pretty routine, wouldn't you say? Anyhow, I have rehearsed abandoning ship and we're prepared for it, in case you're wondering.

Where were we? Oh yes, seacocks. Every boat requires openings in the hull, and the valve that shuts them is a seacock. We have five. One to provide cooling water for the engine. One to drain the galley sink and the icebox. One for the exit of bilge water from the electric pump. One for the manual diaphragm pump. And one for the engine exhaust. Seacocks stick up inside the boat and can be opened or closed with a lever. A broken-off seacock admits a geyser of water that can sink a boat in hours. Against that possibility each has a tapered wooden plug taped to it. With a hammer we could drive the plug into opening and staunch the flow.

The seacocks under the galley sink look all right. Do you see how well our crank flashlight illuminates them? This modern device eliminates the problem of dead batteries. Just crank the handle and light comes out the end. Amazing. Tradition has its place, but I say bring on the new ideas.

The other seacocks are accessed through the helmsman's seat in the cockpit. We'll just put our torso into this opening and hang upside-down until we've monitored them for a good while. We're looking for a tell-tale trickle, any shine of wet. Only one arm and shoulder fit through the hatch, so it's in and out for 15 minutes, cranking the new flashlight each time. They look normal, too. Good.

The packing glands are accessed through the narrow end of the quarter-berth in the cabin. At the moment it's filled with 200 feet of nylon line, a heavy Danforth anchor, nautical charts, fishing gear, fenders and 200 pounds of food in large plastic containers. All of it has to come out before we can go in. It won't do to simply load the contents onto the saloon bunks, for the motion of the boat allows nothing to rest unsecured. It takes half an hour to unpack, and then we can crawl in headfirst and have a look.

Both the propeller shaft and the rudder tube pierce the hull, but must be free to turn. The solution is a fitting packed with greased flax, which when tightened around the shaft remains watertight even when the shaft is spinning. Our shaft uses a new, dripless design, in which surface plates rotate against each other to make the seal.

So, headfirst into the quarter-berth. Get one arm ahead and one behind. In the darkness the reflection of the flashlight fools the eye. The rudder gland seems wet, but when you touch it with a hand it's not, we're only seeing the shiny resin of the surface. Flashlight went out. Well, it's crankable. Just withdraw from the bunk two feet, roll upright, free both hands and crank it again. Good for a whole minute after that.

The propeller shaft also appears normal. In fact, the entire stern of the boat is dry and cool, although oddly submarine-like under the echoes of water passing over and under. Our position is laid out in the dark like King Tut in his coffin, if his coffin were being rolled down the side of the pyramid. And if his flashlight kept turning off every minute so he had to back out of the coffin, crank it again, and then crawl back in. And if the boy king were subject to nausea. Let's get the hell out of here, backwards, fast.

Whose ridiculous idea was a crankable flashlight that requires two hands to make light? Oh, mine.

Now, for an hour, I stare at the keel bolts visible under the rising bilge water. I can see four of them, torqued on to heavy half-inch stainless threaded rods which pass through the lowest part of the boat and into the lead of the 4,000-pound keel. The keel on a sailboat is what keeps it up. It's why Weebles wobble but don't fall down, and neither do we. Without a keel, a sailboat with its tall mast and sails would simply lie on its side in the water. It is possible, over time, for the keel bolts of an older yacht to loosen. Some owners have their keels removed, just so a boatyard can confirm the condition of the bolts. Stainless steel bolts are very strong, and under normal conditions impervious to rust and decay.

However, in a constant bath of salt water, galvanic corrosion can erode their protective shield of chromium oxide. Dropping a boat's keel, as it's called, is an expensive procedure usually commissioned by worrywarts. Can't worry about everything, I always say. Let's get on with it and not overthink things, like we did with this ridiculous crank flashlight.

The last time *Thelonious* was hauled out on land I did notice a gap between her keel and hull. I suppose some might say that would be the first sign of keel bolts coming loose. I asked the fellow who was painting the bottom about the gap, and he just said, in Spanish, what would you like to do? I asked his advice. Well, *señor*, he replied, most times the owners just tell me to fill the gap in. After all, you're not sailing across the Pacific in this old thing.

And at the time, I wasn't. So the gap was faired with something or other, and I stopped thinking about it. Besides, from inside a boat nobody can see the keel joint, since it's under water. But now it's easy to see in the imagination. And there it's dangling by a thread.

After an hour on hands and knees I simply can't tell if the bolts are leaking. The bilge swirls and slops, leaving no high-water mark. It does seems like the leak has slowed. But in 10 minutes the electric pump whines again, sucks, turns off, whines again. The sound is like fingernails on a blackboard. The gear-strewn cabin is an unnatural mess. There's nothing to do but put everything back together, and that takes until the sun is low in the sky and the wind is up to 20 knots and what were once pretty whitecaps now explode across the boat so that we seem to be sailing through a tube of rose-colored spray toward a glowering sunset, quite a cinematic view for dull senses, and if an omen, not an omen I have ever seen before.

Day 2, 2030 hours. Wind 25 and howling. Second reef in main and 50 percent genoa. Seas building. Should eat something.

Half a cookie and some water. It's hard just to hold up my Landmark Edition of Thucydides, the great historian of the war between Athens and Sparta. This edition has maps, which are absolutely necessary to follow the events of the Fifth Century, BC, when nearly every place name is different from those used today.

But under these conditions the thick book is as unwieldy as a box of rocks. I'm studying a photo of a replica trireme from the time of Pericles, a long, light warship propelled by three banks of oarsmen. They could be sailed, but for engagements the oarsmen took over. The idea was to maneuver or trick the enemy fleet into a disadvantageous position, then ram them with the submerged bronze spear fixed to the bow. Triremes were around for hundreds of years, but they weren't really seaworthy. Hundreds were lost when the wind blew hard. They were built for glory. Few of the crews could swim. Triremes didn't always sink, they often just lay broken and defeated, like a sailboat without a keel.

The crews did sink, weighed down by armor and, in the case of the aristocrats who commissioned them, a fatal burden of excessive pride. Well, that's not us. We're more humble by the moment.

Pitch dark on deck. It's weird to sail like this, with no lookout. Oh, I frequently scan the horizon for lights. But the whole project relies on what is, in effect, sailing with your eyes shut. Near land, I wouldn't think of going five minutes without a look-see. Here, whenever we're below decks, the horizon goes on without us.

Let's test the leeward bunk. Pretty comfortable.

Listen to the water rushing by, the wind in the rigging, the whining of the bilge pump. It hums for a while, sucks air, stops, and in a moment begins again. It's hard not to think of hitting something as we career along at six knots. I suppose if a ship runs us down there would be a loud sound of splitting fiberglass, followed by water. OK, grab the emergency locator beacon, hack the dinghy free of its lashings, clip on the lanyard of the go-bag and get into the dink as *Thelonious* sinks underfoot.

In the case of collision with a log or piling, the impact would probably be more localized. Loose pilings tend to float vertically, plunging and rising. A telephone pole erupting through the floorboards would certainly wake me up. Find the hole, stuff something in it, start pumping. Been over all this a hundred times.

The most probable thing for a yacht to hit offshore is an Intermodal Shipping Container. They fall off the decks of containerships and float mostly submerged. An ISC is a truck body that can stack on a freighter's deck and become a wheeled truck again at its destination. There are hardly any crane-loaded freighters left on the high seas. Containers were a revolution that preserved cargo from rough handling, water damage and the dockside pilferage that was once a cost of doing business. A typical one is 40 feet long and made of corrugated Corten steel. It would be like running onto an iron reef. Our forestay might break and the mast come down. Our bow might open and sinking be swift. Or we could glance off, with time enough to find the damage and shore it up with the plywood sheets and drywall screws I stowed for just such a diverting occasion.

Sleep while you can, they say. No moon tonight, just this gray cloud that makes sea and sky the same. No need to rehearse for disasters that are, as I have so often explained, statistically unlikely.

Have you heard the joke? They say that if you're concerned about the yacht running into something in the night, always sleep with feet facing forward.

0000 hours, midnight. Increase anti-siphon loop in bilge pump hose.

A few hours of rest always brings an idea: Maybe the bilge pump hose is siphoning sea water back into the boat. It has a loop to prevent that by creating an air gap. Better check the loop.

So here I am head-down in a cockpit locker, looking at the loop in the hose. There's enough slack that I can make the loop higher, if I haul it up with a piece of light line. It's good to have something to do at midnight, flying through the darkness with white wave crests leaping on either side. There, done. See if that helps.

And instead of reefing, I'll just take the mainsail down altogether. We'll do fine till morning just under the jib. Why won't the sail come down? Because I'm standing on the halyard. Now it's fouled on a cleat, so go back to the cockpit and free it. I forgot to tighten the topping lift first, so now the boom is too low over the cockpit. Go back onto the cabin house and fix that.

Have I ever done any of this before? I'm certainly making a mess of it. And now that the mainsail is down and snapping like a wild creature out of its cage, I have forgotten the gasket ties to secure it down. I took them off so nonchalantly while setting sail like a hero yesterday afternoon. But that was long ago, a million years ago, when I lived on land.

So I bind the mainsail to the boom with heavy dock lines. It works but looks awful, amateurish, clumsy. Rig a preventer line to keep the boom from slamming around. Quit fouling the safety tether. Be aware of where the tether is, don't let it get hooked under a leg. Didn't we practice this?

To reduce the size of the big genoa jib, furl it around the forestay. That's better. By the compass, its red-lit lens blurry through wet reading glasses, we are holding course 220, as planned. Still on a close reach, still on course for Hawai'i.

I'll relax below by hanging from the ceiling by one hand in full foul weather kit, sea boots and all. That way, I can go on deck without further preparation. The violent motion of the boat on this course is quite normal, although the sheets of spray over the bow seem loud. The sensation is of being weightless one moment and 50 pounds heavier the next. But we're dry here below and on course. There are no other crew members to worry about and maybe the leak is solved.

Only an arm's length away is the cabinet with the Hennessy brandy bottle. The stove-top, being gimbaled, swings with the seas to provide the only continuously level surface on the boat. Place a cup there. Time the swing of the stove and pour. The heat of the Hennessy warms everything, and, hanging like a monkey as I am, a banana seems appropriate. There are three in the cargo net of vegetables swinging from the starboard bulkhead.

As we reach for it, the boat falls off a crest onto its side and the cargo net explodes. Potatoes, oranges, apples, bread, linguini, onions, mushrooms and carrots spray across the saloon, bouncing and rebounding. It's like a grenade went off, turning the tidy cabin to chaos. I can't catch the oranges, they roll like tennis balls. The onions shed their dry skins. I knee a banana, squashing mush on the slippery floorboards. As I scramble on hands and knees my foot jams the stove gimbals and the brandy cup on top launches like a missile to shower the cabin with sticky droplets. Never jam the gimbals. Didn't we practice that?

0510 hours. No ships.

We proceed on course. I'm tired of standing and holding on and looking out the hatchway every 15 minutes. There're no ships on the AIS. Obviously nobody out here this wild night but us. The fact sinks in slowly but convincingly. Yes, we might hit something, but you couldn't see it coming anyway. Alertness of mind and the habits of a lifetime yield to the immediacy of circumstance. The risk of collision grows smaller. Is that possible, logically? It is if risk is computation. If phenomena are probabilities. If, as the emotions dull, risk assessment is automatically recalculated. It's not so much a letting go as it is getting a better grip on the moment. The moment is all there is.

Let's rest in the leeward bunk, among the papery skins of lost onions, as false dawn lights the ports. That's not a drip of water from the ceiling, its brandy. Wipe it, taste it.

Dozing, I hear the sound of a motorcycle banking through distant hills. It's a sound from the canyons of Malibu near my bed at home, familiar and oddly comforting. I reach out my arm for a companion but there's no one else in this bunk but a lost orange. The boat speeds on and I labor to keep up, as if with any relaxation of mind I might be left behind in the middle of nowhere.

SEARCHING

D AY 3, O730 HOURS. *Wind 15, seas moderate, speed 5. Leak continues.*

Ah, dawn. Good, we got two hours uninterrupted sleep. So why does the clock show 07:30? Holy cow, overslept again. No lookout for five and a half hours this time. Stumble to the companionway, blinking and bracing for impact. Expect the bow of a ship like a five-story building foaming at the mouth and…nothing but empty sea and sky. On course and the wind is down.

Oh. Yawn.

The sound of the distant motorcycle in the dream persists. It's not a motorcycle but the electric bilge pump running continuously. Under the inspection hatch the bilge is full, sloshing. The floorboards are wet. My socks are wet. We're still leaking.

Twenty strokes on the manual pump and the hose sucks air. About five buckets-full, probably, although it's hard to tell. I'm panting, because moving the lever is work. Got to relax, pump slower, don't rush everything. Thinking is grainy, uncertain. Think. But about what?

Breakfast. Ordinarily something to look forward to, but now a necessity. My stomach is empty but uninterested. Put something in there, why don't we. Coffee and eggs.

The stove moves on its gimbals, keeping the kettle level. The boiled water drips through the paper filter into the cup. The coffee tastes harsh. I fry eggs in olive oil and eat them out of the pan, standing up. Outside the galley portlight the ocean goes by, hazy through the salt-encrusted glass. The heat of the stove feels good. The eggs feel like cement. Forget these clumsy sea boots and wet socks, damp deck shoes are better.

We must be leaking somewhere at the bow. So, harness on. Shorts instead of foulies, better to be wet than constricted. I need to quit doing things by the book, we're sailing to Hawai'i, not Murmansk. And relax a little. Everything's fine, we're just slowly sinking 200 miles offshore and I don't know why.

The bow of a sailboat is the pointy end, and to get there we take careful steps up the deck, secured by the tether as it slides along the jackline; then a scramble along the hand-holds of the cabin house; and after a rest at the security of the mast, a half-crawl along the upside-down dinghy on the foredeck.

Lock an arm around the jib luff, wedge into the bow and feel us rise and fall with the seas. No dolphins up here today, but this is where they play. Ahead, an unmarked horizon. Behind us, *Thelonious* seems enormous. She heels and slides over the waves, her wake straight, the red and white of the United States Yacht Ensign standing out smartly from the leech of the mainsail.

The bow splits the ocean in two, giving birth to new waves on either side that rush away to high-five the wind waves that meet them. Everything here always feel right. The bow mocks analysis or concern as if to say, I know how to do this better than you do, I've done it since I carried the Phoenician alphabet to the world.

Right, but the Phoenicians are all dead, so let's get back to it.

We need to tear into the anchor locker under my feet. It's covered by the dinghy, so I need to move that first. I built this little pram two years ago, and modified it to fit the bow. The crown of her transom curves to match the crown of the deck. She's lashed down neat as a pin, but easy to cut free.

Wrestle the dinghy aft two feet. Unlock and open the deep chain locker. The heavy plow anchor will have to come out on deck. Wait for the bow to rise and fall, and as it falls, lift! Now haul up 50 feet of chain, followed by 300 feet of Nylon line, belaying it along the lifelines. There are no seas breaking aboard so maybe it will just lie there. The chain locker is only three feet deep, but I have to go in head first. Wait for the right moment, between rollers.

The locker isn't designed to be waterproof, because anchors and line are wet as they come aboard and must drain. The drain is a hole at the bottom where a rubber tube descends to pierce the hull. Maybe that's the leak. No, it looks OK. Inspection ports give access to the backing plates of deck fittings, and everything in there looks dry and normal. We didn't strike anything, the bow remains strong and unmarked. But I need to stay here a good while, observing, waiting for a telltale spurt of water from a hidden source. We need to check the anchor locker off the list of possible leaks.

After five minutes hanging upsidedown a leak does spring up—inside me. It's the coffee. But I can't leave the bow as it is, piled with unsecured line and chain. Oh yes I can! Fly now along the deck, the tether dragging behind, to drop through the companionway, unhook, and skid over the wet cabin floor and into the tiny compartment of the head, just in time.

This is humiliating. The pot is a rodeo bull trying to toss me off despite feet jammed against the doorway and hands braced against the walls. Get a grip on yourself, cowboy. But there's nothing to grab. I need a strap to hold on to. A toilet harness. In all the preparations for this voyage I never stopped to think of installing that. Good thing no one's watching.

But if I turn my head, there is. A face appears in the mirror a foot away, close and familiar. It seems irritated to have someone looking at it, so I avert my eyes to protect my own privacy.

Toilet paper clogs marine heads, even fast-dissolving paper designed for such use, so instead of flushing I just toss it out the handy porthole above my head. Wait till the wind eddy is right and each little personal flag of convenience will flap away over the lifelines like a butterfly. But wait till the eddy is right.

To evacuate the bowl, run fresh water into the vanity sink. Turn the blue lever and pump until the bowl is clear. This flushes the bowl with fresh water and expels the waste into the sea. Near shore, we'd pump into a 14-gallon holding tank to be disposed of later, at a treatment plant. That's unnecessary out here, and besides, if the tank got filled I'd have no way to pump it out.

Feeling a little better? Now get back to the bow and re-stow the anchor and the chain.

To check for bow leaks from the inside, we'll have to unload everything from the V-berth forward. After wrestling with plywood, 2x4s, spare sails, lines, life jackets, clothes and cookies, there are no leaks there, either. Elapsed time to inspect and re-stow the V-berth: two hours. Leaks found: none.

It wasn't like this on the Titanic, they knew why they were sinking. We are sinking less, but confused more.

Day 3, Noon Position 31°39'N, 121°16'W. Speed 5+, Wind 20-25, seas moderate. Sent email, got GRIB.

Each day at noon we have a promise to keep: a daily email by satellite phone, with an attached file that gives our location on Google Earth. A computer program called UUPlus compresses our messages to preserve limited sat phone time. GPS, a free gift to the world by the taxpayers of the United States that everyone takes for granted, gives our position at a glance, without a sextant sight or laborious calculation. Yet I find the ritual of the daily position report more and more to resemble that of a primitive religious sect. I assume a kneeling position and tremble. I can fix a toilet but not a satellite phone, so when the ship's clock approaches email time it brings a fear I can't dismiss:

If the transmission doesn't go through, They Will Worry.

First step, open the laptop. Attach the portable GPS. Take the satphone out of its waterproof pouch, unspool the 10-foot USB cable, and power everything up. Place the handset in the cockpit, its antenna pointed at the southern sky. Enter a brief message on the laptop keyboard. Typing is difficult because of the lurching and rolling of the yacht, so, to simplify things, this message will be "All is well", rather than the needlessly informative "slowly sinking from unidentified leak but not abandoning ship at this time."

The satphone in the cockpit begins searching the sky for satellites. I kneel, holding the base so it won't tip over, until with a ping! connection is made. I do truly and with all my heart believe in satellites. Actually, everybody does, it's not really a metaphysical issue. But bent over the plastic handset, aiming its antenna at the featureless stratus cloud overhead, I have never felt more a supplicant. I am willing away all past sins. I am promising better behavior in the future. Below decks, where I can't see it, the screen of the laptop begins a liturgy in the ancient form of call and response:

Waiting for remote.
Yes, satphone, we are humbly waiting.
Sending synch.
Yes, humbly, oh satphone.
Connected.
Yes!
Disconnected.
What?
Retrying.
Modem command timeout.
DCD low, resetting timer.
Error, not enough fields.
Sequence NAK, resending.
Send, wait.
Sequence missing.
Modem not responding.
Call Fail login error.
Ping: trying alternate.
Ping: Off line no carrier, idle mode, resetting.
Timed out.
Timed out: the final judgement we wait all our lives to hear.

The trouble is that I have no idea what the scrolling messages signify or why they occur, so there's nothing to do but try again with a purer heart and a steadier hand on the antenna. As a boy I took a bar of soap left in the latrine at Camp Wawayanda and when its owner asked, denied it. In Presbyterian prayer camp I watched a counselor undress in her dormitory window when I should've turned away. I told my little brother to cross thin ice just so he would fall through and I could rescue him. And as an adult, I have eaten carbohydrates and lied about it.

Today, on the third prayer, the satellite answers and the joyful message scrolls:

Connected

Sending all files

No More Work

Zeus and the other gods have names, and so do the stars. I have put my trust in three celestial Inmarsat globes 22,000 miles above the equator, and I don't even know who they are.

But the message is sent, and at home a new breadcrumb appears on our nascent trail of crumbs across the Google Earth Pacific Ocean. At home they will know where we are, and not worry.

In the same transmission I ordered a wind prediction file known as a "GRIB", for GRIdded Binary concise data format. It shows our sector of ocean covered in barbs representing wind direction and speed. The GRIB predicts continuing 20-25 knots from the north for the next few days. That will keep us on a beam reach, heeled and wet. The west-flowing trade winds are at least 500 miles ahead. When we get there the breeze will move aft, sleeping will be easy, the sun will come out, the flying fish will appear and the leak will stop.

I should have learned the names of the satellite gods.

Day 3, 2330 hours. Seas up, two reefs and half a jib. Hard to sleep. Bilge is overflowing.

Pitch dark outside and I have the running lights off so the white stern light doesn't reflect off the steering vane and blind me. I've stopped looking for ships every hour anyhow, there aren't any and AIS can have the job. Running lights? What ship would even notice us, the dimmest bulb on the ocean? I don't need lights to tell me I'm here, and we can't run into ourselves.

Even wedged into the leeward bunk sleep is impossible because the boat keeps falling off the sides of waves. I'm a princess in a blanket tossed by drunken Vikings. There's a runaway lemon in the V-berth and a pencil rolling on the cabin sole. I'm not getting up for that. The new LED reading lamp works well, but the violent pitching motion fore and aft slams Xenophon into my nose every few minutes. Xenophon is a paperback book about a Greek aristocrat who got permission from the Oracle at Delphi to go off adventuring in Persia. Things are not turning out exactly as Xenophon expected, but he isn't complaining so neither can I.

The ride is like a car driving full speed down a washed-out dirt road. We leap and bound, skid and bottom out, weightless half the time and pulling G's the rest.

All right, all right, I'll go on deck for a horizon check. But I'm telling you right now, there's nothing there.

CHAPTER 11

FOURTH OF JULY

D*AY 4, 0630 HOURS. Leaking. Sore. Low clouds. Lumpy sea.* After a night of listening to the bilge pump whine continuously I'm about out of ideas.

Took up all the floorboards again. The pump is not clogged. If I turn it upside down it stops, just as it should when the float is inverted. Closed all the floorboards up again, 48 screws.

In early morning the wind is generally at its least noisy and the seas most at ease. I need to eat something, so the coffee is on and Spam is frying in the pan and I'll dig out the butter. The best boat butter comes in a tub. It gets soft without refrigeration, and the tub keeps it from running down your arms.

Did you know that butter was invented to preserve milk? It lasts a long time unrefrigerated, weeks and weeks. Eggs do, too. Three weeks is about what you can expect from them in warm weather. Some cruisers coat each egg in wax, or Vaseline, to keep them going even longer. There's no ambiguity. Rancid butter informs you directly. The hydrogen sulfide smell of a rotten egg is honorably forthright. An egg just short of that falls apart in the frying pan, for early warning.

Breakfast is eggs, spam, toast, coffee.

Let's throw it overboard.

In the cockpit is a plastic bag placed in anticipation of today, Independence Day, the Fourth of July. A present. I don't know what's in it yet, but I do know that in my home village today there is a 5K run scheduled for 8 a.m., which would be over now. I wonder how the family did. They'll be at the brunch afterwards, catching up with our friends. At 2 o'clock skydivers will descend to Sunset Boulevard trailing an American flag to open a parade of bands, floats, elected officials, dogs and kids. By afternoon the marine layer will burn off and the sun will be out. It's odd to have such a red, white and blue picture in the mind's eye, yet look over a featureless gray sky and sea.

The bag contains poppers. Each is about the size of a dime, with a string at either end. No instructions. The hull hits a wave and a fine mist of spray passes overhead. Probably what's required is to grasp both strings, and pull. The small objects recall those who packed them. Faces swim up in memory for the first time since departure. No, not faces exactly, more like spaces where faces should be, or turning to find no one there. This must be what it's like to be alone.

Yank the strings.

The first popper falls apart. Try another, same thing. Down below the bilge pump is running continuously. I'm trying too hard. Don't pull like it's the pin of a hand grenade or the stuck chain in a roadhouse toilet. Easy now, happy Fourth of July.

A blob of damp confetti falls to the deck. Pop, pop, pop, more multi-color curlicues listlessly drooping.

Let's do the breakfast dishes.

Day 4, Noon Position 30°32'N, 123°31'W. Course 226°m. Speed 5. Wind down, first sunshine. Happy Fourth of July.

The chart shows that we made 120 miles since noon yesterday. In a car, that would be a few hours in a seat belt. In a commercial airliner at Mach .85, about 12 minutes. Bicyclists pedaling cross-country make 120 miles a day on the flats. Julius Caesar's legions could march it in three days, which was so fast a pace they often attacked before warnings arrived.

One hundred twenty miles a day on a small sailboat is a thing in itself. It is so accompanied by pride and a sense of achievement as to nearly qualify as an emotion. Moment by moment on a boat the crew is occupied by eating, sleeping, trimming sails, maintaining gear or just wondering what will break next. The waves pass, night comes, dawn arrives in a continuum. At home, there is constant punctuation: Kids going to school, schedules to be kept, phones ringing, bills waiting to be paid. We're always behind, or late, or early. We leave the house, navigate the day and return to our bed. Progress depends on us. Any moment of repose sends the world on without you.

At home we must move, but here the yacht moves us.

Waking and sleeping, regardless of mood and independent of intention, the boat carries on. To sail at five knots in a direction you want to go, no matter how tired or uncertain, is to be in the continuous presence of progress. Nothing more needs to be done. We are Newton's billiard ball, in motion until some other force stops us. What happened yesterday, whatever tomorrow brings, we are making good today. At home we hammer the universe into the shape of intention. Here, at five knots, if you take no action at all, progress still comes.

On the chart of the North Pacific that shows both California and the Hawaiian Islands, 120 miles is less than an inch. But it's an inch gained only by wind, free of cost and by cooperation rather than demand. Every sailor feels the accomplishment. Some days, in light air, we might make only 20 miles. Even so, that's something. Maybe progress really is an emotion. How often do I feel it at home—this sense of continuous movement in the right direction toward a goal?

Here, always.

That bright spot in the clouds above is the sun, a dim sphere keeping company. When it winks through, shadows appear on deck and a flood of warmth. We're getting somewhere, leak and all.

1800 hours. Bouncy ride. Still no Ships. Appetite better.

Let's find that frozen container in the icebox, it must be thawed by now. In fact, I'll stow away the insulated lid, nothing will ever be cold again and the food vault next to the sink is the best place to stick anything we don't want to roll around.

Ah, Tracy's homemade sausage pasta. I couldn't have looked at it two days ago, but now it generates its own light. Dump carefully into a pot, heat and stir. There's some parmesan cheese here someplace, I forget where I put it. And a bottle of wine, that's the ticket. Pull the cork and decant into a plastic cup. Never mind fancy, just try to hit the cup. How about holding the cup on the gimbaled stove. Wait for a break in the motion, and pour. Well, most of it hit the target.

I choose to dine this evening at table, gentleman-like. The tabletop has a square of non-stick carpet underlayment on it to keep things from sliding around. My own idea, if I dare say so. An inexpensive solution to the problem of fixed surfaces that are seldom horizontal for more than an instant.

While the pasta warms, some jazz. There are 10 gigabytes of it on an iPhone hard-wired to the stereo. The tune is "Monk's Dream," by that very Thelonious after whom the boat is named. I first heard it at age 18, and thought, man, what is he doing to those chords? They're busted up and stretched funny, with 11ths where you expect to hear 5ths. His left hand is comping a stride rhythm that staggers and lurches with such confidence that it's like understanding a language you don't know how to speak. Thelonious Monk was a big black man nobody understood, whose weird changes at first made other jazzmen laugh, and who made the cover of Time Magazine in 1964 only to fall into limbo soon thereafter. I wonder what he would think to have a sailboat named after him, and to be playing this night 400 miles offshore as the sun sets, toasted with a plastic cup.

It's good to be hungry again. Feels like the first time.

In a seaway you don't just sit down to eat as you might at an outdoor café. It takes planning, and, if you'll permit me, technique. The first challenge is the service of the main course from the swinging stovetop, and the coordination of the beverage. Everything should be ready for the critical move to the table, which I have already set with napkin, fork, and book.

I prepare by refilling the wine cup on its corner of the stovetop. Move the pasta pot into the sink, out of the way. Place one of our new unbreakable plates, with attractive sea-shell pattern, on the swinging stove-top. Now, braced against the roll, smoothly transfer from pot to plate a heaping pile of sausage and spaghetti with pleasing admixture of yellow peppers. Dump on it a snow-peak of parmesan cheese. Follow with a sprinkle of hot pepper flakes.

The masterpiece swings on the gimbals like a picture out of a glossy magazine. Fragrant steam mists the galley portlights. Monk goes in and out of the weeds with Charlie Rouse chasing him on tenor sax, and the unexpected tempo matches that of the waves. I resist a famished impulse to eat standing up like a pig on hind legs. No, we shall move to the table.

Wine in one hand, plate in the other, I glide two steps across the saloon and safely into the banquette. With the wine secured by one hand and the plate secured by the other, there is no hand left to raise a fork. But I manage it. As we roll right and left I dine like a pendulum. A forkful in. A sip from the cup. A moment to marvel at the glory of taste, warmth, Monk and consciousness itself, until suddenly the plate is as clean as if wiped by a towel.

It's still pinned to the table by my left hand and the wine-cup is steady in my right. Only the meal has departed, launched by the last sharp roll from its bed of olive oil like a pasta missile to burst onto the floorboards in a scatter of sausage chunks, red grease and colorful peppers. As I reach to save what I can, the plate and fork follow, clattering. Bilge water rises to join the debris I am now chasing like a dog on my hands and knees, grabbing and gulping.

Olive oil and tomatoes are hard to clean off a varnished floor, and I don't do a very good job. I can almost laugh, but not quite. I almost got enough to eat, but not quite. I almost spilled the wine, too, but not quite, and now I sit on the floor with the bottle in my lap. Excellent pasta, all things considered. I can just sit here and think about leaks.

There shouldn't be any on a fiberglass boat. I thought I had found and stopped them all, even the most mystifying.

{PREPARATION}
Rudder Gland

BILGE WATER CAN BE a riddle wrapped in an enigma that stands you right up out of bed at 3 a.m., wondering what it might mean. Where is it coming from? Can the automatic pump keep up? Most owners don't live on their boats, so if she sinks in her slip you wouldn't know it till Sunday, when the dockmaster telephones with the news.

In my case the mystery was a rudder packing gland that kept sneakily filling *Thelonious'* bilge with ocean while defying my attempts to locate the source. The thing is, the gland is usually above the waterline on boats with spade rudders. So, floating at the dock it doesn't leak a drop. But when under way the boat squats down, the quarter wave rises and the rudder tube fills. Water pours in unobserved and presents itself as a mysterious leak when you come aboard a week later.

When I finally observed the gland while motoring under full power it was spewing a quart an hour. In fact, the entire bronze fitting rotated with the rudder post and I could lift it right off with a finger. The factory sealant had entirely lost its grip and its seal.

Repacking a gland should not be a big deal. However, on my boat the radial disk sits right on top of it and therefore must first be removed. Since the lower flange also needed to be re-seated, a haul-out and rudder drop was recommended. But the job can be done in the water, although it is truly a pain in the butt, rib cage, shoulders, knuckles and neck. However, in performing this penance I discovered Secret Knowledge that may reward you with the pleasure of not having to do any of it, and in fact of stopping a leaky gland in one hour flat. This potential salvation resides in a patent issued in January of 1929 to an inventor named Oscar U. Zerk. What a name to wear through the schoolyard, eh? Always one little letter away from humiliation. But he's a hero to me now.

Getting the radial disk (the "quadrant") out of the way takes patience. First loosen and pull off the steering cables. The disk is two aluminum castings held together by four stainless machine screws. Soak them in penetrating oil, use an impact hammer if it fits or tap-tap-tap on a spanner if not. The long stainless bolt piercing casting and rudder post also comes out. The disk will fall into two parts. Actually, I just loosened the bolts and gently pounded the disk up the post using a hammer. Do note the position of the through-bolt hole, as alignment must be eventually regained. This work is done stretched out in the after berth. But you can't reach everything from there, so it is also necessary to enter the steering compartment from the cockpit.

That seems impossible, and it is, until you perfect the entry technique. First, disconnect the base of the water heater so it can move sideways a foot or so. Now lower yourself into the starboard cockpit lazarette while facing the binnacle. Leave a note in case they don't find you for a week. Squeeze your feet past the water hoses. Lower yourself onto your left hip. Your head does not clear the back of the cockpit panel gauges? Keep trying, you claustrophobic weenie. You have to work your rear end between the exhaust system and the water tank. Then, after falling helplessly the last foot onto your nose, you arrive within easy arm's reach of the other side of the gland. I am 6'1", 195 pounds, and was born the day the Allies invaded Sicily. You can do it. What's that? You forgot to bring tools?

Now the easy part—repacking the gland. This fitting has room inside for three courses of Teflon flax, which I greased liberally. Time for a test.

The engine, with its upgraded wiring, started instantly. I backed out of the slip and proceeded to open water, anxious to open the throttle and observe the renewed gland in all its watertight glory. It was 5 p.m. and the light was beginning to fade. I had grease to the elbows and my hair stood on end, the result of resting my head on a convenient pillow that turned out to be the open grease pot. I crumpled up and threw away the piece of paper that said, "If you find this note look for my body under the starboard lazarette. DNR."

At six knots the stern squatted down and I engaged the autopilot, crawled past the roaring diesel into the after berth, turned on my flashlight, and observed water pouring out of the packing gland at the rate of a quart an hour, exactly as it had done a week before. Hmmm. When I got home neither dog nor spouse asked what happened. They just moved to another room. They knew.

By midnight I recalled that I had tested the job without actually completing it. I hadn't greased the Zerk grease fitting on the lower rudder post bearing. Wait a minute. That bearing is below the packing gland. Wouldn't grease there intercept water before it got to the gland? I hadn't repacked the Zerk because the nipple had long ago rusted closed. Probably hadn't been greased in 20 years. Hey, wait a minute!

The next morning I bought a new half-inch stainless Zerk with a quarter-inch nipple. I drilled a half inch hole in the side of the rudder tube as deep as the Zerk threads, then continued the hole with a quarter-inch bit until there was a path open to the tube. I glued the new Zerk in with thickened epoxy and then excitedly pumped three 3-ounce tubes of marine grease through the new nipple. Pump, pump, pump, filling a void empty for who knows how long, and with a growing suspicion that the whole system relied heavily on grease, lots of it, probably an expected annual application of grease, an application that could not have been made through a rusted Zerk and had perhaps never been made since *Thelonious* was tossed into the test pool in Irvine, CA, in 1984, toweled off and destined, eventually, for me.

I steamed off for a test at full throttle and this time not a drop came in from the packing gland or anywhere else. The leak had stopped entirely. It may be that the gland itself was never at issue, the radial disk didn't have to come off, the gland didn't really have to be repacked....

So, leaky rudder gland? Grease the lower bearing first and see what happens. Mr. Zerk was awarded that patent for a reason.

TEN MINUTES

D AY 4, 0530 HOURS. *Speed 5-6, 20 knots under double reefed main. Tacked for pump test. Hungry.*
Here's today's idea. We have been on starboard tack since departure, which means that the wind comes over our right side and the boat is always heeled to the left. Therefore, more of the left side of the boat is under water than the right side. If we heeled the other way, would the rate of leaking change? Let's try it.

In the cockpit, 20 strokes of the manual pump gets most of the water out. For some reason the remaining bilge water has a new, tan color with small particles in suspension. No taste-test this time.

To tack to the other course I'll disconnect the self-steering vane and manually steer the boat through the eye of the wind. The sails luff a moment but refill quickly as the morning breeze takes them on the other side. Cleat the new genoa sheet and reset the vane. We've changed course 100 degrees, and are headed toward Seattle instead of Kaua'i.

When the boat heels now, the water in the bilge shifts to starboard. It leaves the exposed hull under the floorboards brown, as if the tide had gone out on mud flats. The exposed electric pump is also brown. The whole bilge is brown and definitely funky.

Holy crap. The obvious explanation is simply not possible.

A marine head, or toilet, is a simple system but one prone to issues. On many cruising boats the atmosphere below deck has a characteristic smell that cannot be entirely attributed to mildewed bikinis. It comes from the sewage holding tank. In my usual southern

California world, our 14-gallon tank is periodically pumped out at a dockside vacuum provided free by the County of Los Angeles.

Thelonious can also direct our waste overboard, which on the open sea is perfectly acceptable. The U.S. Coast Guard requires three miles from shore before human byproducts can mingle with the spoil of the fishes. Even cruise ships are permitted to pump sewage overboard when 12 miles from land, discharging the remains of an ongoing smorgasbord attended by 5,000 guests. The ocean can handle it. Biological waste in its place is a natural fertilizer of the world.

But its place is not in our bilge, and that's where it is.

Thelonious has a simple Y-valve that directs sewage either overboard, or into the holding tank. Only for this voyage was the valve set to the overboard-discharge position. But is the valve set correctly? It's hard to see, installed upside-down and hidden under the vanity sink in the head. I can confirm its position by feel. Absolutely correct. So, unload everything from the forward cabin again to inspect the holding tank compartment.

By god, it's full to the brim. I can tell because it's too heavy to lift, and by the smell. Recheck the Y-valve. It was formerly in the left position, draining to the tank. Now it is in the correct right position, draining direct overboard. This makes no sense. And the toilet seems to have back-flow in it, although we pumped it dry after use this morning.

Why is the bilge brown? It's impossible that sewage leaked there. It's equally impossible to tell if the bilge water's rising. It moves too much, there's no high-water mark and so, no standard.

Is the valve set wrong? For an hour I study plumbing diagrams in the repair manuals on board. There's a partial photo of a similar valve and diagrams of other types. But in all the discussions of piping schemes, anti-siphon requirements and maintenance needs there is nowhere a picture of how the valve handle should look when set to overboard discharge.

Because the valve is out of sight and upside-down, I can't seem to visualize the right setting. Have I been filling the holding tank all along, instead of emptying waste over the side? And is it now back-flowing into the toilet? Four hours of trying both positions proves inconclusive. One thing sure, the holding tank is full and I have no means of emptying it. The seas are rising again and all this time we have been sailing the wrong way.

The only conclusion possible is that the valve has been set wrong since departure, and is set wrong now. Since I have filled the tank to the very brim, every new pump of the toilet lever only pressurizes the contents. And all this time, the air intake on the port hull has been underwater, providing no oxygen for the bacteria that biodegrade our waste.

Unbelievable. All right, turn the valve the other way and leave it. Go on deck and unscrew the pump-out cap so and the contents bubble on the deck to relieve the pressure. Maybe we're pumping overboard now. Maybe 2 + 2 still equals 4, as it always did before. It's confusing when it doesn't.

Before changing course back toward Hawai'i, let's sail dead downwind for a spell. Downwind the breeze comes over the stern instead of the side, and we'll stop heeling. The bilge will be horizontal, at least on average, and maybe the water there will hold still long enough for the pumps to work.

It does and they do. In a few strokes the manual pump sucks air, and soon the electric pump stops too. I mop out two more buckets-full with a sponge until only an inch or two sloshes back and forth around the electric pump. I'm greasy with olive and engine oil and don't like my own smell. But if this explains the leak, I'm good with it. Nobody wants to drown in his own crap.

Day 5, 1148 hours. Resumed course 235. Wind 20-25. Y-valve set pointing left. First call home.

Today is Saturday, the day I promised always to call home. I'm even in a clean shirt. All I have to do is stand in the cockpit with the handset antenna aimed south. Wait until "Searching for satellites" becomes "connected." Then dial the number of a phone in a kitchen far away.

"Hi. Yes, great. We made 140 miles yesterday. How's everything there?

"Great. Can you hear OK? Well, the connection broke, but it's great. I'm great. That's right, 140 miles. Great, put him on.

"Hi, son. How's work going? Great. That's right, 140 miles. It's great knowing you're great and mom is great. Put her on again.

"We need to conserve satellite time, so remember what I said, satphones don't always work, if you don't hear from me next Saturday it doesn't mean anything, I'll definitely call, but if I don't, don't worry, OK? Great."

Their voices were dim and far, enthusiastic but determined not to give pause. The allotted 10 minutes had been cut to seven by three failed connections. The prudent thing is to preserve satellite time, everybody knows that.

Maybe being alone is finding nothing to say. I had looked forward to the call as a reward, but was unable to tell them what 140 miles really means, that it's fast but uncomfortable; that it kills sleep and spills food; that an average of six knots would shave a week off my estimated 22 days' passage. The wind made it hard to hear, the spray kept me ducking, I couldn't read the LCD display through sunglasses, and we spoke in platitudes, like strangers. But what good would it do for them to know about a leak I can't find? And if they asked if I should turn back, what would I say?

1920 hours. Pumps keeping up. Dinner Indian food.

That's better, isn't it? A two-hour snooze really changes things. First of all, whatever the source of this leak is, the pumps are keeping up. It was only 10 strokes in the cockpit just now and the bilge level is clearly down. The electric pump still cycles every 15 minutes, but if it keeps working, we'll keep floating. To push on with a worsening leak would be stupid. Just pushing on isn't stupid, though. We can pump all the way to Kaua'i if we have to. We just don't want to pump halfway to Kaua'i.

Second of all, let's have a more careful look at today's GRIB file. I want to stay between the isobars indicating a band of strong wind, and that's why we're sailing crossways to the big ocean swells and getting thrown around like a toy. But we've made progress, and I think we can head a little more south now. That's where the trade winds are, and we should pick them up in a few days. Let's try bearing off 20 degrees and see if that makes a difference.

I disconnect the steering vane and set a new course of 215 magnetic. Yes, the card swings back and forth 10 degrees on either side of the target, that's just the action of the waves. Let the swinging average out. It's no fun to stare at a moving compass, so pick something on the horizon to steer for. A cloud will serve. The lifespan of a cloud is 20 minutes, so after a while just choose another one.

On a crewed boat we might be steering like this every four-hour watch, splitting the job among helmsmen in half-hour tricks. But we can just reset the steering vane.

The boat loves the new course. We have reduced our constant heeling by half, and now we're running more down the waves instead of across or into them.

Look, seven knots! Surfing now, the whole yacht seems to lift its stern and slide downhill with a cheer. Be careful climbing down the companionway ladder. It's a long fall and we don't want a broken wrist. I did bring several pieces of pine the length of my arms, and a Japanese hand saw for further adjustments. With duct tape they'll do as splints. Cracked ribs are more likely, and for that the treatment is grin and bear it. For anesthesia, there's plenty of Jack Daniels.

The best medicine is a good handhold, all the time. Practice that, not medicine.

CHAPTER 13

VOICES

D AY 6, 0500 HOURS. *Hungry. Voices persisting.*
Dawn arrives slowly out of misty dreams and with it
the thought of bacon. So this is what it means to be hungry.
Famished, in fact. For the past days chow has been an afterthought,
but now the 10 pounds I've lost wants to come back, all is forgiven.
We'll see. I'll think about it.

But it's hard to be coy, so let's cook everything that will fit in
the frying pan and then flop down drunk on three eggs, corned beef
hash, ketchup, Tabasco, butter, jam, and 16 ounces of coffee.

The whine of the bilge pump has started again and I don't even
care. I heard it on and off all night, in between the children laughing
on deck. Have I mentioned them before? Maybe not. There was a
moon, our first. It sailed through the northern sky like a sister ship,
in and out of the clouds. But whenever I came on deck the laughter
stopped, as if I was interrupting something.

About 2 a.m. I got up to turn the stereo off.

I had been dozing, enjoying a medley of Glenn Miller tunes
with Ray Eberly as the vocalist. The big bands all had good singers.
Tommy Dorsey had Sinatra, Les brown had Doris Day and Billie
Holiday was with Count Basie. But I have more recordings of Ray
Eberly, and when his voice comes in, sometimes quite late in the
arrangement, it adds a whole new instrument to the tight-fisted
Miller sound. I even thought I could distinguish him from his
brother Bob, who sang with Jimmy Dorsey. Ray Eberly never got

bobbysoxers or his own TV show or a street named for himself in Palm Springs, but he had me, and as beams of moonlight swept the cabin I could make out every word. Fools rush in where wise men never go. But wise men never fall in love, so how are they to know?

Poking groggily at the switch on the instrument panel, however, I discovered that the stereo had been off for hours.

Hallucinations are common for singlehanders. Joshua Slocum once awoke to find a stranger in the cockpit. He introduced himself as the pilot of the *Pinta*, one of Christopher Columbus's expedition of 1492, and offered to steer until Slocum felt more like himself. Robert Manry, who crossed the Atlantic in little 13-foot *Tinkerbell*, was visited by a Scotsman named MacGregor. During the solo trans-Pacific race of 2002, Mark Deppe was accompanied by a voice that repeated the question "Got Milk?" over and over again, until he wished heartily it would get its milk and shut up. Studies of human factors in extended space travel often consult reports of men alone at sea, in lifeboats, marooned, or in grueling singlehanded races. A common result of hardship and exhaustion is seeing things. Robin Knox-Johnson spent 312 days as first to race non-stop alone around the world, and was knighted for it. We left six days ago, and I'm nothing like him. Hardship for us is a well-stocked booze cabinet, a humidor of excellent Cavendish and a library that would keep Thomas Jefferson quiet all morning.

Still, my hallucinations are distracting. One of the most frequent is the voice of a woman calling my name.

Christian.

Sometimes it's so startling that it wakes me up. The voice is sometimes urgent, sometimes pleading. It always makes me turn my head. Just before dawn I got up and walked around the cabin to see if the source could be triangulated. But no dice, so I just lay down again to stare at the overhead. The children's voices in the rigging were playful, and I listened like an eavesdropper while Glenn Miller played in the background. Actually, I knew I was only hearing fragments of familiar orchestrations, as you might from a radio far away, and my ear filled in the missing pieces from memory. But the woman is different. She has a question, or need, for which chivalry demands a response.

Interruptions of REM sleep make for a lot of dreams, and the crazy quilt of characters who populate them are often the source of vivid recollection. But this voice wasn't an extension of any recent dream. It was physically present on the boat. It asked attention in an intimate, almost petulant, way.

For the past two nights I have been running through the vocal characteristics of every female person I know, trying to fit a voice to the gap in the jigsaw picture. None would fit. It apparently wasn't someone I knew well. She was familiar but mysterious, pleasant but a little demanding, neither young nor old, and sounded like she smelled good. Insofar as that seemed to include every woman I could remember, it didn't narrow things down at all.

I have been frustrated by these inconclusive efforts, but also entertained by speculation. The boat seemed filled with friendly voices competing to be identified, and I began to think that, when the correct name was finally applied, all the other voices would be disappointed. That would be shabby treatment indeed for so many interesting companions.

Christian.

This morning, as soon as I awoke, I knew who it was. It was Lindsay Lohan.

Yes? I said out loud.

My response surprised me with its volume, and in the same instant all the other potential identities flew out the open hatch like bats from a belfry, leaving me alone and uncomfortable, and I knew why.

Lindsay Lohan, the prodigy and movie star, has not had an easy time of it since "The Parent Trap," in which she was 11 years old and there were two of her. She grew into womanhood beset by the public misunderstandings that sometimes attend a Hollywood career. Although we have never met, I have always felt that sympathy, tolerance and a natural desire to help were appropriate responses to her plight, and if asked, would have certainly done what I could. However, my three grown daughters and red-headed wife did not agree that all Lindsay needed was the counsel of an older man with wide experience in the world. In fact, they would tell me to shut up when I made my defense of her driving a car into the side of the police station in Santa Monica, CA, which is a very confusing place to find a parking spot, or when some rehab facility once again failed to provide the lasting help anyone has a right to expect from expensive medical professionals. Sometimes, in my house, it seemed to be Lindsay Lohan and me against the world. Maybe that's why she would choose to visit me here.

What might she want?

I waited in the half-light of dawn for an answer that never came, because Lindsay Lohan never returned, and neither did the children in the rigging or Ray Eberly or the entire Miller band. I suppose that today, Day Six, we arrived at the time in a voyage when imagination adjusts to reality and magic gives way to routine.

It must be I who has adjusted, not the ocean or the stars, who have always been here 800 miles from land. My solo childhood is over. Perhaps every form of youth is a hallucination, and we must grow to survive. But I already miss when the wind laughed and the night called my name.

Christian. Got milk?

1200 hours. On course, made 112 miles. Rewired pump. Set clock back. Xenophon resumed.

All through the noon position report and downloading of weather files the bilge pump ran. I refuse to look at it, it's too beautiful a day and we're going six and a half knots. I rarely sit in the cockpit sun like this, but it gets me away from the sound.

The bilge pump is running again right now, hear it? Let's go below and check. All right, I was wrong, it's not on. The other sonic hallucinations are gone, only the whine of the pump remains to drive me nuts. Maybe just as I opened the bilge compartment it stopped, like a wise-guy genii. At least the water level seems stable, more or less, as it sloshes around.

You know what? Let's just turn the pump off. It's currently rigged on automatic, but I can rewire the panel to make it manual control only. Then it'll be off until I turn the circuit breaker switch on. I suppose if I forget to do that we'll sink, but at least that would put an end to the infernal whine.

If you hear the sound now, you're imagining it. Let's see how the leak outsmarts that electrical fact.

1900 hours. Dinty Moore. Rolling.

Too bouncy to cook, but I have an answer for that. Just heat Dinty Moore Beef stew in its can, toss in some raw onion and a few shakes of red pepper. For dessert, a big container of peaches. I like to pour the juice out and fill the can with wine. It's drinking peaches with a fork.

I brought a lot of TED Talks, mostly those anthologized by the NPR program called "TED Radio Hour". Audio takes up very little space on my 12-gig iPhone, and the stereo fills the cabin with human voices exploring offbeat aspects of sensory experience. I could tell them something about that, and about Lindsay and the children and the ghost leak, but it's nice just to listen, for a change. I also have hours and hours of music recorded from KJazz, the excellent public radio station maintained by Long Beach State University. But neither TED nor the captured offhand remarks of host Helen Borgers is ever for a moment convincing. If anything, recorded voices beg the question, is there anyone else left alive, this moment, on the planet Earth?

Recordings are the past and the present is night falling over brooding swells. The isolation is overwhelming.

2100 hours. Course 235, 5-6 knots. Cyrus dead.

It's still light at 9 o'clock, which means we have sailed west into an unmarked time zone. I can set the clock to Los Angeles Time, or to Hawai'i Time, which is three hours different. Or I can leave the clock as it is. Bending the day like this is proof of progress, but dawn comes late.

With the departure of hallucinations I have Xenophon for company, and I'm worried about him. He was a young Greek aristocrat, a student of Socrates with a letter of introduction to Prince Cyrus of Persia. I remember what it was like to be drawn to powerful people, and follow ambition for the adventure of it. Xenophon got himself to Asia, put himself under the protection of the prince, and joined 10,000 other mercenary soldiers in a mission to keep the local peace.

Now, suddenly, Prince Cyrus is dead. Neither Xenophon nor anybody else knew that he had formed the army expressly to kill King Artaxerxes II, his brother, and install himself on the throne. But Artaxerxes won the showdown battle, and now 10,000 Greeks and allies were on the losing side and at his mercy. The Greek leader, Clearchus, was sent to make a deal. But at the peace parley Artaxerxes had Clearchus and his whole party beheaded.

Xenophon was a thousand miles from home, like me, but when new leadership was required he stood up. He told the men they would live or die on their own terms. He reminded them that the bold survive, that their ancestors were watching and that to dally in hostile country with the Mede and Persian women would turn them into lotus-eaters, wiping clean all memory of home.

The lotus-eaters did it for me. The reference is to the Odyssey of Homer, a story told 400 years before Xenophon was born and still told today. Any distance between Xenophon and me vanished instantly. We were from the same earth, had read the same book, and for neither of us was the outcome assured. We were bound arm in arm across millennia, both turning the pages to see what happened next.

The mercenaries have now set off on the long march up-country, starving because Artaxerxes has forbidden any village to sell them food.

I feel bad, because we have enough Spam on board to feed an army.

CHAPTER 14

BROACHING

D*AY 7. MIDNIGHT. SORE.*
    The wind is up. I'd say about 25 knots and steady from dead astern. We've traded heeling for rolling. On deck it's black and loud but the leeward bunk is snug and all I need to do is hold on. The apogee of each roll requires a change of grip, which gets old fast. That's why I'm wedged athwartships, sideways to the bunk. To lie normally is to be dumped unceremoniously on the wet floor every few minutes. Most offshore boats have some sort of containing structure of wood or canvas to keep the slumbering yachtsman mummified in bed. However, upon the cue of whatever sound the apocalypse might make I prefer to pop out of the sack unimpeded. Besides, holding on to sleep isn't so bad, it gives you something to do.

I'm surprised to still feel the impulse to check on the crew in the cockpit when obviously there's no crew there. On previous cruises they were always in a parallel universe. When my watch was off duty, theirs was on, and sometimes it felt like you didn't see each other for days. Bunks are shared, so a crew of six needs only three places to sleep. From below, the watch on deck is a murmur of low voices. At the turn of watch a hand touches your shoulder—"10 minutes." Time to dress, grab a cookie, re-orient to the chart and the conditions. The watches "dog," or change, daily so no one is sentenced permanently to the dark midnight-to-4 a.m. shift.

A deck watch is busy with sails and trim, but tries to keep voices down and clattering to a minimum. The off-watch exists in a temporary limbo, comfortable or not, asleep or listening. A muffled laugh is pleasant to hear. A loud story punctuated with laughter may draw a complaint from below to keep it down a little. But when a long silence extends above, I always feel discontent grow. Especially on family cruises, imagination strains for the smallest proof of human life on deck, safe in their foul-weather gear.

There ought always to be the occasional clacking of a winch, or drum of footfalls, or fragment of conversation. Silence is disturbing because to fall overboard at night is an irreversible calamity. The boat keeps on, every moment another 100 feet. A cry might not be heard over the wind and surge. The deck crew are tethered, but not bound together like mountaineers. It is possible that some might attend a task and return to find the cockpit empty. It almost never happens, except in the imagination of skippers, but there it happens a lot.

More than once in the past I have gotten out of a bunk on some excuse, just to confirm two huddled figures still out there in the rain. I did it once on each of our first nights here, only to find nobody at the helm but the wind vane. I don't do it anymore. I'm used to the way things are, being always on watch and yet never on watch and always somewhere between awake and asleep. It's not unpleasant at all, it's more like an extension of consciousness. At home there's a convention of bedtime. The house goes dark and cold, and padding around it like a horny tomcat brings questions from the family at breakfast. Is everything all right? What's going on with you? Here, all 24 hours are available. And you get to sleep in your clothes.

If this is being alone, it doesn't feel like it. The cabin seems more crowded every day. Every opened book spills out new companions in the full flush of their lives and eager to fill the silence. They slap an arm around your shoulder and draw you with them as if they've waited hundreds of years for the chance, and maybe they have. Not that joining them is always easy, because a book here, held in the circle of light from a single LED lamp, doesn't hold still. It moves as if alive, and following the print with your eyes is like straining to hear a conversation in a noisy room. But even that focuses the attention.

I let one book lead to another, and the rack by the bunk is an easy reach. Xenophon's visit to a villa in Asia guided me to an illustrated volume on Greco-Roman houses. Their houses, like *Thelonious*, were the center of everything, a place to work as well as live and rest. The women made food and clothing, the men had their workshops, and a slave was an *instrumentum vocale*, a "tool that talks." In this floating house I'm all of them at once.

A reference to Cicero makes me reach for his story in Plutarch's "Lives," and as I do the world turns sideways with a violent sound of flapping, loose gear tumbles onto me from the other bunk, and the boat lies suddenly stopped, crosswise to the seas and shuddering.

Broached again, that's all.

We usually broach because a wave turns us off course so far that the sails go aback and pin us down on the wrong side. It feels like being in a car that has spun out in a turn and wound up stopped and heading in the wrong direction.

At dusk last night I had set up the sails wing and wing, with the mainsail and jib on opposite sides of the boat. It's a good way to sail dead downwind because it keeps both sails full and equalizes the forces. Until you broach, that is.

Now the 16-foot whisker pole that holds out the jib is jutting into the sky and the back-winded jib is holding us down like a face in a pillow. Both sails snap and flutter as we labor without steerageway. Waves are blowing over the cockpit where I stand at the wheel, trying to regain course. It doesn't always work out this way, but after 10 minutes a lucky wave kicks the stern conveniently around, the jib turns right-side-out with a bang, and off we go surfing down the waves again.

I had no idea it was blowing 25 knots up here, which is too much for the genoa and reefed main. Running before the wind requires constant attention to steering, and when a cross-swell lifts the stern for a roller coaster ride, keeping a straight course is a lot to ask even of a human helmsman. Do you think maybe it would be a good idea to reduce sail at night, from here on? I agree. I keep forgetting what I already know.

So, shall we read some more Xenophon or just sit here on the wet floor with head between the knees, waiting for the next broach? I doubt I can fall asleep like this, soaked and cold. But don't bet on it.

Day 8, 0635 hours. Chorizo Spam and whiskers.

It's natural to be sore, sorer than I ever remember. It's the holding on, that's all. I just turned on the electric bilge pump and it only ran five minutes. The floorboards are dry and I think less water is getting in on this downwind course. Funny how last night is already a blur. I think we broached a couple more times, and that violent flapping isn't good for the genoa jib. But we can wear everything out, including me, as long as whatever is left gets us to Hawai'i. Anyway, the wind is down to 10 knots now, a gentle morning breeze.

The smell is frying Chorizo Spam, cheerful and spicy. I have on a home mix of Rock Bob Dylan, Jimi Hendrix, Credence Clearwater and a dozen other wake-up anthems. The cockpit speakers blast it so rude over the quiet ocean that somebody ought to call the cops, but there's nobody to complain and it does get the blood moving. A couple of eggs and a dry fleece jumper and everything's good.

I have to remember we're not racing. No need to press so hard through the darkness. We should cruise at 80 percent racing efficiency, as the famous yachtsman Carlton Mitchell said he always did. Make that 70 percent, because we were definitely overpowered last night and the pole is hard to handle. How about 60 percent? When tasks take longer to do alone, shorten the tasks.

Good time for a shave.

My method is to carry a plastic cup of hot water into the head, where there's a mirror. Dip the blade into the cup, scrape away five day's growth. The scent of the shaving cream brings back mornings ashore with newspapers. Waking up starts the day there, but it doesn't feel like that here. Our time is broken up and gives no sense of a calendar page turning. I don't have to shave, so why do it? I can't think of a reason. There's no one to notice, and besides, whiskers just grow back. It must be an impulse to continue civilization, an urge to conform. But conform to what, if not to my own needs? In isolation, I should know what they are. But it's not that easy. I'm a creature of my world, and where I go the world goes with me.

Noon. 118 miles made good. Water temp 66F. Cumulative fuel burn 6 gallons. Rolling.

It's blowing 20 to 25 knots this afternoon, and a double reef and half the genoa is plenty. Late lunch is tuna on sourdough, and the last of the second jar of Vlasic kosher dill pickles. There is something unnecessary about running out of pickles, but it had to happen sooner or later. The actor Peter Sellers was asked what, if he had his life to live over, he would do differently. He replied that he would do everything the same, except not go to see "The Magus," the movie version of John Fowles' masterwork novel.

I wouldn't run out of pickles.

By dusk there are puffy clouds on the horizon. So far we've had only shades of gray: dark gray, black gray, light gray, bright gray, wet gray, dry gray, blinding gray and soul-eating- zombie gray. These clouds ahead are cumulous, individuated and warm, the clouds of summer. The same clouds identify the Grand Canyon when approaching by car over the desert. On the green Atlantic 160 miles off New York they mark the vast oceanic river of the Gulf Stream. A line of cumulous seen from any other sky means change, and change for the better.

It's Day 8, and at 28°25'N, 132°32'W we're seeing the Pacific trade winds at last.

SENSITIVITY

DAY *8, 2100 HOURS. Wind 25 from astern, wing and wing. Light rain showers. Holding on for dear life.*

This rolling is quite natural, now that we're running before the trades. Sailboats have always rolled. I remember watching films of Eric and Susan Hiscock on *Wanderer III*, the boat they sailed around the world from 1952 to 1955. Real pioneers, the Hiscocks were, all British upper lip and kind to the natives and never a complaint about minimalist living on a 30-foot wooden boat. In their home movies, *Wanderer* rolls gunwale to gunwale in such a relentless and dyspeptic way as to make you seasick just watching. Their narration doesn't mention it. Quite to be expected, don't you know. All part of the fun.

Let's have cookies for dinner tonight, it's too hard to cook or even open a can.

We might as well skip sleeping, too, because it's not going to happen. Forget what I said about wedging yourself in, doesn't work. Just stay here on the floor, there's nowhere to fall.

Every boat rolls, but some worse than others. New models designed for downwind racing are flatter under the stern, and under these conditions they plane like a motorboat. The faster you go, the more stable it gets. Other designs, even without the twin rudders and spinnakers of the racers, just don't seem to make such a great show of it as we do. They have more stability. They're fatter, or flatter, or more buoyant in the bow, or anyway they're somehow different from *Thelonious*. They probably have dry floorboards, too, whereas my crib blanket is soaking wet.

CHAPTER 15

But of course it won't do to criticize your boat, any more than a good carpenter criticizes his tools. The case of Chichester comes to mind. Sir Francis was a well-known yachtsman by the time he commissioned *Gipsy Moth V*, a brand new boat specifically designed for his epic voyage of 1966. He was the first to circumnavigate solo west to east, around stormy Cape Horn and the Cape of Good Hope, and it won him international celebrity. But what many also remember is his disappointment in the yacht. It was too tippy. It pounded. It leaked. His recommendations hadn't been followed by the famous designer or the famous builders. He had to stop in Australia so the keel could be extensively modified. Chichester was alone at sea for 226 days, unbowed by weather or seasickness or the news aircraft that chased him, even off Cape Horn, to ask what he'd had for breakfast. After all that it seemed odd to be so irritated by his own boat, and mention it so often. Joshua Slocum before him never complained. Slocum claimed that his boat, *Spray*, was sea kindly and steered itself and was just pretty much perfect. Maybe the difference was that Slocum rescued an old tub from the boneyard and fixed it up himself, whereas Chichester was in the arms of all-knowing and expensive professionals. Expectation varies, and less is more.

So I don't criticize *Thelonious* for this preposterous rolling. I just reduce sail again, even though it doesn't much help. We're now down to a scrap of jib poled out to starboard and still going one ear to the other.

Three times tonight I adjusted sails, the last time lowering the main completely. It's blowing hard up there and the deck feels like a trampoline. Furling the main at night is all patience and technique. It's wait for the moment, keep a handhold, plan the steps. And when the job is done, peel off harness and weather gear and reach for the brandy bottle. Can't put anything down, even on the swinging stovetop. It just flies off—did you see that? The gimbals hit the limit, which has never even happened before.

Yacht design is compromise, everyone knows that. *Thelonious*, a third-generation Ericson 32, was made to do everything well: to sail fast in light air, to perform under jib or main alone, to put up with gales and look good in photographs. If she is rolling like crazy, so be it. Perhaps it is I who needs more practice getting a fork to hit my mouth instead of my eye. Perhaps I am just slow to learn how to live with both hands holding on at all times. Rolling is normal, did I mention that?

But tonight, normal rolling incorporates an infernal corkscrew motion unlike anything reported by Sir Francis or Captain Slocum or in the notebooks of Sigmund Freud, who must've seen plenty of people being driven nuts by the wobbling of their lives. There is an angry jerkiness to this motion, a real nasty streak that abides no gratitude for my year-long painstaking refit.

But it won't do to complain about the boat. If my boat is possessed by demons, so am I. If this violent slewing off course is unacceptable, than perhaps I romanticized the true nature of riding the trades into the setting sun. If the yacht doesn't need sleep, me neither. If the craft does not admit to a bad mood, nor shall I. But if this keeps up, *Thelonious* will sail onto the long crescent beach of Hanalei Bay without me, because I will have voluntarily stepped overboard long before.

Day 9, 0550 hours. Reinserted sensitivity pin. Very pretty morning now.

At dawn I stuck a cookie between my teeth and crawled into the cockpit on the puppet-string safety tether, sullen as a teenager, taking a burst of spray right up the nose.

Spread out behind us lay the evidence of our crazy path through the sea, a line of S-turns which brought back what father used to say before I learned to steer straight: son, it would break a snake's back to follow your wake. The wind vane was flopping helplessly side to side. I made my way to it as the stern skidded, snapping the boat like a whip, and then started off the other way to do the same thing again. Miserable boat!

From the aluminum frame of the self-steering apparatus a slender stainless steel pin dangled from its safety line, swinging free: the "steering sensitivity" pin. That should be all the way in. It seems to have fallen all the way out.

Oh.

I guess the pin came out just as the sun went down. Don't know how I missed it. Let's just stick it back in.

With the pin reinserted, the corkscrewing stopped and *Thelonious* immediately resumed her arrow-straight course. The rudder and keel once again combined to direct us straight down the face of the following waves. From a spine-twisting four knots our speed jumped to seven as the boat woke from its nightmare and resumed its usual frolic.

Make a note in future to check all the systems before it gets dark. That would prevent small problems which may take on exaggerated proportions but are easily avoided by elementary seamanship.

I wonder if a tool has ever criticized the carpenter.

CALENDARS

D AY 9, NOON POSITION 27°58'N, 134°40'W. Course 240°, speed 5. 128 nautical miles.

Today is my birthday. Thank you, I'm 71. You would think I could tell you how that feels, but I can't. It feels the same as ever. You need less sleep, they say, and that seems true. Otherwise, my age just doesn't have much to say. The date you're born matters if the kid soccer team says you have to be eight by January first, or for that first bartender job, or to run for Congress or collect Social Security. Most birthdays, though, don't measure anything you need to know.

A clock is no more help than the date on the calendar. The time at the moment is local noon, since the sun is highest. So, does that mean it's 12 o'clock? Not by the ship's clock, which because it was set in Los Angeles reads 1 p.m. Anyway, if we change our clock to read noon today it won't be accurate tomorrow unless we stay in this same spot. Clock noon anywhere is rarely solar noon. Noon is more a shared idea than a time. If from New York you call a friend at noon in Athens, it will be dark where you are. What you have in common isn't a clock, it's her lunch hour.

The Ninth of July at 12:14 p.m., a Thursday, may be important information at home but conveys little of interest here. Our only appointment is with that cloud far ahead. Or with a sandwich, here timed by whim rather than agreement with somebody else. We have left the markers of the days and weeks behind, along with ringing cell phones and traffic reports. Hawai'i is two weeks away if things go well, but even that estimate seems no more useful than an actuarial table of predicted lifespan. When time is elastic and dependent, measurement fails. What works is to assess the stores. We have 50 days rations left, of the 60 stowed on board. Count down from that.

I never feel this way at home. At home, missing a payment date means a fine, and with a cell phone there's no excuse to keep anyone waiting. At home, every hour has the character of before or after. Consciousness ticks, as if we carry a hundred alarm clocks set to go off at different times. At home, I wear a watch to keep in time with the rhythm of everyone else. Since there isn't anybody else here, I stopped looking at the ship's clock a couple of days ago.

But although the date and the time fade in importance, one measurement has grown to supernatural size, and that is how far we have left to go. Ordinarily, my personal location feels fixed. Even moving at 500 miles an hour on an airliner people are already at their destination. Travel is a limbo between locations, and we define travelers by where they wind up: Marco Polo in China, astronauts on the moon, the Prodigal Son home again. Here, places are undefined. You can't see them, because the ocean doesn't have mile markers like a Roman road. To know your place, you need a chart.

Our chart is Number 530 of the National Oceanic Service, entitled "San Diego to Aleutian Islands and Hawaiian Islands." It's the only one that shows both Kaua'i and Los Angeles. The scale of 1:4,860,700 includes a vast area from the Gulf of Alaska to southern Mexico.

The Mercator projection, necessary to flatten the spherical planet onto paper, is daunting. The Hawaiians are tiny and Los Angeles is a fly speck. Land is an afterthought. The entire three-foot center of the chart is simply "North Pacific Ocean," most of it 12,000 to 18,000 feet deep.

Let's mark our noon position. The GPS coordinates are 27 degrees 58 minutes and 4 seconds North, 134 degrees 40 minutes and 4 seconds West.

Making this pencil mark is my favorite time of the day. To locate it, find our latitude on the vertical scale on the right side of the chart. Measure with dividers and scribe a light horizontal line on the empty paper. Then from the bottom of the chart measure our western progress in longitude and scribe north to where the lines meet. We made 118 miles since yesterday's mark. That's an inch and a quarter on the chart. In eight days at sea we have traveled 10 inches, and Hawai'i is still 14 inches away.

I don't know if there's a chart of life, but sometimes it seems that the figures of history had one. Moses, coming down a mountain with 10 rules for living. The Greek general Themistocles, foreseeing that Athens must build a navy. Lindbergh, knowing all he needed to do was fly east. Maps plot the past, too, and can show folly in six dimensions. Charles Minard's graphic of Napoleon's Russian campaign shows an army of 400,000 men starting for Moscow as a thick band, only to shrink to a thin line of walking dead, retreating through snow less than a year later. The map conveys number of troops, distances, temperatures, locations, directions and dates. If Napoleon had been able to see it in 1812, he would have pulled his boots off right then.

A small-scale chart like NOS 530 shows a large area. It's hard, seeing yourself as a pencil mark in the North Pacific, to get too big for your britches.

Jorge Luis Borges, the Argentine poet and philosopher, told of a kingdom in which cartography was so advanced that, in a quest for perfect accuracy, a map of the scale 1:1 was eventually produced. It was the same size as the world, and of no use to anybody.

It's good to know where you are, and who.

CHAPTER 17

SPAGHETTI

1*900 HOURS. RECHARGE BATTERIES. Still no ships. Big seas, rough ride.*

Now there was a nap right out of the Book of Naps. I fell face-first into the leeward bunk less than two hours ago, and just popped up to find everything right with the world. Popped up and fell right back down, because we're still rolling like crazy.

Sleep is good stuff, but I wonder how much we really need. Not too much and not too little, of course, but the amount seems to vary with people and age. Teenagers sleep forever, and we all know successful adults who rise with the sun but conk out at 9 p.m. Others need only four hours a night, among them Michelangelo, Winston Churchill and Madonna.

We think of sleeping as going to bed at night and getting up in the morning, but is that what happens? If the dog starts barking, somebody has to deal with it. There's the disturbance of a vivid dream, a trip to the bathroom, or just the occasional onset of featureless dread at 3 a.m. I think we wake up more than we remember, and eight or 10 hours of continuous sack time is rare. The question is how we feel while brushing our teeth. Feel good? Slept well. Feel out of sorts? Then not so much.

Singlehanded sailors don't tuck in at night and sleep till the birds sing, but the notion that it's a sleep-deprivation experiment all the time isn't true either, especially when outside the shipping zones. Yes, we're up a lot in the night, but just to trim a sail or check the horizon. Sleep returns fast if nothing's amiss. It's not like being annoyed by a screeching cat or rousted by the sudden recollection of something you forgot to do, either of which can lead to moping around the kitchen for hours. On the ocean the rhythm of the day and night remains different, but the partition is not as clear and there's no worry that failing to fall asleep on schedule will punish you all the next day. The day here is 24 hours, not two 12s.

We're not racing, of course. An ocean racing yacht is driven hard and all gear pushed to the limit, including the least expensive and most expendable gear known as the crew. A racing watch aims for a knife edge of alertness, setting and retrieving heavy sails, grinding winches and hanging over the windward lifelines when not busy. Even family cruisers stand watches all night, and being off duty can result in a sleep so deep that when called up it's like rising from the bottom of the ocean. Solo, I seldom sink that far. It's more like a dive and a swim.

Sleeping for 90 minutes puts the body into the Rapid Eye Movement stage of sleep, which is said to be the most efficient. REM sleep is also the realm where the unconscious mind solves problems and produces those finger-snap revelations later. Sleep at home is a cycle of REMS. A singlehander breaks the cycle into self-contained units, each mini-sleep a new rejuvenation.

Did I say what a great nap that was?

The fact is that we awoke with far too much sail up, which is why I'm swinging like a monkey from the overhead grab rails. But we're making seven knots, and the GPS hit eight and a half surfing down that last swell. Let's keep on like this, it makes up for lost time. And since I'll be tired again in three hours, let's eat. The menu tonight is spaghetti-against-the-odds.

First, a Trader Vic's Polynesian-restaurant-inspired cocktail. The recipe requires a baby-box of orange juice, the kind that comes with a sharpened straw and such a reliable seal that a three-year-old can't spill it. I find this system to equal the aqueducts of ancient Rome, since there's never a drought if I can just get that straw in my mouth. The other ingredient is Meyer's rum.

Although the ice is long gone, there's no need for the cocktail to be warm. All we need to cool it is an old coffee can and a wet paper towel. Instead of a refrigerator, we have on board a dozen aerosol cans of compressed gas "duster," a product intended for blowing cobwebs out of computers.

Wrap the baby-box in a wet paper towel. Place box in coffee can. Invert the aerosol duster and shake. Inject the can with a blast of frosty expanding gas. The paper towel freezes instantly by adiabatic cooling, as predicted by the First Law of Thermodynamics. Wait 10 minutes.

Now we have only to pour the cold juice into an insulated glass, put in three fingers of rum, and for that added sardine flavor, give a quick stir with the rigging knife.

A bold, sweet cocktail builds appetite to go with a building sea. I'd say it's blowing 25 again, with eight or 10 foot swells arriving at an angle of 20 degrees. We haven't broached yet, so on to dinner.

Light the burner on the propane stove. For the pasta pot we can use half sea water and half fresh—no need to add salt.

The mushrooms and tomatoes are far up in the bow in plastic boxes with the other food stores. Dark up there, so I'll wear the headlamp. A bike helmet is a good idea under these conditions, but I forgot mine, so try not to hit your head and get knocked out. Stretch into the V-berth among the stuffed boxes. Now dig through our 60-day supply, examining each label by headlamp. No, those are artichokes. No, that is corned beef hash. No, that is peach slices in own juice. Susan Hiscock made complete lists of where she stored every condiment, jar, can or waxed egg. I prefer a treasure hunt in a submarine being depth-charged.

Success. Now back to the saloon, straphanger style.

There are many methods of peeling fresh garlic, and one way is to watch it fall onto the floorboard and then accidentally step on it. Another way is to use the top of the gimbaled stove. That doesn't work because the stove and I keep parting company with every lurch of the boat. In a seaway like this it wouldn't do to fall backwards and break a rib.

The solution is to clip the safety harness to the rail of the stove. Now we're locked in place, and can lean back in security. I learned the trick from Jane Potts, who was cooking for a crew of 19 in the

Irish Sea under conditions similar to these. The crew was two nine-man watches. She would carve a hot roast beef with vegetables for one watch. When they went on deck the other nine came down, dripping in oilies, to slide into the still-warm seats for the same full fare. I don't know how she did it, tied to her gimballed stove like Cinderella. I was never able to thank Jane correctly, because, being the only woman on the boat, whenever I came near she would pick up a carving knife.

Some wine? Let's open this bottle of Bordeaux from the famous wine-producing region of Kirkland. Strapped in, we can enjoy the sight of garlic, onions and mushrooms simmering in olive oil that laps the sides of the pan just as the ocean laps the sides of our vessel. I add the canned plum tomatoes carefully, breaking each in a squeezed fist so the pulp and the magnificent juices commingle gently with the sauce. The aroma reaches up like hands touching your face, a woman's hands, soft and, but never mind that.

Let's have some more wine and put the pasta in. Or the rest of it, anyhow, since I missed timing the roll and half spilled on the floor. I recommend not letting this two-quart pot of seething spaghetti water tip over onto us, lashed in as we are six inches away, which could happen if our knee stuck in the gimbals. Boil pasta, not yourself.

There's nothing like good wine. Or even inexpensive wine. At the Wedding at Cana they ran out, and Jesus Himself made some out of water. One of the guests noted, insightfully, I think, that ordinary people serve the good wine first, and then switch to the cheap stuff after nobody can tell the difference anymore. But Jesus served the best wine last. That was before Costco, where I get mine.

Ah, the sauce is done and the pasta ready. The method now is to carefully dump the spaghetti into the sauce pan, and mix well with a fork. Lovely. Through the port the sun is down and only an undulating glow remains in the sky. We have achieved a level of sophistication and worldliness few would think possible while careering down cresting swells at 7 knots. Shall we load our plate and make for the table, where awaits on its rubber non-skid surface my book and my pipe? That's what we would do at home.

But I've learned my lesson, so let's dine here, standing up and strapped to the stove, feet planted wide. No need for a treacherous plate or overconfident bowl. Eat right out of the pan. A bit more parmesan, *signore*? Don't mind if I do. Another plastic glass of Kirkland, *mon ami*? I don't mind if I do. We should have music, but there's no way I am going to unclip to turn on the stereo at the navigation panel. We're bucking like a bronco. Now bend, thrust, and lift fork to mouth.

Ah! Compliments to the chef.

Say, this joint is so popular it's standing room only. Pretty witty, and you know it came to me just like that. Standing room, because I'm standing up, get it? And 'only' because it's just me. Or us, I mean. I am not a sentimental person, but I greatly appreciate your company. Thank you for coming along. I don't say that enough, but it is the truth.

Let's finish this bottle before it spills. Here's to us both for getting this far. Have I told you what I believe about people? Well, here it is.

I believe all men are created equal, and also they're defined by a whole bunch of inalienable rights such as it goes without saying. And here also is something else I believe. Even though I may strike you as a white guy from New Jersey, I am also simultaneously Michael Jordan and Herb Alpert and Barbra Streisand, because that's what an American is, you see, all of us at once, mixed up together in the sweat and music of our New World, tolerably OK with each other most of the time and right now standing up strapped in drinking cheap wine out of plastic. Oh, and Rodney King and the cops who beat him up, too. Here's to them because we're all in it together, different but the same.

By the gods, a flying fish just hit the window. Did you see that?

Where was I? Oh, yes, my birthday dinner. Let me pour you a new cup, and ask a favor. Someone needs to go on deck pretty soon and crank in a new reef, and I am feeling full of wine and pasta and quite content, and I was wondering, if you don't mind, if you'd do it.

HALFWAY

D AY 10, 1100 HOURS. *Speed 5, port tack under full main and winged genoa. Finally it seems real. It's glorious to be doing what I said I would do.*

I've been sitting at the navigation station this morning, watching the GPS tick off longitude. The seconds spin by at a good clip, each denoting one sixtieth of a nautical mile. I'm waiting for 138°38' West, with a pencil poised to mark it.

Halfway there.

Did I always believe I'd get here? I told father I would. As a high school kid I blithely informed him that I intended to sail the Atlantic alone. This was about the time of the first singlehanded race in 1960, when the newspapers put such things on Page One and solo sailors were figures of romance and enlightenment, often in beards. I had no beard and was un-enlightened enough to be failing both German and Algebra II. I probably made so many such announcements that nobody even listened. But I was my father's most constant crew, and over the years on night watches the topic of singlehanding recurred in a context of speed records set by exotic multihulls and the new breed of professional sailors who drove them. Solo cruising seemed an amateur waste of time, a remnant of past times.

In the last 20 years of his life we lived on opposite coasts, and the steady advance of Alzheimer's disease turned conversation to silence. I doubt he ever took my offhand statement seriously, and perhaps I didn't either. But I had said it out loud, and I didn't forget saying it. Now we're on our way solo to Hawai'i, almost to my surprise. Ideas are clever. They can bury themselves like mudfish or sleep till spring like a bear. Ideas want to survive. They remember, even if you don't.

Here at Longitude 138° West we're as far from land as it is possible to be on the planet. To turn back would put us against the prevailing trade winds, so keeping on is now the only rational choice. If something goes wrong we'll have to make it right. If everything goes wrong, there's a plan for that, too.

This far offshore the issue is rescue. Even today, distance trumps immediacy. The range of a helicopter is less than 300 miles. I have the number of the U.S. Coast Guard station in Oahu on the satellite phone, but they're more than a thousand miles away. No agency patrols these waters, because that would put assets far from where they are needed most of the time. The Coast Guard would most likely direct commercial traffic to our aid. The law of the sea makes compliance mandatory, despite the expense of interrupted commerce. There are many recent episodes in which giant ships have arrived at the scene of disabled boats, maneuvered skillfully to shield them from howling winds and breaking seas, and taken the crews safely aboard. The owner, before leaving his boat, is directed to open her seacocks so the yacht will sink and not be a hazard to navigation.

It was once very difficult to locate a yacht in trouble, but with GPS it's easy. Even if the boat sinks, our EPIRB, for Emergency Position-Indicating Radio Beacon, would continue to send its position within a hundred feet.

As a child I was fascinated with stories of downed pilots and wrecked sailors being saved after drifting for months at sea. Before GPS, waiting was part of survival. Time was on their side as long as they could keep alive, and staying alive bought time to be rescued. But nobody's good at waiting anymore. Robinson Crusoe was on his island 28 years, which today sounds preposterous. Cartoons of a bearded man alone on a desert island used to evoke "marooned." Now they're ironic, with a cellular phone in the joke somewhere.

The ability to wait can take you far. It's a lost knack. Apollo 11 required four days to travel to the moon in 1969, and a week to get back. Today it takes eight and a half minutes to get to the orbit of the space station. We'd rather go nowhere than wait.

For a small boat disabled on the open sea, rescue is more likely than ever before. A crew of a sinking yacht half way to Hawai'i can expect salvation in a day or two, if it comes to that. Most boats carry a survival raft containing water, food, and a portable GPS. The sight of its canister lashed on deck, ready to instantly inflate in a crisis, has comforted the thoughts of many a worried crew.

I probably should have mentioned this before, but we don't have one.

{PREPARATION}
Dinghy as Lifeboat

A GOOD DINGHY NEEDS to serve many masters. I have no inflatable or outboard motor. No emergency life raft, either. So my 60-pound mahogany plywood Eastport pram needs to be a jack of all trades—sailboat, tender and one-man lifeboat. I wouldn't give it up, but the little pram does have limitations. It sails wonderfully, but floats low if capsized. That's not good for the ultimate function if bad turns worse.

The dink rides securely lashed upsidedown on the foredeck. To make it sit flush, with no wobble, I trimmed the transom to conform to the crown of the deck. A hard dink has unexpected good consequences. It doesn't interfere at all with the genoa or with passage to the bow. The skeg makes for a grand first grab when going forward in a seaway, and the next handhold is an insert in the inverted daggerboard box. The most treacherous journey on most sailboats in heavy seas is from mast to bow pulpit. No more, on our boat.

So, am I making a case for light wooden dinghies on deck? Sure. But I can only carry one other person and a dog, and the water needs to be pretty flat. Rowing them is no fun, although alone you go like a surfboard. Forget a half-mile ride ashore with five guests in blazers drinking prosecco, that's what an outboard-powered inflatable does so well. However, I don't miss dragging a wet mass of whale blubber out of a too-small compartment, pumping it up, and then praying over an outboard motor.

Anyway, how many dinghies can you have? One must serve.

As a solo lifeboat, an Eastport pram will make you

smile. After all, an emergency life raft can be had for under $1,500. A standard inflatable, if pumped up in advance of disaster, does as well or better. I suppose you could have all three, and tow them in a fourth.

More flotation was definitely needed for the lifeboat role. It came in two cans—as two-part expanding foam from U.S. Composites, at about $85 the gallon. The chemical reaction causes heat, but not all that much. So I just lined the forward well of the dink with cardboard, taped black plastic trash bags to contain the expansion in the necessary shape, mixed the components for the recommended 15 seconds, poured like it was nitroglycerine and ran behind the blast wall.

For the foam to rise the ambient temperature needs to be 70F, and 80F is better. Every 10 degrees below 80 means 20 percent less expansion. I did the fill in three pours, since it's difficult to calculate the result. Urged by a heat gun, the foam rose in minutes and was hard and smooth in half an hour. When done in close sequence, each new layer adheres to the old. In three hours out popped a perfectly sized plug of foam that looks like it will support 200 pounds or so. Great fun.

I screwed a piece of 3/8 inch plywood over it to hold it firmly down. Added weight, about 8 pounds. Some lines looped around the gunnels give a lifeboat-like appearance and place to clip on a safety harness.

Are you crazy, going offshore with a wooden dink instead of an eight-man emergency raft? As a singlehander, maybe not. In several gales at sea I've considered what it would be like to inflate and board a life raft in 50 knots of wind, and concluded that success was not assured. At best under those conditions you can expect to clip your harness and EPIRB onto the survival vessel and manage to remain attached to it while departing the wreck in an uncontrolled way. When it's hell in a handbasket, anything that floats is what you need and you'll be in the water with it, not inside it. Later you can bail and climb aboard and wait for rescue.

I conclude that in today's world there will not be much waiting. With a GPS EPIRB, AIS, and a satphone, to survive abandoning ship likely means rescue within days. If you are run down without warning by a containership, well, your raft is probably not as important as your luck. If your boat is sinking after being holed by a telephone pole or an angry swordfish, or otherwise flooding beyond the capacity of the pumps, then if you have managed to communicate your position or at least turned on the EPIRB, you will probably bob off when the time comes with a dry shirt as she sinks out from under your feet. And this you can do in a pram as easily as in a life raft.

Risk assessment is a personal thing. My calculation, made while warm and dry and feeling clever, is based on the premise that satellites have changed everything. The likelihood of 60 days in a raft holding your hat upside-down in rain squalls has been decreased by the swarm of observant grandmas in geosynchronous orbit overhead. What is all-important now is your GPS position and clean underwear. Fail to inform the satellites and the odds of rescue, even today, drop sharply. If you do get off a call for help, no expense will be spared in coming to your aid. It is a little-acknowledged fact that, there being no world war, navies have nothing better to do than speed toward your plywood dinghy with its bleating EPIRB. The whole world is listening and wants nothing more than for you to shut up and appear for penance on the evening news. A lost yachtsman becomes a training exercise. That's good, and better than a penknife. Or anyway, it's what settles for good when disaster strikes.

I hope not to demonstrate any of this, or defend the thesis against a jury of sharks. But it does help justify adding eight pounds to what used to be a very light dinghy.

CHAPTER 19

THE ENGINE

D*AY 10, 0920 HOURS. Wind shift. Jibed whisker pole. Opened second tub of butter.*

The sun rose late today. It didn't come over the horizon until 7 o'clock, more proof of our progress west. I postpone turning back the hands of the clock because I enjoy seeing the change in longitude. The later the sun rises the more distance we have put between us and Greenwich, England. The GPS says it in numbers, but sunrise is a billboard.

I need to jibe the whisker pole before breakfast. The wind shifted 20 degrees during the night, which made *Thelonious* change course 20 degrees too, because the self-steering vane follows the wind. Our course is now 250 degrees magnetic, which is north of the rhumb line, the direct course to Kaua'i. I should have done it during the night, but Xenophon needed my attention in Asia to deal with some pretty disturbing rumors.

I agree with his plan to fight out of hostile country through Armenia, which has friendly Greek settlements on the Black Sea. But Xenophon is a literary guy and an aristocrat, and although the hard-boiled jock troops are fun to play dice with, none of them can read. They tend to follow anybody who waves his arms and promises booty, so that's how the other officers lead them. Greek commanders are good at rhetoric, even when their ideas are bad. They lead by reputation, threats and appeals to pride and the gods. And although they all claim ancestry back to famous men and always sound logical, their real techniques are sophism and demagoguery. As a door-to-door salesman I was trained to use the same Aristotelian rules of persuasion to sell vacuum cleaners, and once, after a three-hour harangue, managed to close a deal on a $300 machine with a family that didn't even own a rug.

That memory left a bad taste, so I was worried all night about what Xenophon was getting himself into. Worried, really? Well, without outside distractions a book becomes the present universe and its events and people take on terrific immediacy. It's as if the biggest clock of all simply disappears and thousands of years of human endeavor exist in the same moment. Nothing a Persian prince or a Thracian mercenary says or does seems exotic or unfamiliar. Times have changed, but people are the same. Expectations are different, but we're not.

In Xenophon's time, events were seen as the result of character. Today we assume that events make character. We ask, what positions does a leader have? Where does he stand on foreign policy, the minimum wage, marriage, guns? But do policies make leaders, or is it the other way around? I was wedged in the bunk about 4 a.m. when it became apparent that the men liked Xenophon's character, but his fellow officers didn't. A rumor started that his own colleagues were plotting to kill him.

So, that's one reason why I didn't get up and jibe last night. The other reason was that I still don't have a good way to do it, which is pretty stupid to admit this far offshore. Come on, let's get it over with. All we have to do is move the pole from one side of the boat to the other.

Bend the knees moving up onto the cabin house, because that helps absorb the continuous rolling. Double the safety tether so it's only three feet long, because that makes some resistance in the hand, for balance. I use it as orientation, the same way a dragged ski pole gives a point of reference to a skier in a whiteout. At the mast, grab the shrouds and relax. Ain't the view grand from up here? I'll say. We haven't seen a ship in seven days. Maybe there aren't any more in the world, ever think of that?

The big, triangular genoa is pulling nicely on the starboard side of the boat, perfectly square to the wind. The telescoping whisker pole is set at 16 feet, which allows us to use all 350 square feet of jib. But if we roller-furl the jib around the forestay to reduce its size, we'd have to shorten the pole, too. If not, the jib will only furl halfway and when the wind comes up that's too much.

Here's the problem I can't solve: the pole extends from 12 to 20 feet long. To change the length, push the release button at the base and reach out 12 feet with the other hand to pull out the pole. Can't do it, right? The pole was designed for two people, one to push and one to pull. Or for Plastic Man. So, there's that.

And then there's the length. Sixteen feet is a lot of lever arm to deal with when standing on tippy toes on the narrow foredeck of a rolling yacht. At least for me.

A control line connects both ends of the pole. Pulling the line releases the jib sail from the outward end. The jib starts flapping. Now unhook the pole from the mast. Hang on, because it's now supported only by a lift line from the top of the mast. Uncleat the lift and lower the pole just off the deck. Crawl to the bow and switch jib sheets. The goal is now to maneuver the pole to the other side of the bow, but it's four feet too long to pass the headstay. My method for that is a hopping, one-handed, hope-for-the-best kabuki theater dance, none of it predictable or efficient, until the pole is on the other side. To reattach the inboard end to the mast takes all my strength, and feels like grabbing a flying arrow out of the air. Now go back and trim the lines and winch the sail taut on its new side of the boat.

That's a sloppy way to jibe a pole and in a squall it's almost dangerous. Meanwhile, Xenophon's men are fighting barefoot uphill in snow against barbarians rolling down enormous rocks.

Now there's perspective.

1400 hours. Speed four, wind 10. Full main and genoa. Water temp 69.5. Lunch Spam on sourdough with banana peppers and a cold beer.

Time for the daily recharge of the batteries.

We need the engine for that, and the Universal M25 is very reliable. There's no key, just pull the ignition switch. The clicking sound is the lift pump, which pressurizes the fuel lines. Now hold down the button to energize the glow plugs and preheat the cylinders. Ten seconds ought to do it. Push the start button and the diesel rumbles to life. If it ever fails to start, the batteries will slowly die and with them all the instrumentation, GPS and AIS.

Therefore, the engine always must start.

{PREPARATION}
Diesel Electronics

FOR SAILBOAT OWNERS, THE diesel engine and its wiring harness and gauges is the deep end of the amateur mechanic pool. Professionals abound, so why bother to understand any of it?

Well, twice last year my engine wouldn't start up again after being turned off. I could jump the solenoid with a screwdriver—if there was someone in the cockpit to hold down the paired glow plug and starter buttons. When it happened while out alone, I had to sail back into the slip through a maniacal fleet of 10-year-old Optimist pram racers all yelling "Starboard!" at me like Transpac lawyers. So, there was that.

And then there were the cockpit gauges. The tachometer jumped like a kangaroo. The ammeter didn't function at all. The faded water temperature dial never got above 160, but was it measuring anything? The switch to test the oil light was quite mysterious, and I eventually understood it only after abandoning Aristotelian deductive logic, which, although it sustained Christianity for a Millennium, is quite susceptible to the false premise eventually identified for me by a consulting electrician. Behind the cockpit control panel was the typical tangle of wiring. The panel looked OK from a bar stool at midnight, but upon sober inspection in the morning had a rode-hard-and-put-away-wet appearance. So I determined to fix the old girl up with two bucks and a pat on the head. This was, as usual, an underestimation.

Aging marine electrical systems wear down but not out. Renewing them is mostly just a matter of performing known safety upgrades, re-terminating wires, improving grounds and replacing instruments and switches. An electrical system should really pose no challenge to anyone who has worked on the space shuttle or dug a root cellar in permafrost.

Attention was needed to the back side of my cockpit instruments. Several ring terminals were hanging by a thread. The ammeter lamp had corroded right off. The push-pull ignition switch and the buttons for glow and start were suspect, and with no lock washers their terminal screws were perpetually loose. An in-line fuse holder, when opened, crumbled to rusty dust. Most panel wires arrived through an 8-pin connector hidden out of sight under the cockpit floor. There were two of these famous "trailer connectors", the other one being in the engine compartment. They allowed the Ericson factory crew back in 1985 to just snap the electrical system together. But over the years corrosion may have introduced unwanted resistance, so time to cut the old connectors out. In fact, I concluded that I might as well replace everything.

I tossed the cockpit ammeter and replaced it with a voltmeter. New start and glow-plug buttons and push-pull ignition switch were installed for bright and shiny peace of mind. I even bought a new oil light test switch, since the old one didn't seem to do anything. Sometimes it lit up the oil light and sometimes it didn't. I tried it with the engine on and the engine off.

When faced with a puzzle like this, what I do is logically think it through. I envision the purpose of an electrical component, trace its circuitry in the mind's eye, and apply logic. That way you avoid the dumb mistakes of inexperienced boobs. For example, the electrical technician who, when I explained my oil light test circuitry to him, admitted he was unable to follow my thinking. He did sell me an expensive switch.

However, when I removed the old switch, I found that it was not actually connected to anything. I effortlessly deduced that this could well be the cause of its intermittent function. But without a wiring pattern to copy, I didn't know how to wire it. Furthermore, the oil light test switch was not on any Ericson wiring diagram I could find. I emailed my personal electronics consultant, Tom Metzger, for help.

"Oil light test switch?" he said. "What's that? There's no such thing on your boat."

"Of course there is," I said testily. "It's the switch right under the oil pressure warning light."

"No, that's the blower fan switch. Do you have a blower?"

"Of course not. I threw it away last year. Who needs a blower with a diesel?"

"Well, since there is no such thing as an oil pressure light test switch, and since you have no blower fan, you can throw that switch away, too." I could hear Metzger laughing a thousand miles away.

My cockpit instrument panel now looked so fresh and shiny that I found myself stealing glances at it instead of pretending it wasn't there. The tachometer didn't bounce, the buttons were no longer corroded, the wiring had new connections good for 30 more years. And I had done the job all with my pretty little hands.

However, when I pulled the brand new ignition switch for the first time, the engine started. This unexpected surprise threw me back three feet. When you pull that switch the lift pump starts, the oil light comes on, the gauges activate. The engine is not supposed to roar to life like carnival in Brazil.

Panic email to Metzger: Now what have I done?

He got back in an hour. Those shiny new buttons you bought for glow plug and starter—does the box say 'Normal Off, Mom on'? Mom is for "momentary." Because if they say 'Normal On, Momentary off', you bought the wrong ones. Just change them. There being no emoticon for "What an Idiot," he closed with a Smiley Face.

With a functioning instrument panel, I could now pull back the insulated cover of the diesel engine and look at it while scratching my head. I had learned from my friendly tutors that, even if neither a diesel mechanic nor master electrician, you don't have to know very much if you know what you're looking for.

So, how did my Universal M25 engine look?

Well, for starters, the wires connected all over it were kind of messy, even if I didn't really know what they all did. The ground wires on the engine block looked pretty random. The ring connectors weren't all the right size. The trailer connector was suspect. A plastic in-line fuse holder appeared original, and therefore 28 years old, and its 25A fuse was one of the most critical on the boat. Many wires were heavy with engine paint overspray, suggesting age. It was obvious that my wiring would never get out of the chorus line. Runs 10, Looks 3.

I took yet another self-directed Internet course, this time in diesel engine upgrades. Twenty years ago it was all a secret. Today anyone can apprentice to the masters.

Success does take getting hands dirty. I performed the recommended upgrades one at a time, ploddingly, but learning something new every hour about tools, gear and suppliers. When I look at the engine now, it's different. The wires are neat and coiled, the replaced components stand out as brand new, the grease and rust are gone, every obvious question has been answered, and all under a new coat of Universal bronze engine paint.

But the most important change is in me. I know what each wire does, where it goes, and why it's there. I'm far from a diesel mechanic, but for the first time I know what I'm looking at. If something goes wrong and the engine doesn't start, I'll know what to do.

Our little diesel is still just a three-cylinder, 21-horsepower tractor engine sentenced forever to plow an ocean that won't hold a furrow. But it's been running for 1,663 hours so far, and with luck and a wink and occasional zinc, might just keep going as long as I do.

WORRIES

D AY 11, 0610 HOURS. *Wind 15, speed 6. Ship alarm for Tangguh Palung, 835 foot tanker bound Ensenada, Mex. Seemed very close under full moon. Many flying fish on deck.* The AIS alarm is set for five miles, but in this perfect weather didn't pick up *Tangguh Palung* until it was only two miles away. At that distance a ship looms large, especially when announced by the ear-splitting alarm I installed so as not to sleep through it. Two miles is enough, though, and we were never on a collision course.

This is the prettiest morning so far. Venus hangs like a bulb on a string, and the moon is huge. Today is Saturday, and at noon I'll place the weekly satellite phone call home. It's something to look forward to. So is coffee and breakfast. The bilge water is where it should be, a few inches gently sloshing. I don't know where the leak went, I sure didn't imagine it.

As the coffee water boils, there's something I can't put off. During the night Xenophon several times mentioned his admiration for Agesilaus, the Spartan king. Never heard of him. But I have two volumes of Plutarch's "Lives" on board, and as I'd hoped, Agesilaus was one of them.

I put off the morning deck work to read, sipping coffee. The king had one leg shorter than the other, but bore himself so naturally it was hardly noticed. Even in the brutal Spartan way of life he was generous and obedient to their laws, and he reigned 41 years, which was very long back then. I left him saddened, though, because the passion of the Greeks had again turned upon themselves. Agesilaus was recalled from a successful campaign against foreign Persia and ordered to lay waste to Thessaly and Thebes, city states of his own region. Plutarch noted sorrowfully this "conspiracy of the Greeks for their own mischief." For an hour that darkened the sea all around me on a lovely morning.

I am sorry to go on like this so early. I know the names are obscure and the blood long dried, and at home a night book closes for the day. Here, it doesn't. My only companions kill each other, pocket slave money for wives and children, and themselves die with awful immediacy. The old books seem not able to contain them, and what's worse, in these kings and traitors, I see all of us with more clarity than before, and the exaggerated history of men and gods seems to lay open the whole human business. Is being alone to join all the ghosts that ever lived? All I know is that it sticks, that lament of Plutarch's: the best of us do mischief to ourselves.

And now to eggs and corned beef hash, a big sizzling pile of it in the frying pan.

How do you feel? For myself, I'm finally starting to relax and enjoy the ride. Good weather helps, and calm waves that let us dine in style on the tabletop with a book. I feel comfortable now in showing the list I have been secretly keeping in the back of the logbook. It might have concerned you, earlier. The list is called:

Things I am Worrying About Now
1. Leak is from the keel bolts.
2. Sat phone breaks, can't call home
3. Steering cables fail.
4. Engine doesn't start.
5. Sailing home.

In former versions, #1 was "Leak," and it was underlined. After tearing the boat apart and finding no obvious source, the underline went away. But "Leak is from the keel bolts" still has an ominous ring. If the bolts fail and our 4,000–pound counterbalance drops off, we will flop on our side in mid-ocean like a tipped cow and we can forget any thought of self-rescue. As for the satellite phone, well,

I just don't know how it works and I don't like trusting something I don't understand. I haven't mentioned the steering cables before, but there's a sound coming from the back of the boat, a grinding sound. We can rig emergency steering, though.

What I should make a list of is what to say to my family. My wife and son will be waiting by the telephone, and my three daughters waiting to hear in Virginia, Colorado and newly arrived to Los Angeles from New Hampshire. If I say I am feeling more relaxed, they'll wonder what the problem was I hadn't told them about. If I tell them everything is fine, they will suspect I'm not telling them everything. Tracy could qualify as a forensic linguist, so alert is she to nuances of speech and tone of voice and the crime of not telling her everything. But what is everything? That there are more flying fish on deck? That Lord Russell's "History of Philosophy" got wet because the mast boot leaked onto the bookshelf? That I love her? Shouting that into a crackly space phone pointed at the equator is not going to happen.

There was something else on the lists, too:

6. Relax, idiot.

I was glad to finally cross it off. I have been ultra-aware of how big the ocean is, and how insignificant the boat and the crew, and how everything depends on me. Now I don't think it really does. Pride just gets in the way. It works better to shrug and do the best you can.

Day 11, noon. Made 105 miles. GRIB shows wind increasing next few days. Called home.

The satellites that carry phone calls are in equatorial orbit, so that's where we are instructed to point the six-inch antenna of the handset. The best place to stand is in the windy cockpit, for a clear view of the sky.

It takes a while for the connection to be made, and then comes a dim semi-familiar ringing, and then someone who has been waiting picks up the phone.

"Hello? Can you hear OK? Yes, good, we're halfway there. We made over a hundred miles yesterday. How are things there?

"Going to dinner at Linda's sound great. News? Well, I'm seeing more flying fish. Five this morning, but too small to cook. And there's nothing wrong with my voice, it's just the wind noise."

Ten minutes went by quickly and I did wind up saying, "I love you." She sounded far away, so I had to shout it to be heard.

On the whole, a satisfactory exchange. We talked about Hawai'i, and our reservations at Hanalei Colony. I'm ahead of schedule and should make it in plenty of time. Let's have a brandy and a warm beer. If you look at us objectively, things really are going well. The good weather is holding. The leak's not getting worse. But a satellite phone brings nobody together. The distance is heightened by the flat timbre of voices and the sense of every word travelling to orbit and back. Stop analyzing, next Saturday we'll be coming down the home stretch.

Funny how nobody mentioned the dog. Well, on the telephone dogs don't necessarily come up. On the other hand, Harley the rescue Labrador is 14 years old, and no longer strong. He tends to whine and limp when any one of us goes out of sight, as if abandoned by his pack. The vet and I went over his X-rays and it doesn't look good. Arthritis, hip dysplasia, sores. We've been carrying him down the stairs lately to get outside. When I asked how much time he had left, Dr. Condello said quickly, "Oh, a long time." When I brought that news home it made everybody happy. But I thought at the time it was a politic answer to a common question about dogs who will probably die soon, if not tomorrow.

I had not mentioned the leak. Why give people you love bad news when they can't do anything about it?

And they had not mentioned the dog.

1500 hours. Lunch tuna. Water 71F, wind astern 20 knots. Transferred 5 gallons fuel deck to tank.

The fuel tank on *Thelonious* holds 20 gallons of diesel oil in a trapezoidal stainless steel fabrication under the quarter berth. The thrifty engine burns only about half a gallon an hour. That's 40 hours at five knots for a range of about 200 miles. Two hundred miles is plenty of fuel for coastwise cruising, and means that in a flat calm we could motor from the Cape Cod Canal to Maine. It's not enough for this trip, though. Not if we want to come back.

The outbound leg is mostly with the breeze from behind, thanks to the trade winds which at this latitude blow predictably across the lower northern hemisphere. In the Atlantic, they pushed Columbus to the West Indies, here they bear us steadily toward Hawai'i or Japan. We ride the lower limb of a vast circle of air revolving clockwise. At the top of the circle, a thousand miles north, the wind blows the other way, from west to east. In the middle of this spinning atmospheric mass lies a zone of calms, the center of the North Pacific High. To return, we'll have to traverse those doldrums.

If you want to make the North Pacific High laugh, tell it you will motor 200 miles across it. It may answer with 500 miles of no wind at all, and yachts sailing home from Hawai'i have been becalmed there for weeks. For coming back, I wanted more range. The idea was to carry four five-gallon fuel cans on deck, extending our capacity to 40 gallons or 400 miles. When I lugged the slippery polyethylene containers to the boat, however, there was no good way to secure them on deck. The 30-pound jugs needed to be accessible but immobile, and able to withstand the forces of breaking seas and constant chafe. After trying several solutions, I eventually built custom racks of heavy plywood to cradle them between the stays of the cabin house, the racks lashed down and the jugs lashed to the racks. Now we have twice the fuel.

There's another calculation to keep in mind. Each day we burn a quarter-gallon just recharging the batteries, and it reduces our cruising range accordingly. Of course, if there's no wind and we're motoring at five knots, then the engine time also counts as recharging time, which stretches the range out again. Therefore, motoring time depends on an accurate estimate of wind in the future, since we must retain some fuel for each of those future days.

Despite a fair amount of study, the whole business of batteries, voltage and amperes still makes my head spin. *Thelonious* may be a sailboat, but she is an electronic one. Attention had to be paid.

{PREPARATION}
Batteries

HOW MUCH BATTERY POWER do we really need? The answer requires assessing the realistic use of the boat, which is one of the hardest questions an owner faces. It is further complicated by the Rubik's-cube challenge of electrical capacity, charge rate and energy expenditure, for which explanations are provided in the Navajo language.

Will you ever want refrigeration, air conditioning or a microwave? Is your electric draw per cruising day 200 amps or 20? Should there be a portable generator, solar panels, or a windmill? Do they make a crank to charge an iPhone? Do you need much electricity at all? It's not a bad question—Chichester won the first solo transatlantic race with paraffin running lights. And since the wind usually blew them out immediately, he used less paraffin than expected.

I took the minimalist approach. Once committed to warm beer after three days the mind is clarified, especially if you only have two Group 27 deep cycle batteries aboard, and will use only one for house loads since the second is reserved as a backup. Why not more or larger batteries? They're expensive and heavy and there's simply no convenient place for them on the E32-3. So be it.

What electronics shall we use on a hypothetical 30-day cruise, and how shall we recharge the one puny battery that will power them? What is the expected daily draw, in amperes? What is an ampere, exactly? What is the nature of the Buddha, exactly? Do you think any Zen master would answer that? Let's keep the irrelevant questions to a minimum.

My daily number turned out to be relatively low,

computed by multiplying the appliance draw times duration, for amp-hours.

> Binnacle GPS/chart plotter.............0.5 x 2 hours = 1
> (No need to keep the GPS on continually)
> AIS...0.5 x 24 hours = 12
> LED running Lights.....................0.7 x 8 hours = 5
> LED cabin lights..........................0.5 x 2 hours = 1
> Stereo..2.0 x 2 hours = 4
> Total 22 amp hours/day

Notice there's no fridge, no single-sideband radio and no powerful autopilot. My single deep-cycle battery is rated at 100 amp hours. Theoretically, a draw of 22 amp hours would take it down to 78 percent, still well over half fully charged and with a mighty fudge factor before zero. We really, really don't want to run the battery down to no charge at all, which shortens its life and possibly ours.

I have a servo-pendulum wind vane for sailing, and only use the Raymarine wheel pilot when motoring. On a slow-response setting, that's only about 2 amps in calm conditions. Not on the list are the batteries of an iPhone, satellite phone, laptop and video cameras, which also have to be recharged daily.

Shall we keep all these numbers in our head? You may. I can't, so I installed a battery monitor which displays current state of charge on a screen, along with draw and remaining duration of charge. The plan is to discharge only to 50 percent of capacity, which is the sweet spot for efficiency, and recharge only to 85 percent, because beyond that the going gets slow.

So, how shall we recharge? There are many approaches.

I chose to use the diesel engine. It's not passive like solar, it costs fuel to run, it has moving parts, and bearded cruising gurus don't think using the auxiliary engine is the best way to go about maintaining batteries. But I'm not living aboard with cats. I'm extending my cruising range and independence. I have an engine and it might as well earn its keep. I'd like to skip a windmill generator or solar power plant overhead.

Most yacht engines come fitted with an alternator for recharging batteries. Mine was rated at 51 amps, but would take hours and hours to recharge even our low electrical usage. More recharging hours means more fuel burn which means less cruising range in the doldrums, not to mention a noisy, rattling cabin. To recharge in less than an hour daily, I need more output, as promised by the more muscular Balmar 100.

But there's more to it than a jock alternator. The Balmar also needed a "smart" regulator. A regulator determines the flow of current, and mine was pretty dumb. Its output was always the same, little more than a trickle, no matter the urgent needs of the half-depleted tub of acid. A smart regulator can pour on the juice when the battery is low, then back off so as not to boil the battery in its own bathwater. Do you notice how I provide these explanations in laymen's terms? Thank you. I am a layman.

The installation of the new alternator was easier than expected. I was encouraged by José, a well-regarded professional I tried twice to hire, but who insisted I could do the job myself. The issue with installation is that a more powerful alternator robs one horsepower from the engine for every 25 amps produced, which puts strain on the bracket, pulleys and the belt—especially, the belt, which can spew friction dust or break if alignment is not perfect. So far, in 10 hours, I have no dust.

I saw José the electrician on the dock a week later. He came over to check my work and nodded, satisfied.
I asked him why he hadn't done the job himself, when it was so easy.

"Lucky for you," José said with a grin. "Putting a new alternator on, that can be nothing but problems."

Much as I would have liked to know that before, it is still marvelous to see my batteries go from 60 percent charged to 85 percent charged in only 45 minutes of engine time. And if the new alternator breaks, I have the old one as a spare and know what to do with it.

CHAPTER 21

FILTER CHANGE

D AY 11, 1800 HOURS. *Lovely evening. Charging batteries.*
I like charging with the engine in late afternoon. It means dinner is near, and the sound of the diesel means our batteries will be up to snuff for the night. I propose Indian food for this evening. I laid in about a dozen microwaveable meals from Trader Joe's, along with lots of pre-cooked rice. No microwave, so I just dump the pouches in the frying pan. What makes it all work is lots of mango chutney. That, and being hungry.

I topped off the fuel tanks from the deck jugs using a rattle siphon and didn't spill a drop. The siphon has a one-way valve on the end, no need these days to risk a mouthful of gas. We're surfing at seven knots under sail, so the propeller isn't engaged. We charge in neutral, the new 100-amp Balmar alternator humming like the electrical power plant it is. It's good to be well prepared.

The battery monitor shows 65 percent charged. It was 85 percent this time yesterday, so we've used 20 amp-hours of juice for lights and instruments and the stereo. To get back to 85 percent takes only about 40 minutes of engine time. The new lift pump I installed has been working perfectly. I even cleaned the inside of the fuel tank, which is one of those jobs you don't bother with unless heading out of sight of diesel mechanics. The fuel tank is 27 years old and has been filled with diesel since the boat was launched. Fuel purchased in the United States is almost always free of contaminants, but even so the tank can harbor strains of yeasts and bacteria. Biomass is a problem for aircraft, too, where it's called jet fuel fungus. As diesel ages, it also creates the chemical sludge asphaltene. Biological growth is only possible with water, so the usual suggestion is to keep the tank full to prevent condensation.

Months before departure I opened the five-inch inspection port on top and pumped the tank dry. When studied with a flashlight, the walls and floor had a uniform deposit of thin brown slime. I spent two hours with my arm in there up to the shoulder, wiping with rags and paper towels. Diesel isn't smelly and volatile like gasoline, and feels to the skin like the very light oil it is. I could only clean half the tank, the other half was blocked by the interior baffle that keeps the contents from sloshing around. But when I finally got to the showers my tank was as clean as anybody's, and I didn't have to take anybody else's word for it.

As soon as the engine roars to life the alternator kicks in. The battery monitor shows we're initially charging at a rate of 75 amps. That's a lot, but the two Group 27 deep-cycle batteries can accept it because they have room. As the state of charge increases, the rate of charge decreases. When it slows to 15 amps, I'll shut the engine down.

The M25 Universal is a little louder and makes more vibration that a gasoline equivalent, but I've become attuned to the subtleties of its voice. It sounds different depending on where you are. From the bow, it's a distant thrumming. Inside the cabin, a loud hum with pots rattling in the locker. On the cockpit seats it's like sitting on an orchestra of kazoos.

Maybe I'm a little oversensitive, because I often think the sound has changed when it hasn't changed at all. For example, just now. Sometimes the throttle setting slips, reducing the rpms a little. If that happens again, I'll just tighten up a cable clamp to increase the friction. Routine maintenance is easy if you keep up with it.

These changes in engine sound are illusions, and I know what causes them. It's me. It comes from formerly not trusting the diesel engine, and worrying that it might stop running for no reason at all. But all a diesel needs to run is air and fuel. They are famously reliable. Let's go below and dig out the tikka masala before it gets dark.

Down here the sound is different from on deck. But it shouldn't be this different. It shouldn't stutter like that. It shouldn't lose 500 rpms and cough.

Before I can get back to the cockpit the engine surges, fades, shudders and stops dead. The sound stops. We coast silently at 6 knots under full sail.

Betrayed.

The last time I felt this particular hole in my stomach was in high school, after I asked a girl to find out if another girl liked me, and got back the message, "maybe." That night in the train station tunnel in Rahway, New Jersey, where we sang a cappella because the echo was cool, I was never in better pitch. Even when we had to stop our rendition of "Blue Moon" to let the Jersey Central Line pass overhead I was still hearing music. But Friday night at the library she was leaning on some other guy like a drunk on a lamp post, laughing at his jokes instead of mine.

That felt just like this. But this betrayal was worse, because if I studied the operation of high school girls half as much as I have recently studied the operation of my diesel engine, I would have been king of the prom and on American Bandstand, too. Quit crying and get busy. Only three hours of daylight left, and we're starting to roll again.

It must be a clogged fuel filter. To access the Racor filter assembly means unloading the quarter berth of its seven-foot cushion, two anchors, coils of line, fenders, chain, sea anchor, floats and heavy boxes of canned goods. They fill the cabin, which now also has to accommodate the long bulkhead board and unwieldy engine box. It takes a long time.

The Racor is installed between the fuel lift pump and the engine. It's the primary filter, there's a secondary filter on the engine block itself. I load all my wrenches into the quarter berth and crawl in after them. The filter is the size of a coffee can and full of diesel. This why we have disposable diapers on board. I can wrap one around the filter like it was a baby's bum and the tabs hold it in place. The filter unscrews using a band wrench. I dump the contents into a bucket, spilling it as we roll.

It takes half an hour to find and install a new R20P filter unit and another half an hour to pump it full of fuel with its awkward miniature pump. The engine still won't start.

I'll have to bleed the fuel line, because air in the system stops ignition. I turn on the fuel pump with my foot while also opening the bleeder on the engine, and wait for something to spurt out. No dice.

Rationally, I know what is going on. The rough seas of our passage have stirred up residue in the fuel tank, and the filter was full of junk. Bleeding sometimes takes a while.

But it'll be dark soon, and I need to reef the mainsail for the night. Both hands are skinned and decorated by trickles of blood. I smell of diesel oil, and there's a pool of it now slopping around under the engine. Tools are everywhere, and the cabin's a mess of gear, all shifting as we roll. The old filter, when removed, showed little outward sign of contamination. Maybe it's a little darker in color than the bright white replacement canister. Maybe it's not the filter at all. The whole Racor filter assembly, in fact, is brand new, and I remember why.

We departed on a Tuesday, and the Saturday before I took the boat out alone for a final sea trial. I sailed for an hour, testing gear and installations, and headed home certain the boat was well prepared. Motoring back to the slip in the Saturday traffic of busy Marina Del Rey the engine quit and died, just like that. I had to anchor in the channel and call for a tow.

The next day was Sunday. I pulled the fuel filter, which was brand new. It was clean. Spotless. But the engine still wouldn't start.

The next day was Monday, the beginning of Fourth of July week. In summer, every boatyard and every mechanic is booked solid a month in advance. I went shop to shop, describing my problem. There was no one free to troubleshoot a common problem on little auxiliary sailboats. The only hope was a guru named Peter, who inhabited a boat yard full of million-dollar yachts and had either gone to lunch or was around here somewhere, or would be back soon or possibly not.

But I'm leaving for Hawai'i tomorrow, I explained to everybody who would listen. Cool, everybody said.

Heading back to my car I noticed a 20-foot ladder resting against the hull of a 70-foot TransPac Race yacht sitting high on its 10-foot keel. I climbed the ladder. A hatch on the stern deck was open into cavernous darkness. I stuck my head in the hatch and yelled as loud as I could, Peter!

Up came a startled face I'd never seen before, and had never seen me. I told Peter I was leaving for Hawai'i, my engine wouldn't start, my filter was new, and I was out of ideas.

"Diesels always start," he said with a shrug. "Air's getting in, that's all. How old is your filter assembly"?

It was 29 years old, and as he suggested, there turned out to be a hairline crack in the aluminum body. By 4 o'clock I found the last replacement, incorrectly marked, in a storeroom at West Marine. By dinner it was installed and the engine bled and running again.

I'm telling all this to remember what I already know. Diesels always start if they get fuel. They won't start if there's air in the lines.

So, after 20 more minutes running the lift pump and operating the primer the supply line at the fuel jets spurted beautiful red-dye diesel. I let it pour into a can until there were no bubbles at all, and then, on the first try, the engine roared again to life.

There was never anything to worry about at all. I knew what I was doing all along, I just didn't know it. Now to clean up the mess and revisit the worry list.

6. Relax, stupid.

POLE LIFT

D AY 12, NOON POSITION *26°19'N, 142°21'W. 140 miles.*
Wing and wing with reefed main. Rudder cables grinding.
Today I confirmed a northern fulmar, a big glider with a
stubby neck. The yellow bill has a sort of lump on top, which I think
is for the excretion of salt. I've seen a lot of shearwaters streaking
low over the waves. They're sleek, but the fulmar is bigger and has
a bull neck. Hard to know if I'm right, but I think I recognized the
coarse grunting call described by Roger Tory Peterson.

No doubt at all about the white-tailed tropicbird, which has long
central feathers that look like the tail of a kite passing overhead. I
listed this morning's sighting as a white-tail because it clearly had a
bold black chevron across the wing tops, and the red-tailed and red-
billed versions don't.

Stormy petrels are everywhere, darting and skimming and walking
on the waves. We always called them Mother Carey's Chickens, a
name derived from Mater Cara, a Latin name of the Blessed Virgin.
I don't know if they can really predict storms.

What do you think about this beach umbrella in the cockpit?
Not very nautical, but the bright colors of red, green and yellow
are mighty cheerful. I taped the base to the binnacle guard, so it's
easy to stick the umbrella in when we've only got about 10 knots of
apparent wind in the cockpit. If it keeps turning inside out, I'll have
to take it below.

Many sailboats have permanent shade installed, and it is true that without our $10 umbrella *Thelonious* is entirely exposed to the elements. What's popular is a Bimini top over the helmsman's seat or a dodger for the open companionway to cut the wind and rain. The two can be connected by canvas to shade the entire cockpit.

We don't have either, because it seems to me that they interrupt the view of the sails and rig and add windage. Windage is anything the wind can press on that isn't driving the yacht, and the last thing you want in a storm. Besides, a singlehanded sailor rarely sits in the sun for long, and when on deck with a tether, the fewer obstructions the better.

Thelonious does have weather cloths, although they're out of style on cruising boats. A weather cloth is canvas fixed to the lifelines around the cockpit. It provides shelter from wind and spray and flying fish, and makes a good billboard on which to paint the vessel's name for easy identification.

The rolling is getting on my nerves again. Lunching from a bowl of canned New England clam chowder feels like dancing the samba in a wheelchair. To cope with the roll I hold the bowl in one hand and the spoon in the other and let them swing back and forth through an arc of three feet. I chase the bowl through the air with the spoon. Every mouthful is a triumph of planning and execution. But we're going fast, surfing the building swells. Shall we put some music on?

To encourage thoughtful digestion, or any digestion at all, I like Marian McPartland. For years she had a show on public radio. She would invite her peers to sit at the piano, discuss their style with disarming accuracy, and then say, "Shall we play something together?" The result was some of the best off-hand jazz collaborations. She could imitate any style and satirize it, too. Her own style was brilliance without guile. At a club in Washington, D.C., I used to watch her go through a pack of cigarettes every set, crushing them out on the piano-top ashtray with the same unselfconscious ease she crushed the standard repertory. McPartland died a few years ago at age 95, I think it was, but her radio recordings will be around as long as the planet has ears. I'll play some for us. Wait, what was that?

There's a banging from the foredeck, hear it? Whoa! Better

dump the chowder in the sink and get up there, fast. This is why I leave the octopus of the safety harness spread out on the clear bunk, so it goes on without tangling. Quickly, up we go.

Oh, it's just the pole lift halyard. The bridle on the pole broke and the halyard is swinging all over the place as we roll. Right now, that shackle on the end is a missile. I need to get forward and catch it as it goes by.

Ow! That was a direct hit on the forehead. Oh well, second time's the charm. First time was a night watch in the English Channel when Rich Rodoreda lost control of a foredeck halyard and the flying hunk of stainless steel on the end came out of nowhere and knocked me clean out for ten seconds. Took Rich 35 years to apologize, but I was tickled that he even remembered. Shake it off and pay attention, please.

There, got it! Just like plucking a bird out of the air. Now let's get the 16-foot pole off the mast and safely on deck without falling overboard in the process. It sure is pretty up here on the cabin house, rolling and surfing, the long swells cresting as far as the eye can see and the sun and clouds sparkling. Good to have daylight for this job. Just let the pole come off and slam on deck and then dive on it to keep it there.

Not elegant, but at least I can still laugh at myself. One of the unexpected factors in being alone is that I still feel eyes watching, and judging. Since there's no one else, I must be watching and judging myself. That's not bad, because who else is there to keep me on my toes? But it's also weird, like telling your hand to stop scratching your nose. The old question pops up whenever it gets the chance. How many of us are on board, anyway? Is a solo consciousness one person, or everybody who ever lived?

Meanwhile, the genoa has been busy wrapping itself around the forestay. No problem, we'll just haul on the sheets and untangle it. But the sheets are wrapped, too. I didn't notice this happening while securing the pole to the deck, because the truth is that everything a singlehander does takes five times longer than it should. And it takes an hour to free the mess, the last resort being to apply heavy force with a cockpit winch and risk damaging the rig. But it worked.

Now, with the pole bridle repaired and the sails re-trimmed, I'm struck by the enjoyment caused by this unexpected development and its successful conclusion. I seem always prepared for some sort of disaster, not so much sinking or being carried off by aliens, but any schedule-busting gear failure. Progress is easy to define—just get closer each day to our destination of Hawai'i. Disaster for me is being disabled, proceeding under a jury rig at reduced speed, having to tell the home front some story that isn't the whole story: A sprung mast, a bent rudder post, a broken wrist. So a minor case of chafe, which is what broke the pole bridle, draws a smile. I can fix that or do without it. It won't break the schedule.

Every voyage promises known unknowns, and every sailor accepts them. When a problem becomes known it's almost a relief. A pole bridle is an easy fix.

1830 hours, wind 25. Lowered mainsail and now under half winged genoa. Dinner canned Argentine beef with potato flakes. Rolling. Toilet backing up.

Xenophon has made it out of Asia, all the way to the Black Sea. I'm proud of how he stood up to the ordeal and the uncertainty. I'm glad to know all the Greeks and Romans that Plutarch wrote about. They took for granted unknowns that in modern times seem risky and unwise.

It was their nature to go forward. They knew nothing was assured. They worried less about what they couldn't control. They put gods or fate in charge of all that and went about being themselves. In Athens it was a crime not to participate in civic affairs. It was expected that the richest and most powerful people would lead at home and in battle, and whether they failed or succeeded the outcome would attach to the family name for centuries. Nobody was promised an afterlife, and yet from foot soldiers to Socrates they died extremely well in accord with tradition and the law.

My world is different. I'm used to a predictable outcome. This voyage has a predictable outcome, based on the many who have successfully sailed solo to Hawai'i and the expensive gadgets and luxury of experience applied. Angry gods or truculent fate are eliminated, and whatever goes wrong for me is subject to the casual critique, "well, he should have known that might happen."

Unknowns have a bad reputation today. We proceed cautiously, waving good sense like a blind man's cane.

I think it's the rolling that makes me go on like this. What a trivial thing it is, and so completely predictable. But rolling builds fatigue and irritation. It makes joints burn with holding on. Darkness now, and a moon scudding low through the portlights. Xenophon, I salute you. Welcome aboard *Thelonious*, Charles Darwin. I read and enjoyed your "Origin of Species" years ago. Now I hope you will tell us all about the voyage of *HMS Beagle*, in which you went around the world as a young botanist. Only 24, weren't you? And whereas we have been offshore 12 days, you were gone five years.

0000 hours, midnight. Rolling. Wind continues 25, seas 8-10. Toilet stinking.

0200 hours. No ships. Moved to cabin floor.

0445 hours. No ships. Bilge sloshing.

CHAPTER 23

DARWIN

DAY 15, 1130 HOURS. *Still rolling. Wanna make something of it?*

Four days of rolling, day and night. I'm not very good company just now, and we have 600 miles to go. The leak seems to have backed off. The overflowing bilge, which could return at any time, is currently replaced by a continual stench from the toilet which is no doubt the result of my early misunderstanding of the valve setting and our full waste tank. Somehow, the contents have overcome a rubber valve that prevents effluent from back-flowing into the bowl. It's shaped like a silly rubber hat and is universally referred to as a joker valve.

It's now clogged, so the joke's on me. I pump 20 gallons of clean sea water through the bowels of the toilet and two hours later my own waste seeps back into the bowl, reeking. You say I exaggerate? Smell is connected to imagination, and imagination has no joker valve. Once apprehended, a noxious odor requires thereafter only a bare few molecules to be remembered and amplified. Even on the bow, where air and spray mix in sparkling purity, I smell it.

Did I say how tired of this rolling I am?

Excuse me, that's a booby overhead. Note the distinct dark shading along the trailing edge of the wings. Not as stocky as a fulmar, and with a longish beak. Also, not as slender-winged as a shearwater. It'll come back, they make multiple passes.

I'll tell you why I'm tired of rolling.

Sending the noon position report is a prizefight in a phone booth.

Typing a GRIB request on the laptop is a game of Whack-A-Mole. My seat at the navigation station is athwartships, and merely keeping erect is a Pilates exercise. It is a good thing I trained myself not to feel human emotions or I might be getting really, really pissed off.

Sleeping? Forget about it.

A relaxing dinner? Never mind. I strap in at the gimbaled stove and eat like a dog stealing scraps.

This afternoon I shaved. In the days of straight razors my head would now be rolling back and forth on the cabin floor, and fine by me because my neck is sore just trying to hold it up.

Bathing? I don't even care.

Rolling through 60 degrees it wouldn't be so bad if we weren't broaching, too. If this sounds like complaining, I assure you it's not, it is objective reporting. You may say that we are once again carrying too much sail for 25 knots. Do you say that? If so, speak up. I'm open to advice, but implied criticism won't get you very far. It's a small boat, people can get on each other's nerves. So then, let nothing go unsaid, but watch what you say. May I tell you why your nerves are on edge? It is because you are not sleeping well and eating hurriedly and moping around, instead of reaching within for the mature philosophy necessary to assuage a week of being tossed non-stop like a wet salad.

Let us both get a grip on ourselves and take a lesson from Darwin.

For five years circumnavigating in *HMS Beagle* he shared a cabin not much bigger than this with his friend Captain FitzRoy. He didn't know anything at all about sailing when he departed, and at age 24 wasn't even much of a botanist yet. FitzRoy chose him, I think, because he saw a companionable fellow about his own age. And FitzRoy was right, Darwin never complained. He was seasick but got on with it anyhow. As a Victorian gentleman he didn't have the heroic standards of Xenophon, but he knew how to think courageously. He observed the physical world with clear eyes, recording it and marveling at what he saw, instead of what he was expected to see. True, he didn't have to try to read the unnecessarily small typeface of his own "The Voyage of the Beagle" in 10-foot seas during a rain squall.

Broached again. How clever of the boat to wait until it got pitch dark and moonless. Harness on, then.

The genoa is aback, pressing on the whisker pole like an umbrella inside out. Clip on to the jackline, struggle forward. It's blowing 30 knots in the squall, which makes a lot of noise and gives the jib a beating. I'm trying to steer us back on course, but it's no go. The 16-foot pole won't come off with all this force on it. There's nothing to do but lower the mainsail. I could just wait, tired as I am, because this will pass in half an hour. But no, in the meantime the jib would tear itself apart.

So, down-mainsail, pulling hand over hand. Ordinarily I would head the boat into the wind a little to ease the pressure and the wet sail would slide down of its own weight. But we're pinned by the broach. And I can only get the main halfway down, it's stuck at an intersection of the mast track. The boom is all the way out over the water, banging against the stays. Nothing I can do about that, but it means there's nothing to hold on to while I work. I'm balanced on the cabin house roof, wrestling with a hundred square feet of battens and Dacron like a kid on the yardarm of a square-rigger. The yacht lurches under foot, I compensate, lean, pull, rebalance. After 10 minutes the sail is down, and with the gasket-ties in my mouth I grope along it, securing canvas, fingernails sore and eyes full of rain. The furl is a messy job, but who cares.

Now to the wheel and steer back on course. Disengage the self-steering vane. But we're still back-winded and the helm doesn't respond. Wait for a sea to break across the stern and knock us around, now spin the wheel and watch the leeward rail go completely under water in a crazy roll as the 300 square feet of genoa jib snaps right-side out with the sound of a shotgun blast. And off we go again, surfing downwind as if nothing had happened.

No problem, standard stuff.

However, I am not only in a black mood but also not as young as I used to be. The matter came up on the cabin roof while lunging for a grip on the mainsail. A cresting wave unsteadied me, and although I caught it in time with a bend of the knees the image lingers of being pitched backwards over the lifelines into the blackness. To fall backwards is the most unacceptable of falls because in the instant of lost grip there is nothing to catch you but the open arms of fate. I would have gone over unimpeded, to drag by my tether. I would shake off the shock, grip the bulwarks as the passing water tugged at my clothes, wait for the yacht to roll toward me again, fling up an arm and a leg, and ride the next roll back aboard under the lifelines. I think I could do it.

But I also know that the yards of tall ships were manned by younger men. They climbed a hundred feet to their station and handed in heavy flax sails while balanced only on a footrope, with no harness at all. In the arctic the sails froze, in the tropics they rotted, and in storms crews sometimes fell, to be broken by the deck or absorbed forever by the passing sea. At times I have felt a kinship with them that comes from the necessity, even on a pleasure sailboat, of hauling in flapping canvas hand over hand. Tonight I feel only a premonition of weightless transport toward infinity.

With the steering vane reengaged we're back on course for Hawai'i. The squall has blown past and we wallow in confused waves, almost becalmed. Was that fear I felt, that moment of lost grip? Not exactly. It lives on more as an almost-moment, an incident that might have gone on to a different conclusion in an alternative universe, but stopped short in ours. An unrealized potentiality, you might say: A backwards glance, a rear-view mirror in which a wreck on the highway diminishes with distance, and could have been you, but wasn't.

Darwin is good on fear, less stoic than Xenophon and all Empire Englishman. In Chile he was present during several earthquakes that devastated villages, during which he observed the servants to run, the women to scream in terror, and the local gentlemen to rush haphazardly for the doorways. In his diary he concluded that "this excess of panic may be partly attributed to a want of habit in governing their fear, as it is not a feeling they are ashamed of." When two Britons were seen sleeping through an aftershock, the Chileans were indignant: "Look at those heretics, they do not even get out of their beds!"

I hope not to have a want of habit in governing fear, or to be ashamed of fear, either. But if Englishmen could sleep through an earthquake, why do I lie awake on the wet cabin floor, remembering a moment of imbalance?

The author's Yacht Design No. 1, circa 1950, a grass sailor.

A more mature design, launched with wet paint. It sank later that day.

All 89 pounds of 10-year-old Williams, hiking out on the Penguin dinghy he capsized.

Expanded foam introduced into the forward section of the tiny Eastport pram. When covered with marine plywood, total flotation equaled about 200 pounds. Lines rigged at the gunwales completed the "lifeboat."

The Sailomat 800 servo-pendulum self-steering vane gear: The white vane at top deflects if the yacht wanders off course and rotates the "oar" extended into the water below. The oar is deflected left or right by the passing water. That force is harnessed to adjust the steering wheel and return to course. The effect is smooth, silent and continuous.

Thelonious's "spare tire." Streamed on a line off the stern, any heavy object helps control a yacht running downwind in a storm. Coast Guard tests suggest a Jordan Series drogue is more effective.

For motoring through doldrums an extra 20 gallons of diesel fuel was lashed to deck boxes. The boxes must withstand breaking seas and the chafe of constant motion.

The settee in the main cabin made variations of sleep posture convenient. Sometimes an L-shaped slumber worked well. When rolling heavily, the floor proved best.

With no dance critics for 1,000 miles, Gipsy Kings on the cockpit speakers at Volume Level 11 makes for a vigorous welcome to the morning.

Homemade spaghetti sauce in a seaway. The trick is to hit the moving pan with the olive oil.

Running wing and wing before the trade winds, which often blow 20 knots night and day.

MILKY WAY

AY 16, 1320 HOURS. Probable sooty shearwater. Raised mainsail to second reef. Speed 5-6, rolling. Steering check.
Just before noon we broached again and I decided to put our back-winded position to use. I furled as much headsail as possible, leaving the pole set, and we were left bobbing like a cork, rising and falling with the swells but no longer bashing through them. It was time for a careful inspection of the steering system.

The spade rudder of *Thelonious* is connected to the boat only by the post on which it rotates. Steering cables are attached under the cockpit floor to a radial quadrant. Turn the steering wheel and cables pull the radial to turn the rudder. It's a robust system, but difficult to repair at sea. I have wood to build an independent auxiliary rudder, but that would put us in the semi-disabled category, so let's preserve the one we have.

I've also been thinking, in the dark mood of late, that our leak may come from the rudder assembly. So, once again, out comes everything from the quarter berth, and in I go. After an hour on my belly, sweat pouring, I can't find any leakage at all where the rudder tube enters the boat. Good. We had a leak last year, and in preparing for the voyage I went to some lengths to fix it.

The grinding sound of the cables comes and goes, depending on conditions, and I don't hear it at all, now. Troubleshooting will require something I am trying to learn from Darwin, which is to observe without presumption. The rudder is locked at the moment, but even so the rise and fall of the seas still makes it turn a little. I've been holding the flashlight on the upper bearing for a long time, and it seems perfectly normal. Only once did it move sideways a hundredth of an inch. That shouldn't happen, so let's keep the flashlight on it five minutes more. When I see the line of lubricating grease expand almost imperceptibly, I know immediately what's going on.

The bolts of the upper rudder bearing have come loose after weeks of constant friction. Tightening them will solve the problem. However, the nuts are down here and the bolt-tops are in the cockpit. It's a two-person job, but one can do it with vice-grip pliers on the nuts. Crawling in and out turns 10 minutes into more than an hour, but finally the bearing is tight again and we're back on course.

Wiping the grease off my arms I notice the beauty of the day. A fulmar circles above, the ocean is whitecapped and bright and I don't feel any of it. I'm sullen and ashamed, because there's no place I'd rather be than here.

Part of it, I know, is that today's noon position puts us less than 600 miles from Kaua'i. I recall the excitement of reaching halfway, and the real sense of accomplishment. We're on the home stretch now, but it feels stopped in the middle of nowhere. It could be another week till we sight land. That seems a very long time with nothing on the horizon, not even the distant spout of a whale. I have let myself forget distance. It was a mistake to unroll the approach charts so early and to study the buoys and channels of Nawiliwili Harbor when the ocean beneath us is still three miles deep.

I have made a premature landfall. I have arrived before the boat.

2000 hours. Rolling. Ravioli. The sail home.
The can of ravioli for dinner went down poorly. It tasted as dull and uninspired as I am. I just listened to a TED talk, the one by a fashion model who comes on stage in a bikini, then changes to a frumpy dress so the audience can reflect on their changed perception of her. I can usually appreciate a bikini even on the radio, but now all I see is frumpy. Has it come to that?

Darwin himself has undergone a subtle change. In the rain-swept misery of Patagonia he was always out exploring. By the Galapagos he was fascinated by everything, even by the habit of thirsty natives to drink from the bladder of giant tortoises, which he tasted himself and found "quite limpid" and with "only a slightly bitter taste." But by New Zealand he was wishing he were home, and by Australia the culture of reformed convicts offended him. It had been five years, and he was tired. His friendship with Captain FitzRoy had deteriorated as Darwin came to believe that living creatures descended one from another, improving and changing over time. To FitzRoy and the Church of England that was heresy, since God, in his celestial sketchbook, had first drawn all creatures as they look today. Thirty years later, when Darwin's published theory shook the world, Vice-Admiral FitzRoy would rise in a crowded meeting hall to denounce his old shipmate as a Satan.

I hope that doesn't happen to you and me.

So now another long night begins. Lamp out, books away. Wedge into the leeward bunk and hold on. Did you notice that the picture on the package of dinner clearly showed five cheese and spinach ravioli? However, when I dumped the contents into the pot on the stove there were no more than four. I examined the sauce in case the advertised fifth ravioli had broken up. There was no evidence of that. Four, not five, ravioli had been placed in the can. I am being as objective as Darwin was when drinking turtle urine. It goes without saying that a bladder has no label. But a ravioli product does, and in my opinion a giant corporation should represent the contents of a dinner accurately, rather than with an outrageous, misleading, indefensible lie.

Maybe my spark has gone out. The clarity of my goal, whatever it was, has blurred. I keep looking in the logbook for notes of better days. What I find is the most recent list:

Things I Am Worried About Now
1. Leaking Rudder post
2. Steering cables
3. Keel bolts
4. Sailing home

Never mind the first three, let's face Number Four.

Sailing home from Hawai'i to Los Angeles is a much longer trip than this. It means bashing into the trade winds, not just letting them push you along. It means crossing the doldrums of the North Pacific High. The route is a dogleg, not a straight line, and I know someone who took 40 days to do it in a boat larger and faster than this one. We are 16 days out and if I'm tired of it now, how will I be after a month alone going the other way? And it isn't even necessary. Many sailors ship their boat back. Just write a check and they'll put your yacht on the deck of a freighter, easy as that. Then fly home in five hours, First Class, with a glass of champagne that doesn't fall off the seat-back table. Sailing to Hawai'i is what we said we would do. Does anybody really care if we also sail back?

Wake me in two hours, if the boat doesn't.

0230 hours. Wind 8, speed 3. Milky Way visible.

I don't know why I just woke up. I guess the pots stopped banging in their locker. No ships. No reason even to go on deck. But all right, I will.

Hook in and climb the companionway ladder. Warm outside. Look up to check the sails.

My god. The Milky Way is spray-painted across the sky. No moon, the night is alone. The stars turn the sea into a shallow river, its wide bed pebbled with reflected diamonds. The constellations could be illustrations in a schoolbook.

To my right, the ladle of the Big Dipper hangs vertical. My eye follows Merak to Dubhe to find Polaris, the North Star, unpretentiously in place as the axis of the pinwheeling dome. Venus and Jupiter are streetlights. Orion's Belt seems physically real, his sword sharp and large. And nearby, glowing like an ember, lies the star Betelgeuse toward which my father, back from the war, once pointed my small hand and pronounced its funny name, the first in the sky to stick: 'Beetle Juice.'

We're nearly becalmed and the night stands still. My discomfort and doubt are gone. Above, the universe stands on edge, a billion stars in the billion galaxies of infinite nebulae. I'm part of it, we all are.

After a while the stars begin to disappear, 10 by 10. They're there, and then aren't. More wink out under the moving eraser of an approaching cloud until a patter of drops on the deck prompts me to pull closed the companionway hatch.

Suddenly we're sailing fast again, sliding over a sea paved by rain, but I'm not going below yet. Let the water wash us. Let this moment be forever, and not even the moon intrude.

CHAPTER 25

RENEWED

D AY 17, 0550 HOURS. *Wind light, boat speed 3-4 knots. Water temperature 78. Sea smooth.*

Six hours of uninterrupted sleep! That's not good for a singlehander, and brings you on deck for a look-see pretty fast. Why am I so relaxed? It's as if yesterday and tomorrow have disappeared and all that's left is the moment.

For a while, Zen Buddhism was a vogue topic that came up so often at lunch it seemed part of the hamburger menu. All my friends and I knew was that Zen worked something like the way water flowed, not striving like we all were, but simply following the contour of the land. This 'watercourse way' was said to be so powerful it could sweep away whole cities. I thought it might also improve my tennis swing. For years I kept a favorite koan over my work table, taken from "Zenrin Kushu," the collection of ancient sayings.

You cannot get it by taking thought.
You cannot get it by not taking thought.

While brushing my teeth it came to me in a flash what "it" was. "It" was nothing. We are all striving for something we can't define, and which has no attributes or properties. The elusive "it," the presumed goal of being alive, is nothing more than a semantic trick of language in which a nominative subject is presumed to exist. "It" was the famous Invisible Pink Unicorn of thought-pranksters, which syntax presents instantly to the mind's eye—you see it right now, the color of a Barbie Doll, with well-known forehead horn—even though we all know unicorns don't exist and this one is supposed to be invisible.

No wonder the world chases "it" with a butterfly net! No wonder we can't get it by taking thought or not taking thought!

You may say that's all either an early-morning mystical revelation or something gone bad in the toothpaste. But it's also the threshold crossed by the psychologist and philosopher William James in "Varieties of Religious Experience," which is a good book to have aboard when alone because you will never be crazier than the people in it.

James chronicled the mystical experiences of all kinds of people, from church fathers to lunatics. Like us, they were often individuals left alone, without supervision. They saw beyond, founded religions, and ranted and raved. James kept all the "exaggerations and perversions" of the search for meaning because he thought that illustrated the common experience. He was cagey about his own interpretation. He concluded that finding something to believe in, no matter what it was, seemed to make people feel better, and get more done. The search was important, even if the goal was elusive.

One of James's subjects, when anesthetized under laughing-gas, was tantalized by a cosmic revelation which he could never remember after he woke up. So he got a pencil and paper to record the meaning of life before it faded from memory. Upon returning to consciousness, and with immense effort of will, he managed to write it down. When the paper was unfolded later it said, "A smell of petroleum prevails throughout."

Oh, did I forget to say "good morning?" Here, I've already made the coffee. The smell prevailing throughout the cabin is that of Spam frying. Good, don't you think? For breakfast we're going to have eggs and buttered sourdough and a tin of peaches, too.

But first, let's punch up the GPS at the helm and see how many miles to Kaua'i. Only 570! At five knots, we'll be there Monday. That's a 19-day crossing and three days early.

Noon Position: 24°08'N, 152°34'W. 115 nm yesterday. No GRIB, "modem not responding." Light rain showers, humid.

The Zen calm continues. No idea why. We're rolling again but it doesn't bother me. All yachts roll. They're supposed to roll. You just roll with them. Why didn't I think of that before?

After lunch I took a sea bath in the cockpit using the red bucket. The water is 78 now, and the sun hot. My procedure uses a 12-ounce bottle of spring water, a bar of soap, a bottle of shampoo and a towel. The bucket is attached to a six-foot cord, just toss it over the side and hold on. It comes back full of warm ocean.

Now pour it over the head and repeat. The cockpit is self-draining, so no matter if everything gets wet. One douse seems to revive all the colors of the world and make the sails whiter and the sea bluer. Soap doesn't dissolve much in salt water, but it does work. Scrub down and rise with bucket. The shampoo goes on next, but sea water won't rinse it out, that's what the bottled water is for. If there's some left over it will wash the salt off our back. Scrub down with the towel to get the salt crystals off. Finished, and fresh as a newborn.

As usual, our privacy was violated by a bird. I don't know what it is, but take off your pants in the middle of the ocean and some ball of feathers dives for a look. This was a brown booby, if I correctly identified a white belly in clean-cut contrast to a dark breast. Boobies plunge from the air like pelicans. Exposed in the sun, you feel like prey.

And now I shall take out the garbage. Well, 'out' may not be right, since the garbage isn't going anywhere. When the inside trash bin overflows I beat the cans and packaging flat with a winch handle. We now have five big trash bags completely filled. The amount of packaging is far greater volume than what I have eaten. Everything gets saved. We throw only paper towels over the side, which I trust to dissolve quickly. A beer can discarded here would sink three miles to the bottom, never to be seen again. Its metallic elements would return eventually to nature. I can't think of a logical reason not to throw them overboard, except that it feels wrong.

I believe in keeping the garbage, and believing makes me feel better, and get more done.

2100 hours. Speed 6, wind 20. Spoke yacht Jam *abeam to port. Listening to Monk.*

I saw the green running light of *Jam* seven miles away while cleaning the dinner dishes. It was dim but unmistakable. Took a long time for our AIS to pick up her signal and the ship alarm didn't go off till 2 nautical miles.

Jam is a sailboat, like us, and the first we've seen since Los Angeles. She's a J160-class ocean racer, 52 feet long and running parallel to us at 9 knots. Probably has a crew of 6 or 8, surfing under spinnaker as the watches change. There will be muffled voices, the occasional stab of a flashlight and from time to time a voice carried off by the following wind. I can see them gaining on the AIS screen, and then passing well to port. But I can't see the boat. For me, other people have become blips on a screen.

But that's all right, because past and future are both present this moment in a way they never are at home. Looking up from the companionway the sky is without stars, but I remember the Milky Way of a few nights past. Although family and friends are far away, I feel them with me. For words I have no immediate need, and for touch a mug of brandy will do. I'm an island, but only for a while. On my island Thelonious Monk plays through the cockpit speakers into the flowing night. I could turn the outside speakers off, but I like it this way. The lights in the cabin lure flying fish who thump the cabin side and end their pretty lives wriggling on the deck.

Thelonious Sphere Monk died at 64 in the year 1982, but he plays forever here.

CHAPTER 26

EASY

D AY *18, 0550* HOURS. *Overtaken by* Manoa. *Wind 8, speed 3. Warm.*

We glide as if over ice, frictionless and silent. The wind and sea are down, so we hardly roll at all. What a change. I'm standing on the side deck, holding my coffee like a commuter waiting for a train.

Manoa passed last night, a big containership headed for Honolulu and therefore on pretty much our own course. I first noticed a white light on the horizon at 2 a.m., dead astern. The AIS picked her up a few minutes later as an intermittent target, range 7.8 miles. Not long after, the screen displayed our Closest Point of Approach: 1.2 miles. That seemed plenty of space between us. Just two of us crossing the sea, and I was glad for the company.

The closer she got the brighter her lights became. The AIS transceiver captures two separate packets of information. The first to come is the location, course and speed of the other vessel, and how close she will come if neither of us alters course. *Manoa* was going 23 knots, which is as fast as any commercial ship I've ever seen. We were hitting six knots ourselves, and that's not too shabby, either. The second packet of AIS data gives secondary information: *Manoa* is heading for Hawai'i, too, and is 860 feet long, 105 feet wide and draws 39 feet of water. We're 10 feet wide and draw six feet.

All right, she's not going to run us over and will pass more than a mile away. However, pretty soon what had been a little light on the horizon became a floating city lit like a used car lot on Memorial

Day. I went below to check the AIS again. Now the Closest Point of Approach was 1.1 miles. I could see no reason to change course, and besides, to do it we'd have to jibe.

I was coolly studying the AIS screen in the quiet of the navigation station when the ship alarm went off in my face. It's loud, and after nearly jumping out of my pants it took a while to find the "mute" button. The alarm is set to go off at two miles range, but when I stuck my head out of the companionway the sound of engines came over the water and that was all it took. I lunged to disengage the self-steering gear and threw the boat into a 90-degree course change that jibed the boom with a crash and sent us heading directly away with sails scandalized, jib aback, whisker pole on the wrong side.

We weren't like that long, because she was by in minutes, throwing a huge bow wave and tearing the water with her propellers. Ships are just bigger at night. I resumed course and watched her get smaller. The AIS lost contact at 5.8 miles, and after 20 minutes it was like *Manoa* had never been there at all.

I guess we'd better get used to this, now that we're entering the Hawaiian approaches.

Noon Position 24°08'N, 152°34W. Made 115 miles. Wind light in rain showers. Humid.

I couldn't get a GRIB wind prediction today. My three requests on the satphone never went through. I think satellite coverage is spottier this far out. No matter, yesterday's GRIB will do. It looked five days ahead and saw no storms. But I'm eager to plot the most efficient course along the isobars, because there's a chance we can make landfall on Monday.

In order not to think about that, I'm bashing beer cans flat with a winch handle and packing away the garbage. This will be the sixth large bag full of packaging and goopy cans. The water temperature is 78F and the cabin is 85, so it's hot now, and I'm sweating.

A bucket bath takes care of that, along with a shave and our last clean shirt.

1730 hours. Jibed pole to port tack. Full sail. Sea calm, speed 3.

We're ghosting along with no fuss at all. Even jibing the whisker pole is easy under conditions like this. Dinner is canned Argentine beef and Idaho mashed potato flakes with cheese. Wherever I put my wine cup down it just sits there. After weeks of being slammed around we can take a deep breath and enjoy what might as well be Sunday on the Chesapeake. It's by far the easiest sailing so far, and I hate it.

Our speed has dropped to three knots. That's only 75 miles a day. We've sailed into some kind of hole in the trade winds, and how did I let that happen? We're probably not going to make Nawiliwili Harbor by Monday. I miss the rolling, the bashing, the sleeping on the floor, the night sail changes, the spilled food and the cross-seas that make a course directly downwind a corkscrewing discomfort.

Aren't we beyond the habit of progress, by now? I thought we were. Now to deal with a sunset that paints the clouds vermillion and water that passes the hull with the swish of a grass skirt.

Sleeping will be easy, if I can stand it.

HALYARD SHACKLE

D AY 19, 1530 HOURS. *Wind is back. Called home. Halyard shackle opened.*
Today is Saturday, and the wind has returned. After a delightful morning sail and a successful satphone call home, the afternoon trades got to blowing hard from astern and it was time to reduce the size of the mainsail. Downwind like this the boom is far out on one side, so the sail can catch the wind from astern. That puts pressure on the luff slugs, so when the halyard is released the sail doesn't fall to the deck as usual, but has to be hauled down hand over hand. It takes patience and some tugging, and we reef several times a day.

I had the sail half way down when the shackle on the headboard opened and the freed halyard wire flew off to leeward, streaming like a pennant in the breeze. I watched it swing out and hang there, disbelieving. Then the boat rolled to the right and the halyard snapped back like a whip to wrap itself around the upper stays. As we rolled the other way it found the whisker pole lift, 20 feet above the deck, and wrapped itself around that. As the mast swung back and forth 40 degrees the remaining wire spun triangles everywhere it touched, as if an invisible spider were weaving a web overhead.

For the first time in the voyage my mouth went dry.

The main halyard is the most important wire on the boat. Without it, the mainsail is useless. The worst thing that can happen to a halyard is that it go up the mast unburdened, because without the weight of a sail it won't come down.

CHAPTER 27

That's why offshore sailors, and especially singlehanders, always have a way to climb the mast to retrieve a lost halyard. With a crew, the job is straightforward: someone gets into a bosun's chair connected to a spare halyard, and somebody else cranks him up with a winch. Climbing the mast is usually a pleasant job, and necessary to inspect fittings and replace bulbs in navigation lights. Our mast is 44 feet high, and the view from up there is grand.

Traditional cruising boats sometimes have steps on the mast to make the job routine, and to encourage going up. A high vantage point is useful when dodging coral heads, which are easily seen from above. Some steps fold against the mast and some don't, but they all make windage, foul lines, and look out of place on a light cruiser like *Thelonious*.

It is quite possible for a singlehander to pull himself up the mast in a bosun's chair using a simple three-part block and tackle. With a 4:1 purchase, a child could do it. But that requires 200 feet of heavy line and the correct tackle. And if you let go, you fall.

For solo sailors a mountain-climbing rig works best, and skilled users can shinny up a taut rope in a few moments flat. The system uses a climbing harness instead of the simple seat of a bosun's chair. The climber rigs separate sliding hitches for harness and feet. He stands supported by the foot hitches, slides up the harness hitch, sits in the harness, slides up the foot hitch, and by sitting and standing works his way up. Mechanical belay fittings called *gri-gris* can replace the sliding hitches, but the system remains a combination of sliders, brakes, webbing and ropes that requires practice to use with confidence. All of them need a separate safety line, which adds to complication.

So, what system does *Thelonious* have to climb the mast?

None.

Right. No mast steps, no 3:1 tackle, no *gri-gris*. And do you know why? Because during preparation I had thought so much about the possibility of a lost halyard, and considered so many means of climbing the mast singlehanded, that I had never been able to decide what to choose and wound up departing with no system at all.

Meantime, the mainsail was halfway down and flapping, the boat was rolling like crazy, the afternoon wind was building predictably and our halyard remained wrapped tight around the upper mast and stays. I got the rest of the main down and furled. We continued under poled-out genoa as I stared up the mast, watching the lost halyard waving back and forth against the clouds.

What a colossal screw-up. As the reality of the lost halyard set in, I sat down to wait. It was a trick I had been taught many years before, when disabled 400 miles offshore in the Atlantic. Our big outboard rudder had come off in six-foot seas and was now lashed on deck, a glaring display of why we were sailing in circles, unable to set a course for anywhere.

My watch captain was Robert Harris, a well-known naval architect who used an FDR-style cigarette holder that tilted 45 degrees whenever he smiled. "Don't worry, we'll fix it," he had said. But how? I wondered. "At the moment, I have absolutely no idea," Bob said, the cigarette holder cocking up. He meant that there was always a way, but the way was not to be rushed. The process was mysterious, but reliable.

Hocus pocus? Bob Harris had been on the Murmansk run in World War II, and watched torpedoed oil tankers explode and burn on either side of his freighter, and he seemed profoundly unconcerned to be aboard a sailboat with no steering. The next morning our crew of four, taking turns in a rubber dinghy, wrestled the 100-pound rudder back onto the stern of the boat in six-foot seas, and after many experimental lashings and one split thumb, we had a jury rig that got us sailing in a straight line again toward Bermuda. If it breaks, find a way to fix it.

I studied the tangle through binoculars. I filmed it with a camera, went below, and analyzed the video under zoom magnification. It took an hour to understand the route of the tangles. They looked bad, but many were redundant. If a few key turns were undone, the rest might follow. I still had a dry mouth, but it felt like Bob Harris was there, cigarette cocked, watching.

I would climb the mast somehow. I could start by rigging ratlines, rope steps on the support wires. Square-riggers used them, and that might get me halfway up. From there, I could try sliding hitches on the mast itself. As a kid I could climb halfway up a mast like a monkey—sweaty feet cling pretty well. Well, too old for that now, probably. But 12 feet up I could get a purchase on the horizontal spreaders, rest, and figure out how to climb higher. If I could get that far I could pull up a long pole after me, and maybe snag the halyard from there. If none of that worked, I would sleep on it and start over the next morning with something new. I had time. I had a goal. I had necessity, the mother, father and whole extended family of invention.

The top of the mast was swinging back and forth through about 20 feet of sky. As I climbed, that motion would attempt to throw me off. This I could prevent with a line to bind me close to the mast all the time. The forces would be strong. It would take hours, but a means for rest could be devised. I would be an inchworm, ignorant but determined. I was sure I could do it, somehow.

I don't know where that confidence came from, but it was unnecessary. After another hour's thought I taped a boathook to a video camera pole, duct-taped a wire-snagger on the end, and eventually managed to snag the shackle and work it down to the deck. I used the same rig to place sender lines and painstakingly reverse the path of all the tangles. Six hours later we had a clear halyard and were back on course again.

Could I have climbed the mast? Who knows. There's always another way. A hundred other ways. Some revelation would come. Maybe a jury rig, using a spare halyard. Or sailing on under jib alone, slower but still in the game. I didn't need to know in advance what the outcome would be. Outcomes get spit out of chaos like watermelon seeds. Just wait, it works. We're more than we know or need to understand.

I did tie a safety line between headboard and halyard, in case the shackle came open again.

2030 hours. Broaching. Wind 25, speed six.
Dinner was a cup of noodles, because we're overpowered now even under jib alone. A cross-sea makes it hard for the self-steering

gear to keep us going straight. It's funny what you get used to, being thrown sideways with sails flogging. On an afternoon sail our guests would be demanding helicopter rescue. But here this commotion is normal. Make sure nothing breaks. Check for chafe. Get her back on course. Lie in the bunk and hold on. Eat a cookie. Read Lord Russell on Thales, the first philosopher, who got so fed up with people saying he lived in another world that one winter he quietly bought up all the olive presses in Greece. When the olive harvest came he rented them out at a high rate, just to prove to his tormentors that a philosopher could get rich anytime he felt like it.

That was a good outcome, don't you agree?

0230 hours. Squalls, fulmar.

Another squall just passed over, a hard dry blast for only 10 minutes or so. There's no rain in them, but they're full of silent streaks of lightning. I need to adjust the setting on the self-steering gear again.

How wonderful! As I trimmed the vane just now the sky lit up and a shape loomed above. There, reflected in the glow of the stern running light, a solitary fulmar hovered 10 feet above us, wings beating slowly. He didn't look down, but only maintained his position over the cockpit. Lightning flashed again and again, white sails, white boat, white fulmar hovering.

Beyond our whiteness was a vast encircling dark.

CHAPTER 28

FRONT

D AY 19, O600 HOURS. *Sky dirty. Decided not to shake out night reef.*

The wide-base, 10-year-old aluminum coffee mug broke during the night, so at first light I drilled new holes in the plastic handle and put it back on with stainless bolts. Stronger than ever now. Silly how much pride there is in saving an old cup, but it's more stable than anything else on board.

When I carried it on deck just now the sky behind us looked odd. At dusk last night I had noted high cirrus, wispy ice-crystal clouds in the upper atmosphere. Now the horizon was dirty-looking, with darkness rising where the sun should be. A glance at the barometer showed that the needle has dropped a little since yesterday. The pointer shows the change.

Breakfast seemed a good idea. Sleep while you can, eat while you can. By the time hash and eggs were finished and I had cleaned up, a dark gray wall had risen high to an altitude of 45 degrees, and the breeze had a new punch to it.

1100 hours. Seas building. Pitot tube reads 30 knots.

At 9 o'clock it was blowing 20 knots. I estimate speeds by how the wind feels and how the ocean looks. Many boats have anemometers at the masthead, with a read-out in the cockpit. They're useful for racing, but just feeling the wind on your face and observing the ocean works fine, too. The sea surface changes noticeably with every number on the Beaufort scale from 1 (calm) to 10 (Hurricane), and sails never hesitate to announce when they want to come down. I once crewed for a skipper who didn't listen to his 6,000 square-foot spinnaker, which was not happy to be flying in a squall in the Solent. It got his attention by exploding into tatters. "Ten thousand bucks!" came the cry of despair.

I do carry a simple gizmo that can gauge wind speed. It's a plastic tube with a pith ball inside, an airplane-style pitot tube that measures simple ram-air pressure. Hold it up to the wind and the entering air makes the ball rise on a scale. The scale reads 30 knots at the moment, which feels about right. We can add another five knots to estimate the wind at the masthead, where a three-cup anemometer would be. But a number is just a number. What matters is sustained velocity, magnitude of gusts, sea state and the design of the boat you're in. No single gizmo knows all that.

Thirty knots is a lot for *Thelonious*, so I lowered the mainsail completely and furled it tight. I reduced the genoa to a scrap, still poled out, and altered course a few degrees so we were headed directly downwind. The cabin needed to be tidied up and the hatches and ports locked closed. It was hot, but even so I pulled on my foul weather trousers and dug out the sea boots put away weeks ago. A stash of bottled water and a box of chocolates went into the cockpit bags. Then I loaded the waterproof pockets of my foulie top with cookies and clambered back on deck.

In half an hour the seas had grown to 10 feet, and in another half hour we had a steady 35 knots gusting to 40 and the self-steering vane could no longer keep us on course. In the troughs of the waves, the wind fell away. At the crests, as the boat rose to expose the full horizon of whitecaps and spray, the wind seemed to slap with an open hand. The changes in velocity flummoxed the automatic steering vane, and made its corrections come too late. We broached right, then left. As the first rain arrived I disconnected the gear and stepped behind the wheel to take over.

It was the first time I had steered since leaving Los Angeles, and I had forgotten how much work it can be. Just going in a straight line was a challenge. To hold the steering wheel in one position resulted in a turn as we sped down the face of a wave and cross seas knocked us off course. To prevent spinning out like a skidding car it was necessary to anticipate, and quickly respond with a correction. I enjoyed it for about 15 minutes before my arms began to hurt and a day of steering started looking long.

That's what the cookies are for. I knew that once at the helm, I might be there for an hour, or all day and night. With a crew, we'd take turns, but singlehanders have no relief when running before a storm. In ultimate conditions, survival can depend on picking a path downwind through breaking waves. You don't let go of the helm for anything, which is why I had water and cookies within reach. But this was a front passing, that's all. The GRIB files had suggested nothing more. Time to settle in.

A big steering wheel on a sailboat—yacht salesmen like to call them "destroyer-type wheels"—is a relatively new development. Boats like *Thelonious* were formerly steered by a wooden tiller connected directly to the rudder. It was a simple system, without the wires and sheaves and chains of wheel steering. The drawback is that a tiller sweeps the cockpit, obstructing the guests. A wheel not only makes for a clutter-free yachting environment, but places the owner in a commanding position aft, from which he gazes upon boat and crew like the guy who wrote the check.

A wheel means standing up to steer, which looks magnificent in photographs but tired me out in half an hour. If I sat down, all leverage departed and the constant corrections felt like lifting weights in a swivel chair. How I missed a tiller. How much better to be braced athwartships in the cockpit with both hands on the lever Archimedes proved could lift the world.

The seas built to 12 feet, which is pretty big, but the size doesn't matter as much as whether they're breaking or not. These weren't, which was nice of them. The crests sometimes toppled over, which as they rise behind you always look like they'll break over your head. Instead, the stern just rises with them.

Tired yet? By noon I was, and while thinking of the next memorized passage to recite aloud, or how the second verse of *Funiculi! Funicula!* went, or how to retrieve the soggy cookie crumbs from my pocket, the wind began to abate, so that by 4 o'clock in the afternoon we were back to a perfect trade-winds breeze, all sails flying and self-steering reengaged. It blew 35 knots, not much more, and with the sun out again I was pleased to sneak below, fill a tin of peaches with wine and spread out the Kaua'i approach chart.

We have 150 miles to go, and a fair chance to make harbor tomorrow night.

The passage of the front made us miss sending the noon position report, so I called home on the sat phone and predicted an arrival time. The enthusiasm from the other end was so great I immediately regretted opening my big mouth.

2100 hours. Too much sail.

Every night two or three tropical squalls blow through, which is why it's nice to reef down before dark. But now that I am announced to be arriving tomorrow night we're flying the full main and full genoa on 16-foot pole. We're going seven knots and only need to average about five. We're rolling again like crazy, always on the edge of a broach, the steering cables are groaning, and I'm looking at the clock and listening for Kaua'i weather.

Theoretically we should be able to receive reports within 200 miles of the station, but there's nothing but static at the moment. The chart for Nawiliwili harbor is pretty straightforward. The water is a mile deep close to the island, then shoals quickly. Follow a few buoys into the refuge, nothing complicated about it. We're still too far away to transfer our GPS position to the paper chart, which only shows a few miles of ocean around the island.

I paid a good deal of attention to the time of local sunset tonight, because success will depend on getting to Nawiliwili in daylight. I'd say 8:15 p.m. is the end of twilight for us, and I don't believe in entering unfamiliar harbors at night. If we don't make it by eight, we'll just heave-to offshore and wait for morning. Nothing wrong with that.

Dinner is a can of clam chowder with lots of oyster crackers, washed down with warm beer. I'll eat the chowder out of the pot, in case we broach under all this sail. You don't have to tell me we have too much sail up.

2200 hours. Unnamed ship.

Just as I was dozing off on the bunk, confident in our familiar offshore world, something made me sit up and poke my head through the companionway hatch.

There, off the port beam, was an enormous ship paralleling our course. I could see her deck lights. I could see the large running light that confirmed that her course paralleled ours. There was nothing on the AIS screen. We were rolling in light rain showers, and I think both factors affect the reception of the AIS antenna. Or perhaps the ship was just at the edge of our range. Still, it was disconcerting to be in the company of something so large and unannounced.

I stayed in the cockpit half an hour to watch her pass silently, an array of carnival lights that vanished one moment behind an invisible swell, then reappeared again. Whatever distance there was between us, it was not enough to set off the ship alarm.

I am used to the ocean being empty.

RACING IN

D AY 20, 0600 HOURS. *Light rain. First radio weather on frequency 162.550.*

The AIS picked up a ship a few hours ago at a range of 7.5 miles. The sighting produced a rule of thumb: a ship which shows separate white lights, on a clear night, is about 7 miles away. Farther than that, the many deck lights of a big vessel are perceived as one. Only closer than five miles do running lights reveal their colors, either red or green. I never had an accurate night range-finder before. AIS gives not only data, but a base line for visual identification.

Dawn brought the first crackly weather report from the Mt. Ka'ala station on Oahu, the island south of Kaua'i. The prediction was for scattered showers and thunderstorms, with a flash flood warning in effect. All I care about is the breeze, which is forecast to be perfect: wind from the east at 15-25 knots.

By 8 o'clock our boat speed was 6 knots under all sail. Forty miles to go, but nothing on the horizon. I knew it was too early to see the island, and tried not to peer through the binoculars every 10 minutes. Six knots ought to put us in harbor about 4 o'clock this afternoon.

A wager on the time of landfall is traditional. So, when will we say, "Land ho!"? Mt. Wai'ale'ale on Kaua'i reaches 5170 feet, higher than most New England ski resorts. That ought to be hard to miss, so put me down for some time after lunch.

1000 hours. No more eggs.

How's this for timing? I noticed yesterday morning that the

two breakfast eggs, when broken into the pan, seemed to lack their normal cohesiveness. That is, the yolks and whites sort of drifted apart. But they smelled OK, so I ate them. Just now, as I broke open the last two into the frying pan, a noxious cloud of hydrogen sulfide rose up and it was all I could do to hold my breath long enough to flip the contents overboard. Eggs are easy. They're either perfect, or rotten, with no in-between. We've gone through four dozen in 20 days, including five or six broken by accident. According to the egg schedule, we are arriving exactly on time.

Unfortunately there's no more Spam, so it will be Dinty Moore Stew for breakfast, with oyster crackers and Tabasco. All the bread is gone.

No need to keep playing with the binoculars like that. It is untoward to get all excited over nothing more than an island and the culmination of a dream. But if we must do something, I suggest that we sit as far aft as possible, which will keep the bow up and may gain us a hundredth of a knot in speed. Yes, we're racing now, hastening toward harbor like a horse to the barn. Therefore, let us also move gently around the boat, so as not to shake any precious wind out of the sails. We might as well do all we can. We might as well admit that the finish line is just ahead. We might as well compete, even if it is only against ourselves.

To paraphrase Bill Bradley of Princeton, the basketball player and later United States senator, who said that if you keep practicing and the other guy quits, then when you meet, you will win; well then, by the same token, if one of our selves just lies around on the boat this afternoon eating Dinty Moore and daydreaming, and the other self hikes out all the way aft and plays the sails like a violin, then when those two boats converge on the finish line off Nawiliwili Harbor, which boat will win?

We will, is the point I'm making.

Put the binoculars down, there's nothing to see yet.

1415 hours. Land in sight. Rig anchor, review charts, nap now.

About 2 o'clock a lump appeared on the horizon, but I cleverly waited to be absolutely sure before crying out at the top of my lungs, "Land ho!"

Then the lump disappeared into an ambiguous mass of clouds, but just the sort of clouds you'd expect to swaddle an island in mid-Pacific. Anyhow, now it's an hour later and all there is are clouds ahead, and clouds overhead, too.

1512 hours. Landfall confirmed.
There! That's Kaua'i, 25 miles ahead, I'm sure of it.

Despite a temporary lull in the breeze we're still making a good five knots, which will put us through the door just as night closes it behind us. I took down the whisker pole and stowed it, because the wind is now a beam reach, coming right across our port side, which is a wonderfully fast point of sail. I've rigged the anchor on the foredeck, ready to go. I doubt we'll need it, but it won't do to approach land unprepared. The charts are out and our course in through the buoys understood and marked. But five hours of sailing remain, and since there are no ships on the horizon I'll take the opportunity for a nap. Entering a port requires well-rested alertness. But of course, one must be mentally equipped to nap under these circumstances, and not lie there stiff as a plank. Grace under pressure, Hemingway called it.

No, I choose not to sleep. I shall only rest, relaxed and confident. I will savor the moment. Say, do I understand Hemingway correctly? He had four wives, and their names were Hadley, Mary, Somebody and Somebody. Was there perhaps a wife named Grace? No, I'm sure "grace under pressure" means that when push comes to shove you remain calm, that's all, like Robert Jordan at his machine gun at the end of "For Whom the Bell Tolls." There is no wife named Grace, I'm pretty sure of that. Twenty days alone and everything turns funny in your head.

That's enough rest, it feels like we're losing our wind.

Low, hot mist is forming around us in a gray netherworld, and stealing the breeze away. We're down to four knots. Still 24 miles to go. It's 3 o'clock, dark starts at 8:15, five hours at four knots equals 20 miles. Not good enough. We need to maintain six knots. Six times six is 36, right? Check that with a pencil. Yes, the calculation is correct.

15:32 hours. Engine on.

We don't need wind. We can make six knots easily under engine power. That's what the diesel is for, and we still have more than 20 gallons of fuel remaining. Why, that would take us 200 more miles, and all we need are 23 miles.

The engine starts instantly, and its job will be eased by the fact that we're also still sailing. We will gladly take assistance from the iron horse. After all, we have ridden the wind alone for nearly 2300 nautical miles. It is no disgrace to motor a little at the end.

As soon as I throw the engine into forward gear and advance the throttle we speed to six knots at 2200 rpms, back on our finely honed schedule. Let's have a warm Mexican beer, to celebrate.

Wait, a terrible shriek is now coming from somewhere under the cockpit. Reducing throttle stops it quick, and I'm not sure what it is. I've heard it before, though. It seems to shriek like that only at higher engine rpms.

There, did it again. What an ear-piercing sound it is, loud and urgent. We're also sailing, of course, and maybe that over-speeds the propeller a bit. We can get 1200 rpms out of the diesel without any complaint, but the problem is that only makes 5 knots. That's not quite enough. However, these are the trade winds, and never before have they failed us. In fact, looking to windward over the port side, I can see a lot more wind coming in about 15 minutes. We will soon be back sailing fast again, maybe right into the harbor itself, with no need for an engine at all.

1800 hours. Wind 10, speed 4, motor sailing at 1200 rpms.
The wind is dying. If I throttle up the diesel beyond 1200 rpms, it screams in protest.

1900 hours. Wind 5 in sloppy seas, speed 3.
We have made only three more miles. Nawiliwili is 15 miles out. The sun is low in the gray, humid sky.

2000 hours. Becalmed. Lights of Kaua'i visible far ahead. Engine off.
We're left slatting helplessly on a sloppy sea, sails flopping and pots clanging in the lockers. Might as well furl everything, we're going nowhere till morning. Oh, I suppose the breeze could spring

up again any minute, but even so it's too late now. And it won't, the air is too hot and still. Too dead a calm.

I have heard that the Hawaiian Islands, located so strategically in the center of the most reliable winds in the world, the wind that sent clippers to China and carried Captain Cook to his untimely death on these shores, make their own wind. That is, the vast mass of this uplifted volcanic chain influences its surroundings, making for local calms and channel gales unrelated to other weather for a thousand miles. Now I have not just heard it, but know it.

We almost made it. On the twentieth day, two days better than my most optimistic prediction, we near sailed into Nawiliwili trailing glory with a chorus of seabirds singing our name. *Thelonious! Thelonious!*

Darkness descends. A bird sits on the water 20 yards away, not looking at us. In the distance, a fishing boat speeds toward the harbor. I have turned on all the cabin lights so the boat blazes like a fireship, and now I will go below and play the hand we are dealt.

I believe that when the world has turned to ashes, when hopes are dashed and bleak reality blinkers the eye, the only solution is to make a good spaghetti sauce. I have not known it to fail. There is something about pasta boiling, even in a cabin stultified at 88 degrees, that reconnects man and the universe. There is something of the gods in garlic, and olive oil anoints the soul.

We will dine in style, sitting at table. We shall read Lord Russell on Nietzsche, of whom Russell says, after explaining him at length, that if the German philosopher still seems inconsistent, "it is not my fault." That wisecrack always cheers me up.

There is no reason not to finish off the bottle of Chianti. And it comes to me only slowly, drifting and listening to jazz on Hawaiian public radio, that this is our last night at sea for a while. It is the strange phenomenon called nostalgia for the present. I live this moment as past, present and future, all contained in a forkful of spaghetti. A question that has dogged me, unrecognized but persistent in the discomfort and uncertainty of the past weeks, swims in view again.

Do I really want to sail this boat all the way home?

Yes, I do. I'm sure of it now.

We slat and bang, suspended in the night off Kaua'i.

CHAPTER 30

NAWILIWILI

D AY 21, 0535 HOURS. *Motoring in. The scent of land.*
At dawn we headed in at 3 knots through sloppy seas and no wind at all. It was the new colors that struck me the most, the dark green on steep mountains rising from the ocean bottom two and a half miles down. Without wind in our sails we lurched and rolled under the vibrating hum of the diesel. The entry seemed ordinary and without drama. There were none of the shoals and currents of Cape Cod, or the gray that shrouds Catalina Island, or the swarm of boats always converging upon Annapolis. I remembered a landfall at Virgin Gorda 35 years before. But Virgin Gorda is a desert hump in the Caribbean Sea, and the island ahead of us was jagged and enveloped in steam. We chugged on. I made a pot of coffee, and then another pot of coffee, as a new world evolved ahead.

A lighthouse appeared in the binoculars: Ninini Point, 110 feet high and flashing every 15 seconds. The isthmus-like harbor took shape. The walls of the mountains grew still greener, thickly jungled. The Pacific changed too, long ocean swells yielding to cross-seas of conflicting direction and wavelength.

About five miles out we entered a wall of scent and stuck in it. It was the smell of mud, wet and fecund, and of trees and rain, rivers and animals. It was sweet and thick, invisible and caressing. The wind offshore had made the rigging howl, hurled spray that stung and tasted, rather than smelled, of salt. This was the nose of earth, and all our landbound history in it. Do me the favor to look away this moment, so I don't have to explain the tears in my eyes.

We will just follow the buoys in, past the seas crashing on the breakwater, to putter through the calm inner harbor and come alongside the Coast Guard dock with no fanfare at all.

11:07 hours. Harbormaster check-in, slip, no ice.
Feel like a walk? It's been a while. The harbormaster's office bears 285 magnetic from here, but I don't think we'll need a compass. Her name is Kristy Kanhananui, and she's famously helpful to long-distance sailors. I talked to her on the telephone from Los Angeles six months ago, when this project was still a secret. Can you forget how to walk? No, it comes back in a few steps. Going in a straight line takes a little longer.

Kristy assigned us a slip on one of the concrete docks, which was not so easy to motor into, backwards. But now we're set, at $10 a day, and no strings attached. I'm sitting at the level cabin table just after noon, smiling over my own questions to her, which rang strange after not talking out loud for quite a while. Where are the showers? We have one cold-water shower on the outside of the public toilet. Where can I get some ice? No ice here, just walk into town. Where is the town? A mile and a half down that road over there.

The martini with three olives I had promised myself was going to have to wait. Back on the boat, I opened the logbook on the cabin table and wrote a new "Things I Am Worried About Now."

1. Keel bolts.
2. Sail repair.
3. Steering cables.
4. Leak source.
5. Toilet backflow.
6. Third reef.
7. Sailing home.
8. Nothing.

Number 8 was true enough, but there did seem to be an enormous urgency to the other entries, starting with Number One.

I dug out a face mask and snorkel and lowered the boarding

ladder. Nawiliwili is on the outflow of a rain-forest river known as Huleia Stream, which is earthy brown in color. I slipped into it and swam down to the intersection of the keel and the hull. Through the turgid water I could see that the connection was smooth, the paint and caulk unchanged, with no evidence of any kind that the keel would fall off to doom *Thelonious* and anyone on board. Of course it wasn't falling off. I always knew that. Do you know that if you smile underwater, it gets your teeth wet?

But it was time to face the fact that our sails had taken quite a beating. The big genoa jib, flogged day and night, had lost its entire foot tape, which now hung like a hammock underneath. The mainsail had chafed through under a reefing point, and two of the sail slugs were badly worn. I wanted a third reef, too, to further reduce sail in high winds. We needed a sailmaker, pronto, because my family would arrive by plane in four more days. The rest of the list I could do myself. Need to rent a car. Need to get some ice, some beer, some food. Need to hurry up. Need to get up and at it, now.

Harbormaster Kristy smiled when I asked her for the nearest sailmaker. It was the same smile as when I asked her where the luxury showers were. There are no sailmakers on the island of Kaua'i.

OK. I went back to the boat and got out the sail repair kit, containing needles, beeswax thread and a sewing palm. Might as well start now. Half an hour later I woke up with my face plastered on the cabin table in a pool of drool. What? After splashing on some water I hurried headed back to tell Kristy that there must be some kind of sail repair facility on the island. Weren't there 50 sailboats all around me? Hadn't they all crossed the Pacific to get here? Yes, yes, but no, she said. But she wrote down a name for me on a piece of paper.

The name was Phil Dobbs, and I found him on his boat a few slips from mine. He was grinding fiberglass in 85 degrees and didn't hear me step aboard and about jumped out of his skin as I touched his back as he worked in a cloud of dust inside his own boat.

From Los Angeles, huh? Phil said, recovering. When I asked what had given me away so quickly, he said it was written all over my transom. Was I that obvious? He said he meant the boat's transom. He had watched *Thelonious* come in. Phil had a sewing machine himself, and would be glad to help me out. That was music to my ears. Do you see how easy it is, even in a new port, to solve these little problems? All Phil had to do, he added, was learn to sew first.

I expressed confusion. Well, Phil's ex-wife had had a bikini shop. She sewed them and he kept the machines working. But he had seen plenty of sewing done, how hard could it be to learn? Having myself sewed all the canvas on the boat, I felt it might take more than an hour.

In that case, Phil did know a real sailmaker who lived only half a mile away. His name is Walter.

Good news. Let's call Walter, right away.

Phil shook his head. Walter has bad hands, he explained.

Ah, bad hands. I see.

However, Phil said after a moment, there is a guy named John.

John is also a sailmaker?

No, John is a plumber. A good one, too.

How would that work, Phil?

Well, maybe Walter could show John how to sew.

I was willing to try anything, but when I asked for Walter's number, Phil demurred. Something about people not answering the phone from callers they didn't already know. But he promised to make the call himself, that night.

I offered a bottle of wine if the plan worked. Make that a case of wine. Any idea how soon we could expect the job completed? I could see him reading "Los Angeles" all over my transom again, and it dawned on me that after 20 days at sea, in which time had not mattered much at all, it had taken one hour on land for time to become my own slavemaster again. I was ticking like a clock. Or, it may have seemed to Phil, a bomb.

"You know," he said carefully, "you just got in from the ocean. There are plenty of those martinis you're talking about in town, and it's not a long walk at all."

A cold shower on Kaua'i turns out to be 80 degrees, which is just about perfect. I stood under the toilet-wall spigot in my shorts as the afternoon trades returned, blowing 20 knots of pure Pacific air over the moored yachts to stir the vines and flowers. A Hawaiian family fished quietly nearby, six of them, the children calm and beautiful.

A few fishermen hosed down their boat after the morning's charter. Several other sailors moved about the docks in the languor of afternoon in paradise, where no AIS alarm goes off like a robbery in progress. I yawned and let it sink it.

We're here. What do you think of that?

Back on the boat, fresh as a daisy, I sat on the bunk to put away the entrance charts and woke up five hours later, legs locked over the table, head against the bulkhead, hands gripping the bunk like a starfish on a rock. Everything hurt, and what didn't hurt was numb. What was I holding on for? This is land. Unless there's an earthquake it rarely moves at all.

Now, about that martini.

2030 hours. Dinner, Lihue. New friends.

Up Harbor Road I walked, flat-footed in wet deck shoes, leaving the industrial quay to enter a tourist zone of motorbikes and wandering families. Their faces were stories of other nations and lives, and children tugged at their arms. I felt out of place, as if dropped by parachute in pajamas. Night was falling and Kalapaki Beach was a white crescent where bronzed surf instructors ended their day in conversation with selected students in bikinis. I approached like a coyote, furtive and alert. Kalapaki is a brochure of paradise, with chickens added. Chickens in the bushes, chickens on the beach, chickens in the parking lots. A muscular young man passed in a T-shirt with a leering Kaua'i Rooster. "Chick Magnet!" read the words on his chest.

The most elegant of the beachside restaurants had a long varnished bar entangled with attractive bodies. One departed as I arrived, so I slid onto her stool. In a moment I had in hand a gin martini, dry, iced in a lowball glass with three olives, and was wondering what the name of this exotic local joint was, with its enormous photo of a Hawaiian surfer and 12-foot surfboard. The menu said he was Duke Kahanamoku, and the restaurant was called "Duke's." Actually, there's a Duke's on the Malibu coast five miles from my house. Same enormous picture. Oh.

By the time the second martini arrived, reinsertion into society was well under way. I was an observer, like Darwin. I learned by listening, and simply being among people again was conversation enough: How they move, and laugh, how the light plays on the human form when reflected off moonlit surf. I was at ease, alone in a crowd, unaccompanied by family or friends, invisible, without a name. Twenty days offshore and, yes, I had craved companionship. But now I had it without effort. It was all around me. I was an orb of reception, don't you see, getting without asking. There was no need to talk, or press upon others a vision of yourself. A sea voyage had taught me that.

After a while I ordered the biggest steak on the menu, interrupted the strangers on the bar stools next to me, and told them the story of my life beginning with the Brooklyn Naval Hospital, where I was born.

They were Jim and Sally, husband and wife on vacation from San Diego, and their eyes got wide. I told Jim and Sally about my several careers, my family, my hopes, my dreams, my height, weight, favorite movies, and about my boat, my preparations, my sails, my self-steering gear, my navigational equipment, my favorite songs, my pet peeves and what I liked best in books, movies and fishing poles, including the insights of Livy, Plutarch, Bob Dylan and Sergio Leone, which if you have not studied his spaghetti-westerns, are more Verdi than Hollywood knew. I ventured into foreign policy, King Tut, the death of the novel, aspects of reality TV, my preference in blazers, what's wrong with yacht clubs and what's right about Lindsay Lohan.

Jim and Sally listened for two hours, nodding frequently and once or twice saying out loud, "that's amazing." And it was amazing, even to me, that after three weeks with nobody to talk to my cork had popped out so fast that I was foaming all over them. I leaned closer, summing up.

"Jim and Sally, how long have you ever been alone?"

"I would hate it," Sally said instantly.

I peered in at Jim, who teaches automotive shop subjects to teenagers and had long ago learned patience.

"I don't know," he said honestly. "A week?"

I waited.

"No," said Jim. "Come to think of it, I guess I've hardly ever been alone. I guess by your definition, maybe--never."

I offered to buy dessert, but for some reason they had to go. Flying home tomorrow, Sally explained. We shook hands. How about some chocolate cake? No, but really, they had never had such an interesting conversation with a stranger, right out of nowhere, and so, uh, complete. Have to get up early. Packing, and all that. But thank you. Thank you.

Walking back to the boat alone there were fewer people out, and in the unfamiliar darkness I lost my way a few times, but eventually found *Thelonious* floating quietly in her slip and slid into my familiar bunk with a vague recollection of talking a long time.

At nine o'clock in the morning the crowing of a Kaua'i rooster woke me up. At first I didn't know what it was, and then I knew by the sound that I wasn't on any ocean any more.

KAUA'I

JOHN THE PLUMBER, USING the sewing machines of Walter with the bad hands, repaired the foot of the battered genoa. However, word arrived through Phil that Walter had denied my request for the third reef in the mainsail. He had no means to install cringles, the large stainless grommets required. I appealed to John, who reported that Walter was adamant. Might I chat with Walter? No, he was hard to reach, even though I could see his house from the dock.

John returned two days later to deliver the repaired jib and found his way blocked by our 200 square-foot mainsail laid out on the grass in front of the dock. On it I had depicted, in blue tape, a no-cringle reefing plan using stainless rings pirated from elsewhere, and to be secured with webbing from our reserve jacklines. No cringles required.

Walter would see, I explained to John, that the force vectors which require reinforced cringles would be assumed by the angulated webbing. Just loop the rings though the webbing and sew the webbing onto the Dacron. John hesitated.

I suggested I explain it to Walter himself.

John looked at the ground. I concede that my experience in this sort of negotiation is limited. Or, if not limited, gained as a youth in New Jersey, where yes or no comes pretty fast, a shrug communicates well and a thumb in your eye means the conversation has run its course. Variations on the basics work in most major cities.

I began to explain that I was in a hurry, but stopped, because

I wasn't. It occurred to me to offer a gratuity, but John was a big guy with a brand-new truck who looked very unlike the maître de at the Carlyle, where I once got a front table by slipping a C-note. The sun was bright and the air smelled of hyacinth. Nobody on this island thought the world was coming to an end before lunch. Maybe it wouldn't.

I asked John to show my reef idea to Walter, and asked how much I owed for the jib job. "No rush on that," he said, loading my patterned mainsail into the bed of his truck.

Gloria, the Hawaiian taxi driver taking me to rent a car, said all the chickens on the island came from a hurricane that had broken their cages. I went to Costco to buy water and ice, and people smiled at me. I had lunch at a grille in Lihue where there were no seats available, and a Hawaiian family gestured that I should sit with them, as if I was a member of the family. By nightfall I had refilled my supply of Cavendish pipe tobacco, and was sitting in the cockpit with a rum and tonic, plotting what to do next. I pulled out all the worry lists, and found two with the same entry.

6. Relax, idiot.

So I did. In a few days my spouse arrived on an airplane. She is Tracy Olmstead Williams, former college debate champion and now president of her own company. She brought our two children, Drake Diana, a scholar of anthropology, and Christian Cadwalader, a recent graduate in philosophy who works for, yes, a hedge fund. We talked on the phone with my grown daughters, Tandy Fleckner in Northern Virginia, and Alexandra Martinez Celaya of Los Angeles, and the six grandchildren. I went from being alone to the middle of the people who matter. Friends called, checking in. They were glad I had arrived. So was I, and to hear from them. It seemed to them that we had had a chance to contemplate the world without each other in it. Was that true? It didn't feel like it to me.

Tracy and the kids and I did the things people do in Kaua'i, which is the most beautiful island I have seen, with the most welcoming population of any tourism economy. We dined in style, snorkeled, hiked the famous Na'pali Coast, waded long reef-lined beaches and bathed in the trade winds. We split up and came back together, drawn by the gravity of family. We laughed at our jokes and at each other, savoring our differences as much as the genes that bind us. We did this and that, lost in our time as I had been lost offshore in mine.

I didn't know why, but often my brother came to mind. His name was Jeffrey Cadwalader Williams, and he died too young a few years ago. We had sailed together as boys, and he knew water and harbors and beaches. He came back from Vietnam changed by his tour in 1967, which was a bad year to be a combat infantryman in the Mekong Delta and I Corps. While my family went off deep into a coast trail, I ventured alone a hundred feet into the jungle canopy, following a rabbit. I remembered Jeff saying how beautiful Vietnam was, if no one was shooting at you. I wondered if it were like this, quiet but alive with the peeping of frogs and the rustle of unseen birds. But he was unwilling to talk about the war, to me or anybody else who hadn't been there. Jeff came back broken and addicted, and the lives of the people he loved were damaged forever, and his own was ruined. I remembered something about R&R, the week of rest and recreation his unit was permitted about halfway through their tour. You couldn't enjoy it, he said, because you had to go back. I was closer to him there, at the edge of the jungle, than ever when we were alive together. I certainly wasn't alone.

Prodded by my impatience, John delivered a perfectly realized third reef in the mainsail right on time, amused to see me check it off my list. My days were not like his. Each day, like a gong sounding, my family and I counted one day fewer on vacation together. We inserted events into our schedule so we wouldn't miss them. We planned and strategized as the next Saturday advanced acceleratingly toward us, the plane tickets in Tracy's purse seeming to tick. Soon the Saturday did come, just as we knew it would, and my son and wife flew off after hugs and a tear, back to their lives at 500 miles an hour.

Drake's plane was later that day, and so we completed the reprovisioning of *Thelonious*, topped off the water and fuel, laid in more potato chips and Hawaiian onions and enjoyed the novelty of father and daughter with a task in common. When we were finished she pronounced the boat ready to carry me home. I put her on a plane at 6 o'clock and turned in the rental car.

In the slip that night at Nawiliwili, checking and rechecking gear and supplies, there was something I couldn't explain to myself. I knew that the sail home was long, and I was glad I hadn't backed out of it. Sea-thinking returned. If conditions were not right at dawn, I would wait. Calendar and clock retreated and a cold logic returned, a selfish determination immune to the needs of anybody else. There's freedom in that. There's pleasure in seeing the jury dismissed, and to plead direct to whatever gods there are.

PEDESTAL

08:55 Depart Kaua'i, destination Los Angeles.
Ready for the second half? It's like taking the field again in high school football, but without a team, a coach or cheerleaders. The starting time is up to us, so why not now? Let's go.

I've rigged the anchor on the bow and sorted the chain and line, ready for quick deployment. The trades are already up and blowing, right into the harbor mouth. That means that we'll be sailing into them, and the land behind us will be volcanic rocks and the breaking surf of a lee shore. The plan is to motor out the narrow entrance, then set the jib alone and claw off. Sailors always "claw off" a lee shore, because that's what it feels like. Wind and waves don't like the idea of anything proceeding into them, they're used to carrying flotsam such as ourselves the other way, where surf can break them into small pieces to mark the high-water mark. But once you get away from a lee shore, the ocean shrugs and loses interest.

We now know that our engine makes unexplained noises, and you might wonder how important that is for a trans-Pacific voyage home. Not very. Any major repair would probably take weeks, and the boat would have to be hauled on the Island of Oahu, since there's no facility for that here. Much as I'd like to motor across some of the doldrums ahead, that's a luxury. The important thing is charging batteries, and even if the transmission is failing we can still do that. Even without batteries, and GPS, the west coast of North America is hard to miss.

So, at a cautious 1200 rpms and barely three knots, we set out from our concrete slip through the inner harbor of Nawiliwili. I wish I had gotten to know it better. Most of the week the family was in Hanalei Bay, at the other end of the island. The water is calm and flat here, but we're steering for the breakwater, beyond which the wind sends six-foot seas to dash heavily against the seawall in clouds of spray.

Rounding the buoy we heel suddenly under just jib alone, and *Thelonious* comes alive. In the bight, the indentation of land between Carter Point on the right and Ninini lighthouse on the left, the waves are steep and short. *Thelonious* plunges into them, dunking her bow and shaking off water like a Labrador retriever bounding through surf.

Let's keep on this course, motorsailing, then tack at the last moment at the rocks ahead. It's daunting, but the best way to make progress to windward. The water is confused, bent by rip tides. The engine sounds fine, but we don't dare throttle up more. The jib is pulling nicely, and this is where the Bruce King design of *Thelonious* shines: our fine entry forward and balanced sail plan means that we heel, slip through the confused ocean, and claw to windward. Keep it up. If something goes wrong, we'll lower the anchor and hope it holds. It does feel like movement by will alone, forcing progress with pure intention.

Two hours later it's the open sea and engine off, we're sailing. The boat is only a few miles offshore but I'm 50 miles ahead, rehearsing the series of tacks up the coast that will carry us into the full force of the trades. Relax, idiot. OK, but it's hard, because mind and muscles are connected and these very steep seas make it difficult even to stand behind the wheel, much less steer with it. In deep water these seas will lengthen and tame. Till then, it's hold on tight to the wheel.

Want to steer? I'm not used to it anymore. It's going to be time for lunch soon, I'll set the self-steering vane after that. Right now the wheel is all that's holding me up as we pitch and slam. It's not just the shallow water that makes the waves so steep, there are also counter-waves rebounding from the land. Without the support of the steering wheel pedestal I wouldn't even be able to stand up back here, and with every plunge of the bow I lunge into the wheel.

I wish you'd take the helm just to feel this unfamiliar movement in the steering. I checked the cables and retightened the rudder post bushings, so it should be fine. Just my imagination, I guess. For lunch, we should have a cold beer. There's only ice for three days, might as well enjoy it. The wheel turns fine, I can alter course right or left with accuracy. But there does seem to be a little movement from back to front. That's not possible, because the pedestal is welded together and bolted securely to the deck.

Yes, the whole pedestal now moves an inch forward, then an inch aft. When I brace myself as a sea tosses us, the pedestal gives way under my hands. Down at the base, where it meets the deck, there seems to be a gap in the weld. I can see the gap opening and closing. I can pull the whole steering wheel toward me two inches. Even Four inches.

When *Thelonious* stuck her bow into the next steep wall of water the impact threw me across the cockpit and everything I was holding came with me. It was like a Buster Keaton movie. You want to drive? Here's the steering wheel. The critical weld at the base had completely failed. The pedestal had broken off and I could feel the steering cables binding, trapped and tangled in bundles of delicate navigation wires.

Kneeling, I found I could hold all the gear together by pressing it against my chest like a bag full of cats. In the trough of the next sea I let *Thelonious* turn herself back toward land. We were sailing under jib alone, downwind now, retracing our steps. The jib was winched in tight, even though it should be eased now to catch the air. But I didn't dare let go of the mess in hand, so downwind we went, sail trimmed all wrong, back toward Nawiliwili Harbor.

There was nothing to brace myself against, so for two hours I bent like a hunchback and held on, keeping the steering cables tight so they wouldn't come off their guides below deck, which would mean no steering at all off the dangerous lee shore. We raced at six knots past the exploding seas of the breakwater, missing it by a hundred yards to skid into the protected harbor mouth. There, in flat water, I dared free a hand to restart the engine and furl the jib, and soon we were back in the same slip we had departed not three hours before.

When I let go of the steering pedestal it fell on its side —wheel, chains, cables, binnacle, compass, navigation screens and an open Diet Coke still in the beverage rack, which now dribbled out its contents to punctuate the joke. I looked around, blinking. Nobody was watching. The same verdant cliff rose overhead, the same birds twittered. It was as if we had never departed. I tried to focus, but looking at the broken pedestal was like looking at a photo of a flying saucer. Sure, it looks like one. But it can't be, because there are no flying saucers.

However, there was a broken pedestal.

Gear breaks, that's part of the deal. But this was different. The pedestal and I were well acquainted. The pedestal was a problem I had already solved. I knew its history inside and out. It was broken when I bought *Thelonious*, and was the first thing I proudly set myself to fix.

{PREPARATION}
Pedestal Rebuild

THELONIOUS WAS IN GOOD condition when she came to me, but one repair job that stood out was the steering pedestal. The original owner, who had the boat from 1985 to 2010, must have watched the base of his wheel assembly slowly disintegrate, filling the corroding aluminum tube with putty and hiding the repair under a rubber boot injected with foam. He didn't have many options, since Yacht Specialties, the manufacturer, was long out of business. Obsolete parts are one of the challenges of yacht renovation.

There are occasional used pedestals for sale, but in the end a friend who was rebuilding an airplane recommended a machinist—"it's a tube, just put a new base on it." I found myself in the hands of Keith, who runs Findlay's Machine Shop in West LA. Machinists are in the subgroup of humans that includes boat owners: they like problems to solve. He took a half-inch plate of aluminum, found a tube that would sleeve the pedestal, and welded them together without seams. I provided a careful template of the holes in the cockpit floor, the orientation of the wheel and the original bolts, so he could countersink for them. I liked Keith, and he was clearly determined to make a pretty job of it.

The pedestal came back better than before, a shiny aluminum tube on a hefty plate, sleeved perfectly and with welds as invisible to the eye as they are on the most elegant lighting fixtures. I brushed on two coats of Interlux Pre-Kote, sanding with 220 grit paper in between. I intended to make the final coating Interlux Brightside, a one-part polyurethane enamel I had worked with in the past. But the bell-shape of the upper pedestal and the right angle at the base cast doubt as to success with rolling and tipping, a brush technique that works better on flat surfaces.

I don't have a paint sprayer booth, and Brightside doesn't come in an aerosol can. But it does work fine in one of those $10 Preval sprayers powered by compressed gas. I thinned the Brightside 40 percent, and after five coats the result was just about professional. That I am not a professional will become very clear, soon.

Pedestal replacement fairly cries out for changing the old control cables for throttle and shifter. This was less trouble than expected, although the hidden connecters do tax the imagination. Measuring for new cables is easiest when you have them in hand, and the Teleflex-brand replacements were an exact match. The run of the cables should be gentle, with no sharp bends. The change is worth it for instant butter-smooth operation of the engine controls.

Like every other yacht owner with a big Ritchie Globemaster compass on the binnacle, I sent mine off to company headquarters in Massachusetts for rehabilitation. It came with a new card and with new fluid, rose and plastic base. Re-installing it made me scratch my head. The compass is mounted above the fuel and shift levers, and formerly provided plenty of clearance for them. The new base didn't, and my shift lever would no longer operate. Ritchie must've put a new underbody on the Globemaster, because it fit fine before I sent it off. But the plastic isn't structural, so I stuck a screw driver up there to break away some space.

The result was mineral spirits running down my arms and into the cockpit. I'd just punctured the brand new diaphragm. Feel dumb? Turns out, though, that it's easy to replace a compass diaphragm. Drain or save the remaining fluid, order a new diaphragm from Ritchie, and pick up a rather small bottle of compass fluid from West Marine for a rather large $15. Use a turkey baster to refill the globe through the screw hole in the side, burping the last bubble out.

To raise the compass up an inch I needed a spacer to match the diameter of the controls housing. A plastic product called King Starboard seemed an obvious choice, but how to make a perfect circle? The answer was a homemade "compass" jig for my router tool.

Most steering pedestals use a sprocket, chain and cable to turn a quadrant on the rudder post. Simple enough, but my cables were swaged within the quadrant, meaning a long reach with a hacksaw blade (or the big bolt-cutter I bought later, which is also handy to cut the rigging away in case the mast goes over the side). I reassembled using stainless cable clamps during an afternoon of grunting curses upside-down in the stern lazarette. Success!

With the new Teleflex cables sticking out of the unfinished pedestal like Martian whiskers I decided to motor around the harbor to celebrate. The slip was very tight, no room for fenders. One side was a concrete barnacle wall, and the other was a line of yacht sterns, one with a delicate self-steering gear. But I am extremely good at this stuff and thought little of controlling shift and throttle by pushing the cable ends while steering backwards in a brand-new-to-me yacht. I was alone, with no one to help, but one learns, when as experienced as I am with, ahem, many miles offshore, many dinghy trophies and a wonderful personality to boot, to take it slowly so the admiring crowds can get better photographs.

What the hell is going on? Almost hit the barnacle wall! Now sideways across the lagoon, climbing on somebody's transom to fend off! Could this boat have an offset prop shaft? Oh, torque—that's it! Must correct. Get up some speed and then neutral—wait, not working, turning the wrong way again! Fend off!

Yes, I had failed to cross the steering cables inside the pedestal. All helm commands were therefore reversed. At half-a-knot speed, I can tell you, that is impossible to deduce from sensory input. Only stuck crosswise in the tiny slipway did I start to laugh, realizing what I'd done. I had studied an old diagram of the steering system which showed uncrossed cables. Later I realized that the quadrant in the sketch was installed facing forward. Mine faces aft. Well, I eventually figured it out.

I had a new stainless rail guard made because I was unable to get the old rail tubes off the binnacle connector plate. The stainless and aluminum had gotten to be very good friends in 27 years, and nothing could break their bond. I sawed off the ends and made a shelf to connect guard to pedestal. It bolts on to the remains of the old plate and will be a platform for instruments.

After two months on the *Thelonious* restoration project I already know more about this particular boat than anybody else alive. The price is time and money, with a discount if you can laugh at yourself.

WELDING

IT WAS SUNDAY. No one had noticed my departure from Kaua'i and no one had noticed my return. There was some coffee left on the stove, so I drank it. OK, what now? We need a welder. Maybe we can flag one down on his way home from church, get the job done, and be off tomorrow. There's a plan.

On the next dock were two commercial fishermen cleaning their boat after landing two big wahoos for happy clients. I could see aluminum rails on their bridge and aluminum fishing pole racks on the stern, all custom made. They'd know what to do. I stepped over the shambles in our cockpit and hurried to their dock. It's funny how quickly we can adjust to a new condition, and with every step I felt a growing confidence that a minor setback would soon be overcome. I had on board every tool I would need short of a heliarc welding machine. I wouldn't have to grovel through a boatyard, looking for a mechanic willing to let me cut in the line of his waiting list. And it was a beautiful day.

Bearing that in mind, and aware that my interaction with Kaua'ians sometimes caused them to scratch their heads, I composed the following question to ask: gentlemen, if you had a weld break on a Sunday, who would you go to fix it?

"Good luck!", the charter captain said.

"Yeah, not here," said the deckhand. "We go to Oahu for stuff like that."

I explained that I had no steering, so that getting to another Hawaiian island would be difficult. Surely there was a welder on the island?

"If you can get them to answer the phone," the skipper said. "Which they don't."

"They don't even go to the mailbox," the deckhand said.

Fly to Oahu, was the recommendation. And good luck with it.

Nawiliwili has no Internet service, but the small Web browser on my cell phone eventually returned the names of three welders on Kaua'i. The telephone of one was disconnected. Another just rang and rang. For the third, the listing was 10 years old, but the woman who answered wanted to help. She was sorry to hear what had happened, and concerned about how I would get home. I told her all I needed was a welder. She understood completely, and was so crestfallen not to be one, or to know anybody who was one, that I apologized for taking her time. Sorry, she said, and mahalo. Mahalo is Hawaiian for "thank you," with an implication of gratitude. Everybody says it, and it never seems to be meant as a wisecrack, so I decided to start saying it, too.

It takes about four hours to disassemble a steering pedestal. Compass off, navigation devices removed, engine controls disassembled, steering chains disconnected. I recommend taking smartphone photos at every stage, to know how things go back together. It gave me an excuse to put off calling home with the news that I was up a creek, literally one called Huleia Stream, and no luck finding a paddle.

But there was convenience in not getting very far before the pedestal broke. Turning back early for repairs was better than facing 3,000 miles of ocean under a jury rig. Now call home and tell them what happened, and make it sound like you planned it this way. And get off the phone before they think up questions.

On this pretty evening Doug Tiffany arrived to tend to his own sleek yacht a few slips from mine. I introduced myself and mentioned that I would be flying to Oahu, and how unusual it seemed that a seagoing island such as this one had no welder with a working telephone.

He smiled, reading "Los Angeles" on my transom. What's up with a business that doesn't answer the phone? I went on. How's anybody make a buck? Meantime, the lowering sun was turning the cliff above us from emerald to teal, which seemed unnecessarily beautiful.

"Well," Doug said, "I had a welder do some work on my boat a couple of years ago."

"Got his number? I'll call him right now."

"Better if I do it," Doug said, stepping away to look at the index in his phone.

"No rush!" I added hastily. "No pressure, no problem. Tell him that."

Doug spoke about three sentences into his phone and the call was over. My spirits fell as he walked back.

"Bob says, how about nine o'clock tomorrow morning?"

Mahalo. Double mahalo.

0900 hours, in harbor. Bob the Welder.

I set out early in my newly rented car, so as to be there before Bob the Welder arrived at his own shop. An early departure is a recommended procedure at home in LA, where the 405 may be jammed, the 10 may have a Sig alert, and Waze diverts drivers from freeways to surface streets. I intended to put the welding shop in my iPhone GPS, but Doug had said it probably wasn't on a map. It was only three miles away, so he gave me directions:

"Follow this road out of the harbor, take the first right past the Kaua'i Inn, follow the sugarcane fields although it has been a long time since they were actually sugarcane fields, skip the dirt road, take the second paved road, look for the Suzuki place and go all the way in, past the forklifts. I have trouble finding it myself."

Bob's shop was in a palm-lined industrial park where I circled for half an hour, reinterpreting my notes. At 10 in the morning, few businesses were open yet. I went door to identical door. Finally I heard the sound of a grinder behind one and just went in. It wasn't Bob. Bob, he said, was a few doors down. I asked why nobody's door had a name on it. He said everybody knew where everybody was.

Bob's door didn't say anything on it either. When his truck rolled in an hour later I was waiting like a cop on a bust, and as he pulled out the door key I stepped forward with my identity and ability to pay.

He just smiled, and welcomed me in. The shop was neat. The welding equipment was shiny. He took the broken pedestal from my hand and examined it.

"These were tack welds," Bob said.

I said that the machine shop in Los Angeles had asked if I wanted invisible welds, for appearance, and that I had eagerly said yes.

Bob explained that so-called invisible welds were good on a lamp, and showed me the five small spots that formerly bonded my pedestal tube to its all-important base. But for a steering pedestal intended to cross oceans, full-strength, deep-penetration aluminum welding was required, and he would do it by this afternoon.

Mahalo, Bob. Triple mahalo.

It occurred to me that on an island where everybody knew each other, doing business involved a relationship as well as a transaction. It seemed an unwieldy system, and unlikely to catch on back home.

1400 hours, in harbor. Weather on the radio.

NOAA weather radio is reporting two hurricanes making their way west from the coast of Mexico. They are called Iselle and Julio. It's hurricane season in the waters closer to the equator, and storms naturally blow west with the wind. But hurricanes hardly ever hit Hawai'i, and the last one to arrive was 23 years ago. We are at latitude 20 North, and the water isn't warm enough here to sustain them. That's one of the factors that makes the Hawaiian Islands such a safe and felicitous vacation destination.

By late afternoon Bob the Welder was finished. There were now thick, highly visible welds on every sleeve of the pedestal tube. He was certain it would hold, and his bill was a bargain. We chatted a while, and I wanted to ask whether my developing theory was right: that islanders, adopted or native, shied from the urgency of tourists. That they seemed happy to share Kaua'i, as long too much Mainland didn't get on them. That they liked living here. I had been to other islands, and on each of them, under the sunsets and the piña coladas, ran a deep strain of tension between visitors and residents. I had felt it intensely in the Caribbean. I had sensed it in Bermuda, despite the legacy of British culture. Even on the Isle of Wight, where yachting began, I had seen reticent English shopkeepers frown on boisterous international customers. When I lived in the sailing center of Annapolis, Md., my favorite season was winter. Cold sleet left City Dock deserted, and you could meet friends in a taproom and hear yourself talk.

Bob knew what I was getting at. He'd had seven employees in the shop once, and now was down to one. His health wasn't good. But Kaua'i was a special place. He thought listeners understood it better than talkers.

Good luck on the sail back, and mind the hurricanes, he said.

That night I painted the tube and base with spray cans behind a makeshift barrier of trash bins. In 20 knots of wind I applied three coats to the pedestal, the bins and my own bare feet, then carried it back to the boat half-dry.

Bolt it on in the morning, re-rig the steering and instruments, return the rental car and shove off at 4 o'clock in the afternoon. That would be a personal record for a pedestal rebuild.

CHAPTER 34

DECISIONS

SINGLEHANDED IS SINGLE-MINDED, WE know that by now. The goals are ours, no friends or spouse or boss involved. To be put in charge of yourself is liberating, but unleashes a difficult taskmaster. So it is that at 5 o'clock this morning, well before dawn, I found myself reinstalling a pedestal on which the paint wasn't even completely dry.

By noon I had it all hooked up again, the last of the new provisions stowed, and the weather forecast intentionally not checked at all. First things first. There are always reasons to delay setting off to sea, which is why most people never do it. The last step of the steering re-assembly involved the placement of four large stainless bolts that hold the pedestal to the cockpit floor. I was tired and sweaty and not looking forward to the numerous awkward crawls under the cockpit by which one person can do a job that is much easier done by two.

In the days since our unanticipated return to harbor I had hardly looked up from my lists. I did recall, in memory recorded from the corner of an eye, that there was a strapping young fellow a few boats over who tended to lounge in his cockpit deep into the morning, until a woman stuck her head out of the cabin with some need. Well, I had a need, so I put down the wrenches, scraped the grease off my arms, and sauntered over there.

He said his name was David, and he'd be glad to turn the bolts while I went below to hold the nuts. A head popped up next to him out of the companionway.

"Of course he will. Get up, David!" That was Rosie.

We did the job in 10 minutes, while David surveyed *Thelonious* in its state of readiness. He had noticed my activity, and wondered if I were leaving soon. I was, now that the pedestal was finished. And before dark, with plenty of time for a long tack offshore and a good start on the night's sail.

"Weather OK?" David said.

Oh, the hurricanes? I said I would consider them, of course. A prudent mariner always gets the latest reports before setting out. But conditions change, no need to worry early. I have gray hair and David was 26, so he nodded to my seniority. I said I had no Internet connection for weather on the laptop, but would drive into nearby Lihue to complete my forecasting study.

"John Tebbetts has a connection," he said helpfully. "Have you met him? He's the boat next to mine."

After David left I turned on NOAA radio. The mechanical voice boomed loud through the cabin: Hurricane Iselle, Category four, 500 miles east and south, moving west at 10 miles an hour. Followed by Julio, a second hurricane, with winds to 60 miles an hour moving west at 16 miles an hour. Five hundred miles was two days away. The rotation of the storms would influence the trade winds, giving us a welcome push north. Leave tonight, and we'd be 200 miles north of Hawai'i, where hurricanes never go, and safely on our way.

I wandered up the dock to a boat not unlike my own, where John Tebbetts was coiling lines with his shirt off. He knew who I was, he just hadn't heard a name. I was sunburned like him, approaching from a yacht rigged for sea, unshaved, and collecting information. Who else would it be but a fellow singlehander?

John has been cruising alone for five years, and tells everyone he is having too much fun to stop. He's 61, a former commercial captain and Coast Guardsman. Together we combed weather sources and found that Hurricane Julio was projected to pass north of Kaua'i, with winds declining to 35 knots. I was surprised to see Julio pass north of us, since that was exactly where I was heading. Didn't they usually peter out before reaching the islands? Well, yes. The trouble is, nobody knows what hurricanes are going to do.

John said there was no way he would set out with two hurricanes anywhere nearby, although others might. One skipper on our dock was leaving tonight. But he kept to himself, so nobody knew his level of experience. You'll probably be all right, he said. It's a decision.

We finished our beer and went topside to watch a new arrival from the Mainland. It was a husky 46-footer that looked right off a showroom floor, no wear or tear and with a shining blue hull. The crew was a husband and wife, and they looked tired. The jackline harnesses and foul weather gear showed they had just come in from offshore, and they were motoring down the narrow slipway a bit too fast. From nowhere other sailors appeared, noticing the speed. Sailboats take time to slow down.

The husband threw his engine into reverse, which only turned them. As the unblemished hull slid toward a jagged pier he engaged the bow thrusters, too late. The boat struck hard and the woman burst into tears. As the yacht rebounded with a deep scratch in her side, six of us manhandled her into the narrow slip, safely moored. Judgement was reserved, because coming into a harbor you're always tired. They seemed quite relieved to have made it.

"I think that's the last available slip," John said.

I looked around and got the point he was making.

"Leave now, and you won't have any place to come back to," he added.

I drove the rental car to Rob's Sports Grille in the village of Lihue, where the Internet connection was strong and I could study the GRIB and Surface Analysis charts. I concluded that by slipping away tonight I would soon be well north of the storms. There are always hurricanes in the North Pacific in July, I knew that before we departed Los Angeles. To wait might mean weeks of similar conditions—a parade of storms passing well to the south, as new ones developed off Mexico to do the same thing. The cycle was normal. The decision was mine to make. The window for departure was open, and would close soon.

But if analysis showed a window, the television screens blaring over the bar did not. The local news anchors were tense and the tone of their coverage dire. Large animated charts showed Iselle and Julio as angry red pinwheels spinning toward us. The possible tracks were several, but two suggested a direct hit on the Hawaiian Islands.

The Hawaiians lived here, and they were concerned. In the absence of facts, the TV reporters covered emotions and found them running high. How about mine? Effective risk analysis is cold-blooded, but one of its important factors is a subjective judgement of how you feel at the moment. For 10 years I flew hang gliders with no injuries at all. Twice in those years, standing on a mountaintop with the wing lifting on my shoulders and red tail hawks advertising good thermals in the valley below, I had called off the launch and headed home. That day, that moment, it just hadn't felt right. I was proud of my ability to make a conservative judgement, even if correct only for me. I was sure I could sail away this afternoon and beat the storms, but something was wrong. I tried to think what it was. It was an El Niño year. California was in drought. There were fish kills in Santa Monica Bay, and at home the summer was unusually warm. The weather patterns were crazy. Maybe that was why. But I didn't need a specific reason. Not if, after rational thought, it still felt wrong.

With a shrug I closed the laptop, ordered a beer, and called home. When I mentioned offhandedly that I would delay departure another day as a matter of prudence, a shriek of joy came out of the phone. The storms were on television there, too. Footage was being shown of Hurricane Iniki, which made a bulls-eye on Kaua'i in 1992. It arrived with 140 mile-an-hour winds and caused $2 billion in damage.

I hung up and ordered another beer. Looks like we'll be here a while.

CHAPTER 35

ISLAND LIFE

NINE DAYS HAVE PASSED since the family flew off, nine days moored in the path of two hurricanes. The storms are gone, the sun's out and the trades are back to their steady, white-capped breezes. In the end there wasn't much damage and the islands are getting quickly back to normal. I'm grateful you have chosen to come along on the sail home, which will be long. And the sail here was long enough, wasn't it?

We depart in two hours. The boat is ready and so am I, but maybe talking will help me shake off this strange feeling of—I don't know what to call it. Not foreboding, that's too strong. Not the jitters, or even butterflies, because we know what it's like out there by now. I guess leaving any safe harbor to cross an ocean in a small boat always has the character of choice. By which I mean, volition, or you might even call it willfulness. We leave because we say we will. It's not an assignment. It has none of the qualities of duty. The time of departure, the day, the moment of casting off are unconnected to anyone else. It feels predestined, a decision made by someone else. But part of me will always be here, where the twin storms converged and the Venn circles of other lives overlapped my own.

After aborting departure I finally noticed the other people also living on sailboats tied to low concrete docks, bobbing in an open harbor toward which storms were approaching. All any of us could do was wait.

The approaching hurricane named Iselle had reported winds of 156 miles an hour. She was being chased by Hurricane Julio, with winds of 85 and increasing. I know hurricanes well. As a boy in New Jersey I had seen my favorite climbing trees blown down and the banks of the Rahway River littered with broken boats, including our own. Hurricane Andrew, in 1992, destroyed 25,000 homes in Florida, including the house my wife grew up in, which disintegrated with her mother and brother cowering inside. In 2012, Hurricane Sandy killed 233 people and erased the Barnegat Bay dock where I capsized on my first solo sail. There is no defense against their power. The energy in an average hurricane is equivalent to 200 times the electrical generating capacity of the entire world, and produces enough rain to fill 22 million Olympic swimming pools. Every forecast is hedged with uncertainty as to path and strength. The Indians of the Caribbean called them *urikan*. We name them like people, as if they were like us, which they are not.

So came, loping west from the south of Mexico, the siblings Iselle and Julio. Our sky continued puffy cumulus, but the energy on the docks increased hour by hour. Like everyone else I quietly headed off for the Kaua'i Kmart, a large facility a few miles away. To my surprise, the entire 50-foot rack of bottled water was empty. A stock clerk raised her eyebrow: Sir, do you not realize a hurricane is coming?

At Home Depot, sheets of plywood moved out the door like a food chain of ants. Overhead, big television screens showed weathercasters intoning warnings. Everyone was buying something, so I purchased a bolt cutter to snip away the stays if the mast went over the side, and anti-chafe gear for the dock lines. If the storms were a false alarm, Home Depot didn't think so.

That morning Brian Cline, a young man in a 24-foot sloop, sailed into the protection of our harbor from nearby Hanalei Bay. I helped take his lines, and that night found myself at dinner with six new friends. Three were long distance cruisers who had shoved off semi-permanently from mainland life. Three were singlehanded racers from San Francisco. I'm not in either category, but we had much in common—the coming storms, small boats, and our wary looks at the sky.

John Tebbetts, originally from Toronto, plans to sail on for the

South Seas, singlehanded unless the right mate comes along. He is alert to candidates. David and Carolyn "Rosie" Krisch are in their twenties, and have been cruising on a Contessa 26 for a year and a half. It's a small boat for two people. They took a sailing course together, and set off "knowing nothing." David is 6'4", and the whole thing was Rosie's idea. Their boat is named *Crazy Love*. John, David and Rosie are voluble, interested, and able to extract social nutrients from any atmosphere. Cruising people are like that.

Brian Cline is a tall, gliding fellow out of a GoPro commercial, who raced to Kaua'i in the famous Singlehanded TransPac from San Francisco on his Dana 24, a miniature classic yacht. He appears calm and easygoing, but I doubt it. Brian Boschma owns an Olson 34 sloop, works in the development of "all those electronic things people buy," and was the Singlehanded TransPac race committee chairman this year. Steve Hodges sails an Islander 36 out of Santa Barbara. A bearded physicist with guarded eyes, he won first-place honors in this year's grueling race, arriving in Hanalei Bay after 14 days.

Brian Boschma had flown in to sail home with Steve, which would put two solo personalities into a short cabin for a long time. Each smiled when I mentioned that, and pledged to give each other space. I knew how different their offshore world was from mine.

I was showing Brian some video of *Thelonious* in a 30-knot squall, rain battering the lens, double reefed and on the edge of control. I asked how racers handled such conditions alone. "We'd be flying a spinnaker," he said quietly. Spinnakers are large downwind sails designed for full crews. What happens if you broach?

"Steve and I were talking about it. We agreed that we both wind up putting the mast flat on the water at least a couple of times each TransPac." Singlehanded racers are like that.

I wish you had been with us, gliding restaurant to restaurant, beer to beer, as Iselle and Julio tracked closer, never deviating, straight toward our tiny harbor. By day we rigged double and triple dock lines on our boats, removed sails, battened down whatever could not be moved belowdecks. Our slips seemed suddenly vulnerable concrete piers that rose only a few feet above the surface of the water, for there is little rise and fall of tides in Hawai'i.

Doug Tiffany, my welding advisor, arrived to rig his boat for the storm. I watched carefully, because local knowledge beats any book of tricks. I asked him about the low docks and the storm surge which is often the most destructive force of hurricanes. Were our boats not vulnerable?

He looked around at the many crews laboring in preparation. Near us was a storage yard for shipping containers that were usually stacked four-high, tall as apartment buildings. Huge forklifts were spreading the 10,000-pound containers on flat ground so they wouldn't blow away. At the breakwater beyond them seas were exploding higher than before.

"During the last hurricane this whole harbor was under water," Doug said. "Just about every boat was lost."

So, at dinner that night at the Kaua'i Beer Company in Lihue, we all agreed to a plan. We would stay with our yachts until the storm surge began and the hurricanes closed in. When the sea rose over the docks we would gather on shore, walk together to high ground, and watch. Don't forget shoes and your wallet. "It's a just a boat," John said. "Lose it, get another." Outside it started to rain, and when I got to my rental car the sky was black and moving horizontally.

But Hurricane Iselle faltered as it neared the Hawaiians, and the downpour the next day was only a tropical storm. Roads washed out and there was flooding, but that night as we gathered in the cockpit of John's boat it was pretty clear our luck was good. As rain cells pattered on the canvas we worked through a case of beer and entertained ourselves with first impressions of each other. Clouds raced past overhead in a hurry to be somewhere else, but none of us were.

About 11 we ran out of booze and I unfolded myself from the animated cockpit in order to contribute from *Thelonious's* liquor locker a half-gallon of Meyer's rum. It was black as pitch and I nearly fell off the pier, but eventually returned with the bottle and was welcomed with a cheer. A while later the Meyer's bottle was empty, too.

That night a shiny moon cast weird shadows and I lay helpless to understand why triple dock lines could not stop a 12,000-pound sailboat from so dizzily revolving. In the morning an 80-degree cold shower did little to cool my head, but all that was left of Iselle was puddles in the parking lot to remind anybody of our plans for wallet, shoes and escape to the hills.

Hurricane Julio, meantime, had turned north. It would just brush Kaua'i in favor of scouring the sea in the very direction I needed to go. North is usually into the trade winds, but Julio had temporarily changed all that and the winds were now in our favor. I liked the idea of following in Julio's wake. Hurricanes usually move at least 12 miles an hour, so there was no chance of us catching up to the beast. We would be drawn behind her like a toy boat in the hand of a giant. The sea would be confused and uncomfortable, but the reward would be fast downwind sailing, not pounding into an opposing breeze. John thought I was crazy. Steve and Brian, the racers, understood the idea, and they were in contact with a meteorologist on the mainland.

His advice was, not yet. Maybe tomorrow. Meantime, new hurricanes were forming off the Mexican coast and beginning their own 2,000-mile march toward our islands. So we drank some more and the next day the word was, "go." I had a question: If hurricanes don't usually go north because the water is cooler there, why did Julio? The probable answer was an eddy of warm surface water, perhaps the result of El Niño. And my next question was, if Julio followed an eddy north, why wouldn't some new hurricane do the same thing? Because north was where we were heading.

In the absence of an answer, I went with what Steve's meteorologist said: "Nobody knows what hurricanes will do, not even the hurricanes."

That was yesterday. Today, Julio is 400 miles north of Kaua'i. There she crossed paths with a 42-foot sailboat named *Walkabout* en route to Oahu from Northern California. The main hatch of *Walkabout* was ripped off by a massive wave and she began to flood. Her life raft was blown away in 100-knot winds. She called for help and the Coast Guard diverted the Matson containership *Manukai*. In a bar that night we watched images of *Walkabout* wallowing in 30-foot seas, sails in tatters, listing and helpless.

Captain John Bloomingdales managed to position the 661-foot *Manukai* to windward of the sailboat, float lines to the wreck and draw it close to cargo nets rigged on the ship's side. The yacht crew of three climbed up, but their boat was lost. Captain Bloomingdales had changed course to avoid Julio. Then he headed his ship right back into it to rescue sailors who had not.

Ready, then? I'll start the engine and cast off the lines. The transmission seems to work if we keep the rpms low. We have food again for 60 days and water for 75, new welds on the steering pedestal, and ice for three days. Don't look back. I've already said good-bye, and it won't do to make a fuss of it.

We'll follow Julio's path. What happened to *Walkabout* won't happen to us. Never mind the new hurricanes off Mexico now spinning west along the El Niño highway.

The author posing for a camera at mid-passage. The safety harness tether is clipped on before leaving the cabin, and unclipped only after returning to it.

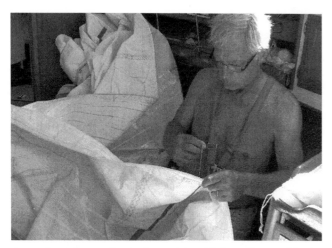

At work with a sewing awl, repairing 25 feet of genoa jib. At one lock stitch per quarter inch and a leisurely pace, the job took a week to complete.

Becalmed in the North Pacific High. The photo was made by a GoPro camera lowered 100 feet on a fishing line.

Thelonious *moored in Nawiliwili Harbor, Kaua'i. Note the double dock lines and wrapped mainsail in preparation for Hurricanes Iselle and Julio.*

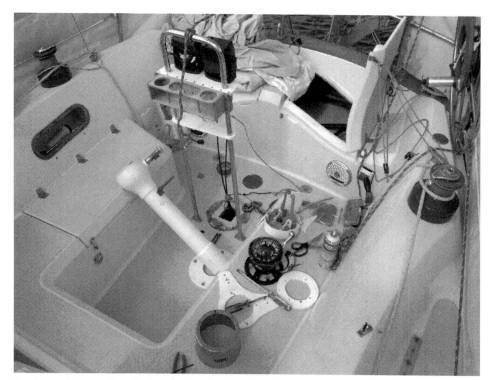

Broken steering pedestal after the forced return to Hawai'i. Now to find a welder.

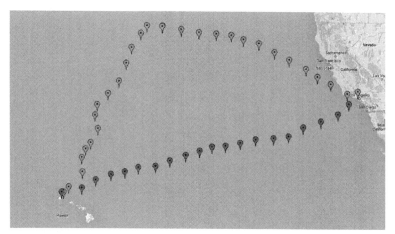

Noon positions for 48 days: The route to Hawai'i is essentially a straight line, but the return required sailing a thousand miles north to find a favorable west wind toward home.

Thelonious *homeward bound on a beam reach in 30 knots gusting to 40. The near gale lasted 50 hours, a definite contrast to the previous week of calms.*

From left: John Tebbetts, "Rosie" and David Krisch, Brian Boschma and Steve Hodges in the cockpit of Crazy Love, *the tiny Contessa 26 that Rosie and David sailed to San Francisco, Mexico, and Hawai'i.*

Project manager Tracy Olmstead Williams, with daughter Drake Diana and son Christian Cadwalader.

The author upon his return, newly washed and in a clean shirt five minutes before the arrival of nine friends and multiple bottles of celebratory prosecco.

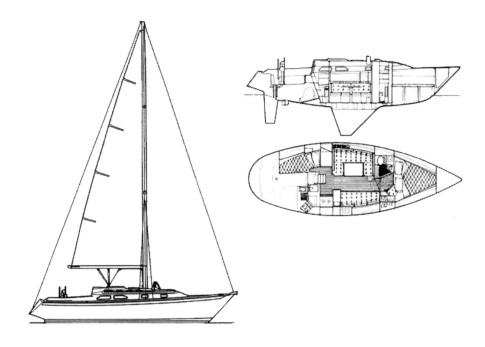

Thelonious *is an Ericson 32-III, a classic example of 1980s yacht design by the naval architect Bruce King. As a 32-foot cruiser-racer she is a compromise of speed, accommodation and affordability. Her fine bow makes for excellent windward performance, but unlike today's boats her hull is not optimized for downwind sailing. The extensive use of teak belowdecks is no longer to be found on production yachts. Ericsons were built in Southern California during a time when American yacht manufacturing set the standard for the world. Profit proved elusive, however, and the company went out of business in the late 1980s.*

CHAPTER 36

NORTH

R ETURN DAY 1, 0940 hours. Second reef, full genoa. Course, north.

Once again I wonder where I left my appetite. Work is the answer to a hollow stomach, so let's remove the anchor from its ready position on the bow and secure it in the quarter berth below. I need to rig the lines which loop along the topsides to help climb back aboard in case I get tossed over the side and dragged by the tether. The little tasks put things back to normal. Back to being alone, and trying to figure out what that is.

Tacking up the green coast of Kaua'i is great sailing. We head offshore for a few hours, then back almost to the land, zig-zagging into the opposing wind. Another six hours ought to put us clear. I want the land behind us. I want the horizon empty again.

To sail back to Los Angeles from Hawai'i, you first sail north. That looks all wrong on the chart and points the boat toward Kodiak Island, Alaska. Home is due east, but that's where the trade winds come from and sailboats can't sail directly into the wind. So it's north we go, at right angles to the breeze, until the gods look elsewhere and the wind swings favorable.

The chief god here is the North Pacific High, a vast circle of air rotating clockwise around doldrums at its center. The southern limb of the circle brought us to Hawai'i in the wake of the trading ships that gave the trade winds its name. The top of the gyre, far to the north, blows east, and there we must reach before turning for home. In the middle of the circle lies 500 miles of calms. If the North

Pacific High were stationary, our route would be predictable. But the High advances, retreats, and elongates like an amoeba. If the center shifts south, we may catch the eastward flow in a week. That would be nice. But not even the powerful algorithms run by meteorology computers can tell us whether it will, or won't, or when. So go, as Captain Cook did, and don't look back.

But I do keep looking back, don't you? It's hard not to, because behind us is where a north-turning hurricane would appear to chase us down. I couldn't get a weather prediction on the sat phone today, which doesn't help. My requests came back "incomplete data."

Return Day 2. Noon position 100 miles north, intermittent rain cells. No GRIB.

It's wet on deck and steamy hot in the closed saloon. I have just managed to find and replace a broken wire to the electric wheel pilot. We don't need it yet, but we will to motor through the calms ahead, where a wind vane is ineffective.

But never mind that, I just can't stop looking over my shoulder. The barometer has dropped a bit, and I've started entering the readings in the log to track the speed of change. It's probably nothing. But although Hurricane Julio has petered out far north of us, it took this very track. Are we sailing in a surface eddy, a hot bath drawn for the pleasure of every next storm to come? Our top speed is six or seven knots. A hurricane might approach three times that fast, and arrive in two days.

It's uncomfortable not to have an "out." I learned the term flying airplanes. At 15,000 feet a light plane can glide 25 miles. Keep an airport within that range and if the weather deteriorates or the engine sputters you always have a place to land. That's the out. Gliders can land almost anywhere, and while soaring I always searched the ground below for a golf course, school yard or dry river bed. Having an out means control. It tempers risk and keeps the world on our terms. If a hurricane catches us from behind, it will be on the hurricane's terms.

I've been studying the things we can do in my water-stained old edition of K. Adlard Coles' "Heavy Weather Sailing."

The first sign of an approaching hurricane will be cirrus ice clouds that stretch across the sky and appear to converge on the horizon behind us. If we can see them moving, the winds aloft are at least 80 knots. They will thicken into altostratus, and the barometer will plummet fast. The sequence is: cirrus, cirrostratus, altostratus, then nimbostratus with rain and scud.

In the early part of the storm's approach the cirrus clouds will come to a point on the horizon. That is the storm center. Observe its path.

The storm revolves counterclockwise at perhaps a hundred knots. But it also moves across the water, like a spinning top moves across a table. Its progress may be 15 miles an hour. If so, then on one side of the storm the wind will be felt as 115 mph. On the other, the wind will be 85. That side is the so-called navigable sector. We will gauge the direction of the center, and sail as fast as we can to the navigable side, to be blown away from the eye. On the other side, we would be sucked into it.

Hurricane winds make sailing impossible, and can tear even furled sails from the boat. We will continue as long as possible. I have drawn on the chart the likely track of a storm following the path of Julio. The left side is the navigable sector, so that's where we'll head if cirrus converges in the sky. But I'm tired of looking over my shoulder. The barometer hasn't moved. These are just rain squalls coming through. In a few days more we will be too far north for tropical storms.

1800 hours. Unscheduled satphone call.

At dinner I broke satphone discipline and called my son, who had agreed to follow the Pacific storms using the landbound sources of computer modeling, NOAA weather and graphic projections. He had an answer I liked hearing: no hurricanes reported to be deviating north. Even so, after the three tries it took to get through and the usual difficulty hearing, I was left dull and out of sorts. It was a while before I figured out why.

My two days without an out had revealed, brief as a glimpse, the difference between our endeavor, with its predictable discomforts, and the everyday experience of highway cops and firefighters or my brother in Vietnam, or doctors in epidemics or coal miners working for a paycheck. Their contract with risk was fundamentally different from mine. They agreed to face it without an out. If danger came, it was what they signed up for out of duty or necessity. For us, risk is a spice. For them, it's the main course.

Let's open the last of the cold beer.

Here's to them, and to the difference.

CHAPTER 37

SUNDAY

R *ETURN, DAY 6. NOON position, 600 miles north. Smooth seas, Sunday service.*
        There is so much time in the North Pacific. Time to think, read or learn to play the bagpipes. I knew a bagpiper once, and he had to go to the city dump to practice. No problem here, but reading is quieter. At the most western book store in the United States, Tall Story in Hanapepe on Kaua'i, I restocked on books. For some reason I bought several I had already read. "Treason's Harbor" is one of Patrick O'Brian's 20-novel saga of Captain Jack Aubrey in the Napoleonic wars, many of which are just plain superb. Another was John Updike's "Couples," a best-seller in the 1970s, when people were interested by wife-swapping. Updike was a keen observer of America, but I found myself turning instead to lives recounted by Plutarch at the end of the First Century AD: Julius Caesar, Themistocles, and Artaxerxes, "among all the kings of Persia the most remarkable for a gentle and noble spirit, surnamed the Long-handed, his right hand being longer than his left...."

I hadn't opened "Moby Dick" on the outbound passage. I wasn't ready yet to join Ishmael, Queequeg and Ahab on their ocean. Now I am. And it's Sunday.

1000 hours. The canticle in the fish's belly.
I have decided to read Father Mapple's sermon aloud to the birds and the clouds. We coast along at five knots, close-hauled with the sun shining. I really have nothing else to do, except listen to a TED

Talk or go back to scrubbing away the dirt-line the shrouds make when they press against the white mainsail. Besides, I miss talking out loud, and declaration into this warm wind will loosen my throat and remind me that human conversation, ordinarily, is audible, not just voices in the head.

It is Chapter Nine, early in "Moby Dick," when Father Mapple climbs the man-ropes of his lofty pulpit to address a congregation of New Bedford whalers on the Book of Jonah. To read it I climbed atop the cabin house, restrained by the tether, facing the wind with the heavy volume in hand and proclaiming into it:

"Shipmates, this book, containing only four chapters—four yarns—is one of the smallest strands in the mighty cable of the scriptures. Yet what depths of the soul Jonah's deep sealine sound! What a pregnant lesson to us is this prophet! What a noble thing is that canticle in the fish's belly! How billow-like and boisterously grand! We feel the floods surging over us, we sound with him to the kelpy bottom of the waters; sea-weed and all the slime of the sea is about us! But what is this lesson that the book of Jonah teaches? Shipmates, it is a two-stranded lesson; a lesson to us all as sinful men, and a lesson to me as a pilot of the living God."

I read on about how Jonah hopes that a ship made by men will carry him to a country where God doesn't reign, but only "captains of this earth." I recited how he books passage for Spain, his captain and crew aware he's some kind of fugitive, and how a storm springs suddenly up. But after a while my throat got hoarse from preaching, and so as not to lose my audience of whitecaps and bow-wave, closed the book as if it were a Bible, which in literature it surely is, and carried it back to its dry shelf below.

I know that many people can't stand Moby Dick, which I have read every five years since I was 25, each time to find more in it, or maybe more in me. We are all due our tastes. Besides, Melville's story is about a ship and a crew, and of natural appeal to anyone who sails. But if it has no appeal for you, fine by me. I myself cannot get 10 pages into Proust or Jonathan Franzen without a strong impulse to hurl the book against the nearest wall. Give me that, and I forgive any yawn at Melville.

But one thing I can't abide is a tin ear, especially in a popularizing scholasticus, by which I refer to Clifton Fadiman, for 50 years a judge of the once-powerful Book-of-the-Month Club, who in his reading of "Moby Dick" finds the author a gloomy Gus and the work unjolly, unchristian and subject to various faults of taste. Unjolly? That is his verdict in the case of a story which opens with an eager young man and a cannibal harpooner in the same bed, and who go on to become fast friends, and in which every character save Ahab revels in the delight of being alive and trying to stay that way?

I just now discovered Fadiman's grudging, offended remarks in the introduction to my Easton Press edition. If we have luck to see a whale, I plan to tear the pages out and feed them to him.

1600 hours. Stereo has stopped working again.

All right, I have stopped fuming over Uncle Clifton. The Whale ("Moby-Dick, or, The Whale") does not need a solo yachtsman to come to its defense, any more than Darwin or Thucydides does. Life is good. The stereo stopped working this morning but I have re-crimped the wire connections I made two years ago when I didn't know what I was doing, and now it works perfectly again. Father Mapple's sermon has quieted the waves, at the expense of a throat sore from shouting.

Do you feel the serenity? Yes, we have a long way to go, and yes, I too am beginning to wonder how far north we'll have to go before turning the correct way. The lesson is to exhale. Allow time to stop. With dinner tonight we'll have Alcibiades, by Plutarch. He was a traitor to Greece, Sparta and Persia, but you can't help but love the guy for trying. And we're heeling so nice and steady that the plate will stay on the table.

The Polynesian cocktail comes first. As you recall, we wrap a wet paper towel around a baby-pack of orange juice, then freeze it with liquefied gas. While that's cooling I'll get the rum out. *Thelonious* has both a liquor cabinet and a wine rack, both of varnished teak. I suppose in 1985, when Ericson was churning out high-priced boats for doctors and lawyers and aerospace engineers, that was a marketing ploy. But I have often smiled to imagine prospective owners stepping aboard a showroom boat. Why, Ralph, a cabinet just for your Glenfiddich! Why, Camilla, a wine rack for your Puilly-Fuisse! Their hands touch as she writes the check.

I don't suggest that our hands will touch, all I mean is that we seem just now to be sailing through a sales brochure, sun setting colorfully, motion easy, dining in style.

The rum is in the back of the cabinet, behind the bottles of lime water and artichokes and pickles and whatever else fits. Is the juice pack cold? It is. Pierce it with the rigging knife and empty into our insulated cup. Any juice will do. The irreplaceable element is Meyer's rum, with its aroma of many a darkened bamboo booth at Trader Vic's.

The Meyer's bottle is shaped not unlike the large bottle of olive oil I have just pulled out, and which now sends a forbidding shiver down my spine. For the past week I have noted the brown cap of this brown bottle, hidden in shadows in the locker, content that it was a half-gallon of rum. But it's not, it's olive oil. The rum bottle was there all the way to Hawai'i, hidden behind a companion of Jack Daniels. In the reunion of family on the island I contributed the whisky to our shore-side lodging. But not the rum. Perhaps I have stored it somewhere else. But where? It's a small boat. I know where everything is.

As I closed the liquor locker the dustbin of memory swung open. It contained a foggy recollection of the rainy night the hurricane passed over Nawiliwili. We were on John's boat, celebrating. It was late, David and Rosie were laughing, Steve and Brian had to shift as I rose up to announce that were not out of booze after all, there was a full bottle of Meyer's rum on my boat. Their faces lit up. I returned to cheers. By morning the night was a blur.

I forgot to replace the bottle. We have no rum. We also have no whisky. A new inventory counts only two bottles of Chianti and 11 cans of beer for the weeks and weeks that lie ahead. Chichester had his whisky with lemon, but we shall not.

Rationing begins.

1900 hours. The field of brit.
For the next desultory hour I sat in the cockpit as a man in mourning,

postponing dinner and everything else. Thousands of miles lay ahead, with no booze. Even the water had changed.

Earlier I had seen on the surface some sort of pollen-like substance, yellow in color and unfamiliar. It came and went in patches. It was odd to see the spore of plants so far offshore, in so remote a place. But the wind of the gods blows everything before it.

Now the sea was covered in the stuff. Long streaks stretched to the windward horizon, lined in wind rows the way spume is by a gale. The ocean was a golden field and the particles dispersed by our bow were infinite in number. The lowering sun turned their gold to red, and out of empty thought came, as by a clanking of slow gears inside my head, the beginning of recognition. What was this stuff? I had never seen it before, but I had heard of it.

And recently.

I went below, past the trickster olive oil bottle, to where "Moby Dick" lay open upon the saloon table. I paged through until there it was: Chapter 58, entitled "Brit."

"Steering north-eastward from the Crozetts, we fell in with vast meadows of brit, the minute, yellow substance, upon which the Right Whale largely feeds. For leagues and leagues it undulated round us, so that we seemed to be sailing through boundless fields of ripe and golden wheat."

Through the brit came whales.

"As morning mowers, who side by side slowly and seethingly advance their scythes through the long wet grass of marshy meads; even so these monsters swam, making a strange, grassy, cutting sound; and leaving behind them endless swaths of blue upon the yellow sea."

I saw no monsters swimming, for the right whales so prized for the whalebone of their baleen jaws are all but extinguished by the hand of Man. The ocean was empty, but the harvest of brit remained.

Only *Thelonious* was left to mow the field, leaving one blue swath through the yellow sea.

LATITUDE

Return, Day 10. Calms *and squalls. Every day the same.*
And so we sail north, north and more north. Today we reached the latitude of Los Angeles. Draw a line due east on the chart and it's only 1200 nautical miles to our slip in Marina Del Rey. We'd be halfway there, but we're not. Although Hawai'i is 900 miles behind us, we're closer to British Columbia now than to home.

The days and nights are almost perfect. With the trades far behind the breeze is now a steady 15 knots over gentle seas. When the sun goes down it turns the sky flaming red, and shortly after that the windward horizon darkens irregularly. By the time I'm washing dishes the first squall appears as a hole in the stars moving toward us. A few days ago I stopped reefing at night, so our speed wouldn't drop below 5 knots. Sometimes the squalls miss us by a few miles, and I sit in the cockpit and watch them sweep the water with rain like a broom. The clouds tower high and in the distance seem foreboding. But they move slowly, without thunder or lightning, and rarely contain more than 25 knots. At the first sound of raindrops on deck I close the companionway hatch and dog down the ports. Sometimes I linger in the cockpit, in foulie top and shorts, just to feel the rain. Often, instead of reducing sail, we just bear off to run before the wind with waterfalls streaming from the sails. And then it's over, and we turn back to north.

Always only to north. Never east, toward home.

Most nights have two or three squalls, and at midnight the breeze dies and by dawn we lie becalmed, drifting. It is if I have always been here, on this boat, in this placid ocean. The sameness of the days, and especially the gentleness of the sailing, gives uninterrupted time to remember everyone I know, even those not present for many years, and sometimes it seems the boat is full of people. Some have to introduce themselves we've been so long apart, so many years without our thoughts touching. In turn, I introduce them to Darwin and Xenophon and Stubb, second mate of the Pequod, who had the temerity to ask Captain Ahab, who paced the deck all night, to pad his ivory leg because the sound of the whalebone stump kept the men awake. If this is alone, it's crowded. If this is lonely, well, join Ahab for his stroll on deck, if you dare.

Just now, as I went up to adjust the steering vane, it was utter black. I had been in a reverie below, no lamps on, neither sleeping nor waking. A squall came down, more sudden than most, and the boat headed up into the wind to make the genoa flap in that urgent way it has. I clipped in and rose in the hatchway. Our running lights were off, no need for them in this empty sea. No star, no moon, no phosphorescent wake made a reference point, and for a moment, eyes wide, I was blind and it didn't matter, I could feel it all, the whole universe, complete.

As I stood gaping, *Thelonious* bumped a wave and I took a bucket of salt water in the face that went up my nose and peeled back my eyelids. A whoop of laughter and astonishment escaped as if from someone else as I scrambled below to grope for the cabin lights and a towel. I laughed again twice that night, just thinking of how consciousness tantalizes us: at the moment of enlightenment, a bucket of cold water in the face.

For dinner we have Indian food, with papadum fried in olive oil and Beer Number Nine. No whisky.

Things lost are sought. Things rationed, most enjoyed.

Return Day 11, 0610 hours. Change jibs. Lifted briefly.

This is good sleeping, don't you think? I put in six hours last night, out cold, and woke to find the sun rising on the horizon dead ahead. The sun rises in the east, not the north. We were pointed home for the first time.

The speed is only a few knots, and the wind barely rustles the waters. But we're moving, and that's better than usual lately, at sunrise. I moved the sheet block of the genoa a few inches, as if to encourage another tenth of a knot in our speed. I drew a new line on the chart depicting this sudden shortcut home. It was the lift we had been waiting for. The wind had gone south, and we'd be home in nine more days, which meant we were already halfway there, which meant I could open a rationed bottle of wine and make a spaghetti feast for dinner.

The change lasted an hour, and then the breeze turned steadily until by noon we were actually heading west of north, toward the Bering Sea. Oh well. Nice while it lasted.

There's just no way to know when the wind will change. Maybe the North Pacific High will move. Sometimes it does, sometimes not. And so, we must plan on waiting. A day, a week, two weeks, a month. We will sail north as far as necessary, and that's the way it is. It's why we left with 60 days food and so many books. I predicted 30 days, and we're right on schedule.

The sail repairs in Kaua'i have worked out well, but the genoa has been looking poorly, like a sick friend. John the plumber and Walter of the Bad Hands had fixed the horizontal foot tape, and it was still securely fastened. But the furling and unfurling and the night squalls had beaten up the trailing edge. Each day the reinforcing tape there had detached a little more, and now 25 feet of it stood out in the breeze like wash on a tenement clothesline. Time to fix our loyal headsail one more time.

Genoa jibs are larger than standard jibs because they overlap the mast. They take their name from a regatta in Genoa, Italy, where in 1926 a racer unveiled one for the first time. Changing a big genoa on a furler is a tedious job for a singlehander, but in an hour or two I had a smaller sail on and the genoa below for repair.

The 350 square feet of white Dacron made the cabin look like Hugh Hefner's bedroom on laundry day. The repair was to fold the detached four-inch –wide leech tape back in place, and resew it. With no sewing machine, I'd use an oak-handled Speedy Stitcher Sewing Awl, a 1909 patent with a grooved needle. Push the needle through, then withdraw it slightly to create a loop in the waxed twine. The other end of the twine goes through the loop, and the needle is pulled back out the way it went in. A tug on both ends makes one lock stitch. A foot contains 48 quarter-inches. I had 25 feet to sew, which is 1200 stitches.

In military school I learned to sew by attaching my new corporal stripes, and then how to rip stitches out by taking them off every time I got busted back to private. Odysseus sewed, so did Robinson Crusoe and Joshua Slocum. My grandmother had a sewing machine, and I wish I had paid more attention. Over the years I came to realize that a sailboat has canvas in many forms, from the sails to the cushions to the hat on your head. So before setting out upon the fabric of the sea, I sat down to teach myself to sew.

{PREPARATION}
Sewmanship

SEWMANSHIP, AS POPEYE AND I likes to call it, is a manly art dating way back. On the other hand, Lord Nelson didn't make his own hats. Can a modern sailor learn a trade that once had a long apprenticeship? Yes, thanks to Sailrite, an Internet supplier which gives away every trade secret of the canvas-workers craft in hundreds of free instruction videos. Why? So we'll buy materials from them. But the real lesson is that sewing cloth for a boat turns out to be as enjoyable as varnishing or changing engine oil, jobs for which we could also pay.

A sailor who takes an interest in sewing suddenly notices the canvas on every boat around him—the semi flat-felled seams, the triple stitching, the taut fit (or not), the placement of darts, the color, the material, the hardware, the design. There's a lot of cloth on a boat besides the sails: the bunk upholstery, line bags, sail bags, ice bags, sunshade, wind funnels, boson's chair, dinghy tarp, curtains, and all the covers for teak, varnish, fenders, pedestal, jib, main and lifebuoy. All need ongoing repair or replacement. How hard can it be? Only one way to find out.

Sewmanship starts with a sewing machine. I chose a 1963 Singer 237, a home machine with a manual that begins, "Everything for the woman who sews." Hats off to those '60s women. The 237 weighs 35 pounds, has all metal gears, and requires weekly oiling at 12 separate points. For the cost of only about $100 on line, it is one of the most complicated and well-made machines I've ever owned. I later purchased a 1953 Singer 15, which is somewhat more powerful, for about the same price. The main difference between these antiques and a new walking-foot sailmaking machine is the length of the straight stitch. They do about an eighth of an inch; the real thing can do three-eighths or more, which is what you usually see on a sail cover.

Sewing machines send a threaded needle down to a shuttle, where it picks up a second thread from the bobbin. When all is working well the result is a chattering high-speed stream of perfect stitches. To lock, just reverse for half an inch. For most boat sewing a #18 needle is used, with UV resistant V-92 polyester thread. This stuff is so strong you could hang from the ceiling on it, and it unwinds vertically off big 250-yard spools.

It took me a week to get confident with basic sewing. Many times I Googled my problems: stitch not tight, "machine jams with nest of bobbin thread below," fabric puckering, "machine jams with double threads," needle bends, and so on. In the end, all my issues, even the most persistent, were caused by lack of experience. The "something wrong" was my technique, never the machine.

The first project was a cover for the pram, to be supported using its mast as a ridge pole. Ten feet of Sunbrella fabric seemed to fill the room, until I learned to roll one side into a tube so it would fit through the machine. I came quickly to pay attention to the thread path from spool to needle and careful winding of the bobbin, but I kept getting bird nests under the cloth and many unexplained jams. In a few hours I knew the old sewing machine for what it is—a complicated and sophisticated piece of machinery in which many tensions and gears work together, or don't. I fiddled with every possible thread and bobbin tension, but couldn't find a pattern to my problems.

Hatch covers were next. I used shock cord instead of

line, and they came out pretty well. The corners weren't right, but I discovered small revisions in design to be easy. Just cut the unwanted stitches out with a razor blade or seam ripper and re-stitch as needed—sewing mistakes are not permanent. And if you go really wrong, there's always a patch. I found I was beginning to enjoy myself.

On to the pedestal cover. My old one was not only faded, rotten and the wrong color, but no longer fit. The cover, however, was a complex three-dimensional shape that I had no idea how to measure for—just the sort of job we pay pros to do right, using their hard-earned skills. They still have the real skills, but the secret of how to pattern an irregular-shaped cover is now free to everyone as a Sailrite instructional video.

I decided to think for myself, and, instead of using their method, to deconstruct the old pedestal cover and use the panels as templates. In fact, I continued this plan through subsequent projects, in line with my motto of "When Wrong, Keep Being Wrong." You'd think time would be saved, but ripping out seams is tedious and the old panels are hard to measure due to wrinkles and bias and stretch. People have been sewing since the first time Adam ripped his pants, so maybe I didn't know better.

For the 14-foot long mainsail cover I once again laboriously deconstructed the old one, laid the parts out on the living room floor, and cut to the pattern. Now I needed to make long flat-felled seams, which have two stitch lines so one is protected from sunlight. Sewing is done inside out, so the seams don't show. With half a dozen panels and a large mass of cloth, keeping the correct sides together jangled my brain. Long runs tend to pucker and therefore shrink, and a professional machine makes long stitches to reduce that effect. With a home machine, it's necessary to keep constant tension and plan on some minor shrinkage. There was a lot of sewing involved and I still couldn't predict a jam-free experience.

And yet, the jams went away. Over time I'd come to see that if the material catches under the table, it bends the needle and creates problems. I learned not to raise the presser foot unless the moving arm is in top position. I learned to automatically check the thread path for hang-ups, to start a stitch only with the needle buried, and to bury when rounding a corner. I was now alert to when the bobbin would run out and knew to concentrate on keeping stitch lines parallel. It took about six hours of actual sewing to feel confident. The machine seemed to know it and began to hum fast and true, the tough polyester thread running fast off the big spool, the chattering canvas pouring steadily forward into finished piles and the birds chirping admiringly from the window.

When I finished the sail cover the aft ends did not meet and the horizontal line under the boom had an unplanned curve in it for five feet. On the boat, I made corrective marks, then ripped out my mistakes, refolded, re-trimmed and re-sewed. The final result was as neatly sewn as most of the commercial products you see on the dock—and better than some.

Then, increasingly at ease with a new found skill, I made a big cockpit shade and moved on to replace the tops of the V-berth cushions and a worn-out zipper. I taught myself to darn rips in the 14 individual cushions of the boat. The estimate for all new cushions was $6,000. My cost was $75 in fabric and thread.

Using leftover Sunbrella I added a companionway hatch

cover, snap-on covers for all exposed teak, and shields against salt water for the winches. Oh, and new covers for the lifeline comfort tubes, too. And line bags for the cockpit, to keep the halyard tails neat. And weather cloths to surround the cockpit against offshore spray—where I painted on *"Thelonious"* writ large, in the old tradition of easy identification through binoculars.

I repaired our many ice bags, the heavy canvas carriers that are perhaps the most useful item in yachting. Two were from the 1970s, stained, battered, and reminiscent of summer days, young children and good times. I fixed boat shoes, belts and household backpacks.

I made flags. I let out my own tuxedo pants, obviating the need to reveal to a tailor all too many recent helpings of linguini. I hemmed curtains, repaired a fancy bicycle pack, manufactured several ditty bags, invented a pouch for a radar reflector, and I tell you without exaggeration that if you gave me the right materials and a day to think about it I could probably make you a damned pretty set of doilies and some lace underwear, too.

Am I become like unto a god? In modesty, that's not for me to say. Or, in Ian Richardson's refrain in the British original of "House of Cards," "You might well think that, but I couldn't possibly comment."

Ah, sewmanship. It changes you in so many ways.

CHAPTER 39

EAST

ETURN *Day 14, 0500 hours. Collision alarm. Changed headsails.*

The AIS audio alarm I installed sounds like an alarm clock having a nightmare. I can't sleep through it, which is good, because when it went off at dawn this morning the message was: "Collision Alert." Rather quickly did I stick my groggy head out the companionway to see approaching, six miles astern, a fully laden tanker. Both red and green running lights were plainly visible, which means she was heading straight for us.

The air was light and we were hardly moving, but I took a moment to splash water on my face and start the coffee. Before the advent of the Automatic Identification System, I would've waited a while to confirm the course of the tanker, and to decide which way to turn to escape her path. But the IAS screen provided the situation at a glance. The time to the Closest Point of Approach was 25 minutes. The CPA itself would be .10 miles. That's a direct hit, given the vagaries of course computation. It seemed odd, on this huge ocean, that two vessels should align on a collision course, but the obvious is quite persuasive. Our sailing speed was about 2 knots, which left only a small reserve for escape and no chance for aggressive maneuver. So I just started the engine, spun us 90 degrees, and in half an hour the long, low profile of the ship passed in the early sunlight a mile or so away, pushing a bow wave like a waterfall before it.

I thought of Joshua Slocum, run down and sunk, or so history assumes, for no trace was ever found of man or boat. Ant (for "Anthony") Stewart, who sailed around the world in a 20-foot modified day-sailer, was struck in the Indian Ocean by a freighter going full speed. His open boat was shouldered aside by the bow wave and sent scraping down her barnacled side, dismasted. The freighter never knew it had hit anything. And I thought of one of my first night watches, alone in the cockpit of our Herreshoff ketch off Montauk Point en route to Martha's Vineyard. We slatted on a misty, windless sea, and from all around came engine sounds. I could see the lights of ships, sometimes red, sometimes green, passing in the distance. I was 15, and determined not to wake my father with any evidence of unsuitability for solo command. I endured the sounds and the lights for hours, until out of the fog two running lights appeared heading straight for us.

There was no wind. Our engine was started by turning a crank, like a Model T car, and half the time it refused to start. I swallowed my pride and went below to touch father's shoulder and call him on deck. He came up slowly, more tired than I had seen him, and squinted into the dark for a while, but the lights had turned away. "Keep an eye on it," he said, and went back to bed.

When dawn came we were surrounded by fishing trawlers. They circled us with engines gurgling, lights always moving, as they had been all night. Whether they had seen the oil lamp hanging off the mizzen boom behind my head I didn't know. I just knew I had seen theirs, and had no answer for it.

In the wake of the tanker a new line of wind waves appeared on the smooth water. We were headed north, but the masthead fly, a wind-pointer I look at every 10 minutes day and night, now pointed south. Delicately, as if not to disturb the intention of the universe, I disconnected the self-steering gear and turned our steering wheel to the right. *Thelonious* curved east from north, right into the rising sun. The compass wheeled from 000 degrees to 090 degrees. We heeled almost imperceptibly and our speed crept from two knots to three, and held there. I reset the vane and she sailed herself again, in a direction we had not seen in two full weeks.

It was the turn toward home, at last.

Return Day 16, 0935 hours.

Last night I finished the sewing job on the leech tape of the genoa. Twelve hours total work time, and it gave me a good idea how it was to make sails by hand in the old days. I could stay at the job only about an hour at a time before tedium set in. But now that it's up and drawing again, I feel like we're both stronger. We may need that in the days ahead.

Noon position, 40°53'N, 147°27'W. The provisional self.

Today's GRIB file confirms that we're entering the center of the North Pacific High, and the projection five days ahead is light breezes and calms. The barometer is higher than I have ever seen it in my life: 1030 millibars, or 30.42 inches of mercury. It doesn't change, which means the weather won't change either, for a while. But that's all right, we have enough fuel to make a good dent in these doldrums, even though the calculations make my head hurt. I just topped off the 20-gallon main tank from the deck jugs. Ten gallons remain in jugs. We should reserve 15 gallons for engine charging. That leaves 15 gallons, or 150 miles, for motoring. Not bad. But not yet. We're still sailing, if you call two knots sailing. At that speed the wind vane no longer works, but the electric wheel pilot keeps us going straight.

It took much longer to get to these doldrums than I expected. I thought we might turn for home a week ago, and when we didn't, I just waited another week. Is that laid-back persona really me? Something has happened to the old way of thinking about things. Have you noticed it, too? It's part of being alone, but not so easy to put your finger on.

I call it the departure of the provisional self. The provisional self is alert to others, conditioned for approval and judgement. It's provisional because it's always changing, adapting to the moment and the people and the situation. One single self wouldn't do, really. The provisional self makes us good citizens, parents and friends. It's on offense or defense according to situation, it's wary and brave, and in some people is highly tuned to the nuance of others. We're different selves at a funeral, when flying a kite, when buying a car.

We have to be. There's a provisional self for giving birth or playing a video game. I hope there's one for dying well.

Since the provisional self is about other people, it's us at our least alone, and it's the way we usually are. It grows with us as we grow up. The self of a small child isn't provisional, it's pretty much who he or she is, unfiltered and singular. But kids grow fast.

Here, alone in a calm, provisional selves are unnecessary. All we need is one. Do you feel it? It feels like it takes no effort to exist. But without effort, who are we?

Night is falling and squalls will come. We will sail east, or maybe have to turn north again. Home is too far away to think about, and Kaua'i left behind in a dream. Here is all there is. A minute, an hour, a day are all the same.

Never mind latitude and longitude, "now" is our current location. We and the boat and the stars aren't parts, but the whole. We exist with no explanation required.

CHAPTER 40

CALM

ETURN, DAY 17. COURSE *due east, winds declining.*
We had a breeze two days ago, less of it yesterday, and now we languish on a mill pond. This is the famous center of the North Pacific High, the lull around which the winds turn. I've been becalmed before, and I admit, I like it. The water temperature is down to 71F now, and although noon is hot on deck the nights call for a sweater. The ocean is polished, undulating, and each day the shallow hills lose stature without winds to rebuild them.

The usual sounds of a sailboat are of rushing water and straining lines, of blocks clicking and halyards ratting. Without wind, rolling in slop, the sails and lines slat constantly, a sound that has driven many a sailor half mad with frustration. But I lowered and furled the mainsail completely early this morning, so the swish of limp Dacron is gone. No cup clacks in its cabinet. No pencil rolls in the navigation bin. The last of the leftover waves were gone at dawn and now the ocean is as still as the air. And so we sit, a toy in a bathtub.

Alexander the Great has come to the end of his story, one march too far into Asia and monomania. I've been following the maps in the Landmark edition of Arrian, the Second Century historian who is the best original source on the Macedonian hero. Arrian saw himself as the second coming of our companion Xenophon, who lived 500 years before him. But I don't recall Xenophon mentioning Arrian, not even once. It amuses me to think of us all as contemporaries. It comes from losing track of days, months—and centuries. You can't run a railroad like that, but it works for being becalmed.

After a long time without a breeze the ocean lies naked. Waves and whitecaps and wind are the clothing it takes off, one by one, until it lies with you, skin to skin. I sit on the boarding ladder, trailing my legs overboard and watching sun shafts penetrate the water. Nothing moves. The bottom is three miles down. We float among reflections of clouds.

A glass ocean is a window. Below us, in the shade of the hull, swim lively pilot fish. They've been with us since Hawai'i, perhaps mistaking *Thelonious* for a cruising shark and waiting for meal-time leftovers. At least that's the theory, because nobody really knows why these quick little striped fish adopt boats and stay with them across oceans. On the water near my knees flit tiny insects borne by the surface tension. I have no idea what they are or how they live out here, and they can only be seen from a few feet away.

There is no plant life, as there is in the Sargasso Sea of the Atlantic Gulf Stream. Years ago I was becalmed three days there, and lay on the deck in a torpor, pulling sargasso weed on board with a boat hook. A few shakes and the residents would fall out, worms and buggy things and miniature crabs strutting with their claws upraised. We marveled at their ecosystem, and always returned the creatures back to the water alive. It was hot 300 miles from Bermuda, and it was my first time since boyhood with nothing at all to do. I enjoyed it until I got home. It was July, 1973, and I was a Washington Post editor on vacation. I had missed the entire televised Watergate hearings, John Dean, Alexander Butterfield, Haldeman, Ehrlichman, the whole spectacle. The gap persists to this day. When my colleagues recall Maureen Dean's memorable pearl button earrings, all I flash back to is seaweed.

Each day I sit here on the cabin house for an hour or two, in morning or late afternoon, just watching the water. We are in the so-called convergence zone, also known as the garbage patch of the Pacific. This is what I've been seeing, in three categories:

Fishing debris: Tangles of one-inch poly line and all manner of floats made of foam, wood and exquisite globes of glass. Brian Cline arrived in Nawiliwili with one on his foredeck, as a souvenir. I've seen two dozen, so far.

Household debris: Plastic trays, cups, toys, spoons, and water bottles. A few days ago my own brand of plastic water bottle floated by, label fully intact. I have a case of it aboard, although I doubt I ever will again. Some of the junk has barnacles. Some looks like it was sold yesterday.

Foam: My notes, made while sailing slowly during the past week, show that in any given five-minute period I could record one or two white pieces of what appeared to be Styrofoam. Each is two square inches or less, and stands out bright white against the blue of the ocean. Our view of objects that small extends only about 50 yards, suggesting that the ocean is littered for hundreds of miles. I retrieved a few specimens, but their original form was unidentifiable. Some had growth, some were marked by oil, some were crumbly, some not.

Two years ago it was different here. The Tsunami that destroyed Fukashima, Japan, in 2011 provided an obstacle course for my new friend Brian Boschma as he sailed his Olson 34 yacht home from Kaua'i. He saw an overturned 20-foot skiff, many pieces of house or office buildings, a refrigerator, and twice his bow struck massive encrusted logs. He described the sea of floating water bottles as "endless." Fukashima debris still blows onto the windward shores of Hawai'i and long since reached the United States. But now most of it has sunk.

Out of sight, out of mind, but I was aware that eight million metric tons of plastic trash enters the world's oceans every year, about five bags for every foot of coastline. I had read the University of Georgia study that listed cigarette filters as most common, followed by food wrappers, plastic drinking straws, beverage bottles and bottle caps, each of them a single-use disposable product. And I knew that common plastic doesn't biodegrade, but fragments smaller into microplastics, so that a sample of the purest water under our keel, if examined closely, would reveal a slurry of manufactured trash.

On a boat, trash becomes personal.

We now have five plastic bags full, filling the farthest reaches of our limited storage. The packaging far exceeds in bulk the food I've eaten, and the microwavable pouches, tinned cans, waxed cardboard, hot-molded display packs and the aluminum of our few remaining beer cans makes a pile higher than I knew.

As you recall, we agreed not to throw anything overboard. And so, arriving at Kaua'i, I unloaded seven heavy bags of saved garbage and put them in the trash bin provided by the Hawai'i state harbor agency. It was days before I realized what the big, former sugar-cane processing plant on the hill above us was. It is the trash disposal plant of the Island of Kaua'i. There, the recyclable garbage we sailed to Hawai'i was packed into bales, loaded on a ship, and sent to the somewhat larger Island of Oahu.

Oahu had contracted to send its trash back to the mainland United States, but the deal fell through. Stacked bales started to stink in the sun. So trash there is burned, some energy extracted, and the ashes and nonflammables dumped in Hawaiian landfills, which are filling up.

It has been educational to live with my garbage for a while, instead of putting it to the curb in Los Angeles, where it magically disappears.

We are what we eat. Or are we what we throw away?

1155 hours. Motoring. Reading with feet facing forward.

I am trying to get used to reading with the diesel engine running a few feet from my ear. It is quite dark outside and we are motoring blind and deaf through the very patch of water where Brian Boschma ran into two tree trunks.

Alexander the Great is dead, and in Appendix "O" of the Landmark Edition of Arrian, Eugene N. Borza, professor emeritus of Ancient History at Penn State, is trying to figure out what killed him. I have always preferred to believe that handsome Alex (see his profile on any coin of his realm) expired after having the last word in a stupendous wine-drinking competition in the Asian desert, going out like a Welsh poet with some line like Dylan Thomas's, "I've had 18 straight whiskies, I believe that's the record."

But apparently not.

Professor Borza examined the evidence at a pathology conference at the University of Maryland's School of Medicine that had previously weighed in on the deaths of Beethoven, General

Custer, and the Roman emperor Claudius. What killed Alexander wasn't wine, or even the lead in wine cups. He had a fever, and lead poisoning doesn't do that. How about deliberate poisoning? No, his reported symptoms don't match known ancient poisons. It wasn't malaria, because malaria patients don't complain of severe abdominal pain, as Alexander did.

Prof. Borza's team did eventually get around to considering the terrible wound Alexander received while attacking a walled city in India. As usual he was first up the ladder, but while busy slaughtering people was struck by a big arrow right above his breastplate. Air and blood hissed out of the wound, and his men carried him off thinking he was dead. He survived, but that may have weakened a constitution already oppressed by fatigue, stress, multiple injuries, malaria and heavy drinking.

What got him, after conquering the world at the age of 33, was most likely typhoid fever.

But not before he saw a lot of it.

FOOD

eturn Day 20, 0900 hours. Fuel allotment expended. Teakettle rhythms.

R I motored 24 hours, noon to noon, and was glad to turn the engine off after 100 miles of it. Eight gallons of fuel remain from our 40 gallons, and the deck jugs are empty. Eight gallons gives us 16 days of battery charging, which is a large reserve. It pretty much assures an additional 100 miles under power, if we need it in coastal waters. It's a relief to rely on sailing again, even slowly.

The ocean remains flat. Yesterday was Sunday, so I finished Father Mapple's homily for the education of fishes: "But oh! Shipmates! On the starboard hand of every woe, there is sure delight; and higher the top of that delight, than the bottom of the woe is deep." The actual bottom here is 2839 fathoms, the chart says, or about 17,000 feet or more than three miles deep.

The woe isn't the ocean, but rather days and days more of being a ship in a bottle. It takes a better man than myself not to let the past intrude on this silence. It takes a better man to be alone, if alone means not populating every silence with people. If we are trying to figure out what alone means, this windless cathedral of thought is our main chance. Who are we, when no one else is there?

I cannot get out of my mind a wonderful book by Douglass Hofstadter called, "I Am a Strange Loop." Hofstadter thinks we are creatures of feedback, which is the sound a microphone makes when too close to speakers, or the strange patterns of a video camera set to record itself recording itself. Personality, he says, is endlessly correcting consciousness. Even alone, I find the feedback continues. Memory repopulates emptiness. The clamoring crowd never recedes. What is the creature we call the self? I fail at every attempt to pin myself down like a specimen for study. No hypothesis fits, except Melville's: On the starboard hand of every woe is sure delight.

1400 hours. Raw water pump seal failure.

Three days ago I noticed water pooling on the cabin floor in front of the engine compartment. Observation of the running diesel revealed a light spray from the raw water pump. The pump turns an impellor which draws ocean water to cool the engine. After another day or so the spray became a stream, and it was clear that the seal had failed. The pump assembly is connected by a shaft to the bowels of the engine, and not serviceable at sea. I shut the diesel down and took a nap, content to sail without an engine.

An hour later I was awakened rudely by an idea. It was irritating, because I knew it was the loop intruding with feedback from an unconscious source. An hour after that I had dug out some latex rubber strips, packed for no reason other than their ability to conform to irregular surfaces. I wrapped them tightly around the base of the leaking water pump and secured them with hose clamps. That slowed the leak from the water pump to a drip. To deal with the drip, I modified a large funnel to fit under the pump, and piped the funnel to a receiving jug under the sink. The leak was reduced by 80 percent, and I could now monitor the intake water loss by observing the jug. Once more we were on our way under power, clattering over the featureless water.

1800 hours. Provisioning.

In earlier times, sailors had to do with salt pork or cod, with roaches for flavor and scurvy for dessert. Yachtsmen have never seen fit to continue that tradition, and the cruising diet has improved even since I was a kid.

Captain Slocum, singlehanding at the turn of the century, ate potatoes and fish, and when he salvaged barrels of tallow from a wreck, made fresh doughnuts. In 1969, when Robin Knox-Johnson became the first to sail around the globe non-stop, he carried 1500 cans of beef and sausages, 350 pounds of potatoes and 250 pounds of onions in a boat the same length as *Thelonious*. Near the end of his 312-day expedition he was so tired of his food he had to force himself to eat it.

By the early 1980s, freeze-dried food was the ticket for serious offshore racing. It could reduce the weight of one crewman's meal to two pounds a day. Nobody liked the taste, but ocean racing crews are there to suffer and break records. Chichester, and most solo sailors, have a more measured approach: Sir Francis liked to keep a keg of beer tapped at the ready. Nowadays, cruisers carry frozen sirloin and ice cream in galley freezers, and warm their leftovers in a microwave oven.

But they have larger yachts than ours, and I have never felt the lack of a Sub-Zero refrigerator on a sailboat. Our provisioning was mostly done by Project Supervisor Tracy Olmstead in the aisles of a supermarket called Trader Joe's, pushing a cart past underemployed movie actors, entertainment lawyers and gourmet children. Such shopping is not very nautical, but easy to load into a Prius.

As you know, the featured main course aboard *Thelonious* is spaghetti. Therefore our 60-day inventory began with 10 pounds of pasta, 10 cans each of plum tomatoes and mushrooms, 15 onions, six containers of powdered parmesan and two containers of crushed red pepper. Everything else was an afterthought to carry us from sauce to sauce. I don't say it's right, only good. We had:

Thirty-six supermarket eggs, good unrefrigerated for 20 days. Three tubs butter—which lasts longer. Ten heads of fresh garlic. Various cuts of cheese. Cheese, invented to preserve milk, does well warm for a long time. To accompany the eggs we had six cans of Spam in imaginative flavors, each of them still reassuringly Spam.

I had remembered bread going blue with mold after a single week at sea. But sourdough lasts much longer, and was simply gone, rather than gone bad, when we arrived in Kaua'i. We should have brought more bread, and not so many bags of potato chips, oyster crackers, bagel chips, wheat thins and generic crispies. None is any good for mopping up sauce.

For luncheon we had 11 cans tuna, two of peanut butter and jelly, three jars mayonnaise, sardines, chowder, salsa, pickles, fried onions, banana peppers, salsa roja y verde, and, just in case, 15 cans of Cuban black beans.

Of fruit, 40 cans of pineapple, mango, pears, peaches, fruit cocktail. For snacks: three bags of yogurt pretzels, two of oatmeal raisin, and one each of dried apricots, raisins, granola, chocolate almonds, chocolate peanut pretzels and Oreos.

Dinner was precooked in cans, or in pouches designed to be microwaved but also easily warmed in a frying pan. We had six tins of Dinty Moore beef stew, four of Argentine roast beef, three of hash, four of mac and cheese, two of ravioli. Instant mashed potatoes blossom with only water. For variety we had cuisine that stretched from the Punjab to Old Siam, including Palak Paneer, Jaipur vegetables, Pad Thai, Kung Pau and vegetable biryani, all cut from plastic wallets and poured steaming over a bed of 12 kinds of instant rice designed, I think, for people in office buildings who have half an hour for lunch before the boss gets back from her noon Pilates session. The portions are small, which is fine, because here we are always one squall away from our perfect weight.

Of spirits, wine and beer, the mistake we made is to run low. Beer is not so important, I find, without refrigeration. Whisky, rum and wine carry the day, with a good brandy when wet or discouraged. It is true that a scarcity of booze, like a scarcity of company, engenders appreciation for it.

1100 hours. Sailing easily. "Pannonica".

Five days we motored or sat waiting for wind. Now there is a breath of air on the water. I can't see it in the darkness, but it touches my face on deck. The sails are up and drawing some. We have just enough speed for the self-steering gear to work again, which is about two knots.

The GRIB forecast shows good wind lies ahead, and from a favorable direction. Whether we reach it tonight, tomorrow, or the next day—does that matter? We have a full belly, and the cockpit speakers send Thelonious Monk's "Pannonica" out over the empty waters. The composition is named for a patron of bebop, Kathleen Annie Pannonica de Koenigswarter (nee Rothschild). In photos with Monk, Charlie Parker and Miles Davis, she looks delightfully compatible.

Here's a good name for a jazz tune, if Monk were alive to write it: "North Pacific High."

Only we know how it sounds, and how the rhythms match our own.

CHAPTER 42

WIND

R ETURN D*AY 21, 0900 hours. Course 080m under genoa and
single reef.*
What lies ahead is the last leg toward the cold waters of
the California coast, where gales spawn and it's not good to linger.
The breeze came up in the night, so that at 3 a.m. I took the first reef
in the mainsail. The yacht is alive again with motion, and to celebrate
I'm playing Jimi Hendrix loud. We even had pancakes to go with the
eggs and Spam. The batter mix comes in a jug, just add water and
shake. Only one more day's worth of maple syrup, though.

It is remarkable how quickly I forget the way the world is, or
was. The past five days have been beautiful and weirdly silent except
for the hours of engine drone. I read everything on board, and felt
bereft. Two days ago I discovered the entire July 17th New York
Times downloaded on the iPhone, and read it the way a dog eats a
bone, chewing till nothing was left.

Just yesterday I saw *Thelonious* from a new perspective. At
noon I lowered a waterproof GoPro camera 100 feet beneath us,
watching it diminish in size but never disappear. Didn't think much
about it, since the GoPro has no viewing screen. But last night I
downloaded the video file onto the navigation laptop, and there
we were, suspended in space, hovering high over the camera. The
underwater profile of the boat was surprisingly lovely. I could see
the line of growth at our waterline, proof of long immersion. I could
see the fineness of our bow, and the deep spade rudder, and the fin-
like keel. From below, *Thelonious* looked like the smooth-skinned,

elegantly finned sea-creature she is. Near the stern the two pilot fish were suspended, lazily swimming, dressed as if for their portrait in brilliant pin stripes.

I had passed the week of calms in my own calm. I had reminded myself that an intelligent person is never bored, and so, to my surprise, I wasn't. For hours and hours, as the boat lay motionless in the sun, I accompanied Latin jazz on the stereo with kitchen knives on the stove-top teakettle. My best work was sitting in with Bobby Valentin and Mambo DJ Planet Salsa, a cut called Zip Zap. After five hours I got good, and added tuned coffee cups to my percussion set. At any time I could have called home on the satellite phone, but there seemed no reason to interrupt the lives of my family, and they would seem no closer, and maybe further away, if asked to say words through a tin filter bounced off the edge of space.

What is different, sailing again, is re-engagement with progress. In the calm there hadn't been any, life just quietly was. But once moving, the calm became the past and the future demanded attention. Change is progress. Progress must be measured. With luck, we'll make a hundred miles today. Progress is an upstart, Age of Enlightenment idea. In Medieval times people didn't make progress. God had made the world and that was that. You lived it as it was, and waited for the reward later. For a week I lived as they had, past and present together in the sun, unchanging.

Now the future is here, and it's wind. The GRIB files show steadily increasing flow from the north, and then the northwest. The velocity barbs are strong. Our course home is southeast, but we don't want to turn south this far out, in case of gales ahead. So it's hold this latitude as long as we can, headed 200 miles north of San Francisco.

1300 hours. Spoke sailing vessel Aeriagnie.

The noon position shows us 1100 miles from Los Angeles, and after recording it in the log I stuck my head out of the hatch to see a sailboat ahead on the horizon, the first ever since we left home nearly two months ago. I tacked to head right for her through the line of scudding clouds and building seas. She was a pretty boat, larger than *Thelonious*, and proceeding under double-reefed mainsail and storm jib. I was surprised at how small she appeared against the panorama of the ocean and clouds, and how she rolled and heeled. After half an hour I could see her crew looking at us through binoculars, as I was looking at them.

The yacht was *Aeriagnie*, out of Oahu on her return from the Pacific Cup Race from San Francisco Bay. We had a nice chat on the VHF radio, and I was surprised to learn that her destination was Marina Del Rey, like mine, and her slip almost within sight of my own. I could see her crew on deck, probably finishing lunch, and thought for a moment how nice it might be if there were someone on board to hand me a sandwich. There was a gale off San Francisco, and *Aeriagnie* had abandoned plans for a stopover there. We sailed in company together for a few hours until the sky lowered and a line of rain squalls came in, and *Thelonious* was once again alone on the darkening sea.

2000 hours. Third reef, seas building.

I strapped myself to the gimballed stove for dinner and managed to heat up some rice with jodhpur vegetables and chutney, and hold on to remaining beer Number 5 long enough to get it down. We're on port tack now, which means I lean over the stove, instead of away from it. Leaning away was better. The sky is very dark and I estimate 20 knots of wind directly over the left side of the boat. We're making six knots, but the sea state is lumpy and short. This is where a traditional design like *Thelonious* does well. We're tippy, with quick motions, but we carve through the bumps like a mogul skier. Many new-model cruising boats are wider and higher, for more interior space, but in these conditions they part the waves like a rock jetty. *Thelonious* gives with the punch.

But this will not be a night for easy sleeping, I don't think.

0200 hours. Gale preparations.

I don't know what it's blowing now, probably gusting to 30 knots. It would be easier on the boat, and us, to head downwind a little on a straight line to Los Angeles. But this is no time to take it easy. I want to keep to Latitude 41 North as long as possible. As we approach the coast we can bear off if the going gets rough.

Gales, yeah. I don't like them, but ahead is where they live. Our water temperature is already dropping. That's the first sign of the Pacific current that sweeps the coast from Alaska to San Diego and Mexico. It makes the water cool and the flow adds energy to the gyre. Even without a gale, the waters ahead are subject to fair weather gradients that can peg the wind at 40 knots for days.

Today I checked my gale procedures and thought them through for the hundredth time. If sailing becomes impossible we can heave to. You put one sail aback and ride sideways like a duck, going nowhere. That works for some types of sailboat. If it doesn't work for us, I'll stream the 12-foot sea anchor, which opens underwater like a parachute. With 300 or 400 feet of springy nylon line deployed, some boats ride well, bow to the wind. Some don't. The next alternative is to trail behind us the large truck tire lashed under the dinghy on the foredeck. We will run before the wind, dragging the tire like a brake, and in success that will keep our stern to the waves and the breaking seas. I've dragged anchors, chains and even a set of mahogany companionway stairs, and they just skipped uselessly across the ocean behind us. The tire may work better.

Gales are all different, depending on the strength of gusts, the height of the waves and how long they last. There's no one answer. The answer is to find something that works to prevent catastrophic damage from breaking seas, and to remember that gales always pass.

Hurricanes must be avoided, but gales can be endured. It's likely that any sailor who ventures offshore will eventually meet one, so let's make peace now, with all gear still intact.

We have had no secrets between us, and so I will share my personal preparation for what may lie ahead. It is just a few loose sheets of paper in the navigation drawer: Skip Allan's story. Allan, like me, is a veteran of the 1979 Fastnet Race, in which a full gale off the west of England scattered the fleet of 300 boats and drowned 15 competitors. In 2008, Allan was on his sixth return sail from Hawai'i, and I am on my first. His boat was *Wildflower*, which he had built himself, as I have renovated *Thelonious*.

He was alone, but in these dog-eared pages I am always with him, and we are at his latitude now.

{PREPARATION}
The Loss of Wildflower

By Skip Allan

TEN DAYS AFTER LEAVING Hanalei Bay, Kaua'i, we were halfway home to Santa Cruz with 1190 miles to go. We had passed the Pacific High, and were running in the westerlies at 38°38' N by 147°17' W. So far the passage had been going well, and was my sixth return from Hawai'i aboard *Wildflower*. But an ominous note on the thrice daily weather fax charts was the notation "GALE" between our position and the Pacific Coast.

I began to plan for this possible gale by increasing latitude, slowing down, and closely monitoring projected GRIB files out to 144 hours. It appeared from all forecasts that we needed to slow down at least 48 hours to let the gale ahead abate. However, it is against my instincts to try and slow a boat down, and so with difficulty I reefed the main and dropped the jib in 8 knots of wind, reducing speed to a sedate 3.5 knots in smooth seas.

On Wednesday, the morning GRIB file showed the area of most wind ahead was between 124 and 128 degrees, with no weather abatement until at least Monday, Sept. 1, at the earliest.

On Friday conditions began to rapidly deteriorate. I changed to the 75 percent short hoist jib and storm staysail, dropping the main completely.

The following day, with Santa Cruz 365 miles on a bearing of 095 T, we ran off due south in winds of 30-35 knots. By 1530 hours the sail combination proved too much, and I dropped the jib, keeping only the 39-foot storm staysail and began towing a 30-inch diameter metal-hooped drogue.

It was uncomfortable, windy, and rolly that night, with the cockpit filling about every five minutes and the boat being knocked down to 70 degrees at least half a dozen times. *Wildflower's* shallow cockpit and oversize drains allowed full drainage in about 90 seconds, and this was not a problem.

The electric Autohelm 1000+ tiller pilot was doing an amazing job steering, as it was being continuously drenched, even submerged. The Sailomat wind vane was useless preventing or correcting breaking wave induced broaches, and I retracted its oar to avoid fouling the drogue rode.

On Sunday the wind was 30-35 with a confused wave train from the northwest, north and northeast. At 0915 hours I winched in the drogue to change from a high-tech spinnaker sheet to a stretchy nylon anchor line. Unfortunately, I found the drogue had split and was no longer effective. I deployed my spare drogue, but without a metal hoop it would periodically collapse astern in a breaking crest.

During the long night, my third in this particular gale, breaking crests would poop the boat about every five minutes, filling the cockpit and surging against the companionway hatch boards. Even though I had gone to lengths for many years to insure fire-hose watertight integrity of the companionway hatch, I found the power of the breaking wave crests slamming the boat would cause water to forcefully spray around the edges of the hatch boards and into the cabin.

In the wait for daylight I had more than enough time to ponder what might happen if the autopilot was damaged or was washed off its mount. I had two spare tiller pilots. But it would take several minutes, exposed in the cockpit, on my knees, to hook up a replacement in the cockpit, on a dark night, when the boat was being periodically knocked down and the cockpit swept. In addition, I pondered the fate of *Daisy*, a boat that was lost in the Lightship Race [in San Francisco Bay] when presumably a large breaking wave crushed and sank her. I also reminded myself I was responsible for not only my own life, but was also a family caregiver at home.

There was no doubt that if *Wildflower's* tiller pilot was lost we would round up and be at the mercy of the breaking waves, some of which I estimate to be in the vicinity of 25-35 feet, and as big as I had seen since the 1979 Fastnet Race storm on *Imp*.

The anxiety and stress of this night, with the whine of the wind in the rigging, the wave crests slamming into the hatch boards and 70-degree knockdowns that would launch me across the cabin, created serious doubts that we could continue like this for another night, much less the three or four more days the conditions were expected to continue.

The boat was fine, and had suffered no serious damage yet. My physical health was OK, but I could see that, with minimum sleep, my decision making could be beginning to be compromised.

At 0715 the following morning I sat-phoned my longtime sailing friend, ham radio contact, router, navigator and weatherman, Joe Buck, in Redondo Beach. Joe and I had maintained twice-a-day ham radio schedule since leaving Hanalei Bay, and he had instant Internet access to all forecast weather and wave charts. I explained the current situation to Joe: that I'd had a difficult night and wasn't sure I could safely continue. Joe's weather info had the highest wind and wave on my current drift southward continuing for at least another three days, with continuing gale force winds and 18-22' significant wave height.

Joe called back an hour later on ham radio 40 meters and said that Lt. Saxon at San Francisco Coast Guard Search and Rescue (SAR) reported no military assets within 200 miles or 20 hours, that *Wildflower* was 200 miles beyond helicopter range, but that *Toronto*, an inbound container ship, was coming in my direction at an undetermined distance. Joe helped me to understand if the boat were lost, I would likely be lost also. If I left *Wildflower* proactively, only the boat would be lost. I told Joe of my hesitation to put my life in the hands of a possibly foreign crew on a big commercial ship in a transfer off *Wildflower* in these conditions, especially at night. We agreed that a decision had to be arrived at soon, before 1130 hours and before *Toronto* passed by.

I spent the next hour sitting on the cabin sole on my life raft, debating whether to ask for assistance in leaving my beloved *Wildflower*. "Fleur" was my home, the consort and magic carpet I had built 34 years ago. I cried, pounded my fist and looked out through the hatch numerous times at the passing wave mountains, remembering all the good times I had shared with her. And I came to a decision.

At 1200 hours, like a gopher popping out of its hole, I slid the hatch open to get a clear satphone signal and called SAR. Lt. Saxon already knew my details and position, and only asked "what are you requesting?" I replied, "I am asking for assistance to be removed from my boat."

We kept the conversation short and to the point, due to my exposure topsides with the satphone. She said that *Toronto* would be requested to divert, and that I was not to trigger the EPIRB but to take it with me when I left *Wildflower*. Lt. Saxon also said that if I left my boat she would be considered "derelict" and broadcast as a hazard to navigation. I assured her I would not leave my boat floating.

An hour later, at 1300, *Wildflower's* AIS alarm rang. *Toronto* was showing 30 miles away, closing at 23.4 knots from the southwest. I had to do some fast planning. With no idea how the transfer would be made (jump, swim, climb, hoist?) I didn't know what I could pack into my bag. I decided on my documents, wallet and passport, laptop, camera, cellphone and satphone, logbook, EPIRB and a change of clothes and shoes. All this I bagged into waterproof bags. And in a moment of whimsy, I decided to try and offload the two Singlehanded TransPac Race perpetual trophies, as they had 30-year historical and sentimental value to our race.

At eight miles, the captain of *Toronto* rang on the VHF radio He spoke perfect English, and as I had a visual on his ship, directed him to alter 20 degrees to starboard to intercept me. He explained that *Toronto* was over 1,000 feet long, that he would lay her parallel to the waves and make a lee at a forward speed of Slow Ahead, which is six knots.

The captain also explained that I would board his ship from a rope ladder that led to the pilot's door, on the aft starboard side. I asked if he could slow to a speed between 3-4 knots, and he willingly agreed to try. At five miles, a sharp-eyed lookout sighted *Wildflower* ahead. *Toronto's* radar did not identify us until 2.5 miles, under the conditions.

At 1415 hours, one of the world's biggest container ships was bearing down on us less than five boat lengths (125 feet) dead ahead, the huge bulb bow extending 20 feet and making a five-foot breaking wave. With my heart in my throat I motored down the starboard side of a gigantic black wall, made a U turn, and pulled alongside the pilot's door and rope ladder.

The crew threw a heaving line, and in the next five minutes we transferred three bags. Knowing I was next, I jumped below decks, said a final quick goodbye, and pulled the already unclamped hose off the through-hull fitting of the engine salt water intake. Water flooded in.

Back on deck, I reached for the bottom rung of the Jacob's ladder. It was alternately at head height, then 10 feet out of reach, depending on the ship's roll. I grabbed hold, jumped, and did a pull-up onto the ladder and climbed up wearing a 15-pound backpack with my most valuable positions and EPIRB.

At 1429 hours, on Monday, September 1, 2008, at position 35°17'N x 126°38'W, *Toronto* resumed its voyage to Long Beach, leaving *Wildflower* alone to bang and scrape her way down the aft quarter of the ship and disappear under the stern. I watched, but could barely see through my tears.

For the next 24 hours I was treated with the utmost kindness and compassion by Captain Ivo Hruza and his 24-man crew. We stood watch together, ate together, told stories, viewed family photo albums, discussed the world situation, and toured the ship and the engine room with its 12-cylinder, 93,360- horsepower diesel. By the time we came down the Santa Barbara Channel and docked at Long Beach, I felt a part of this happy crew of six nationalities. I could not have been assisted by a better or more professionally manned ship. On Tuesday afternoon, after clearing customs and immigration aboard, I shook hands with each and every crew member and descended the gangway alone to meet Joe, my sister Marilee, and begin new beginnings.

I will never forget *Wildflower*. She took a beating in the

gale. She never let me down, and took me to amazing places where we met wonderful people and made new friends. In this time of loss, a most wonderful thing is happening: many loved ones, friends, interested parties, and people I've never met are closing a circle of love around the mourning and celebration of *Wildflower*. Time will heal a broken heart. I look forward to seeing everyone. I apologize in advance if at times I have to look away and wipe my tears.

Treasure each day,

Skip

NEAR GALE

R ETURN DAY 23, 0600 hours. Position 38°12' N, 129°55 W. Wind 25, seas 8.

So, in we go. Dawn looked like a tunnel through mountains ahead. Now we're in it, watching scudding clouds through the vortex of spray that curls around us when the wind comes all from one side. This is Force 5 on the Beaufort scale, a Fresh Breeze of 18 to 24 miles an hour. The scale give attributes. At Sea: "Moderate waves of some length. Many whitecaps. Small amounts of spray." On land: "Branches of moderate size move. Small trees in leaf begin to sway." That sounds about right.

Force 5 is an invitation to push off for a sail on a fast dinghy. With some athletic hiking you'd be planing and surfing, having fun and a good workout, too. A dinghy wouldn't be a good choice here only because the seas are too big and confused. *Thelonious* does fine, although we have too much sail up even with a third reef in the main. We had Force 5 behind us much of the time on the outbound leg, urging us forward. But wind over the side, a beam reach, makes us heel. We jump to seven knots and then fall off a wave, roll, pitch, and climb the face of the next one. I can drink my coffee in the companionway hatch, as long as I duck when 50 pounds of blue water passes overhead.

I thought about the fate of *Wildflower* last night, but when I woke up the barometer was holding steady. The gale off San Francisco is 800 miles away, with no influence here. This wind will build, that trend is clear. But I think it's a fair weather blow, just the ocean doing what it does. We may be uncomfortable for a while, but we've gone over our plans. They're good, or at least the best we can do. Now back to the moment. A sip of coffee, a duck beneath a sudden sheet of spray, a grin.

1300 hours. We made a hundred miles since yesterday. Not bad, considering.

That crash was the kerosene lamp flying through the air. After 4,000 miles of hanging over the saloon table, the shock-cord that restricts its swinging came untied. Amazing that the glass chimney didn't break, but came to rest on a pillow on the leeward bunk. But the cabin floor is wet with slippery kerosene, which I'm mopping up on hands and knees, spraying cleaner with one hand and wiping with the other while sliding all over.

We need to get the mainsail down completely. Good deck shoes are important today. The cabin house will be rolling, so we'll take it slow. The sequence of actions isn't critical in a calm, but now everything will go better if I think through the steps in advance. Shall we head up into the wind to relieve pressure on the sail? I don't think so, in this wind. We'll free the main sheet and let her luff a little, not too much. I don't want the flapping sail to shake its battens out, or flail its lines into knots. I can wedge myself against the mast and haul the sail down hand over hand, while the boom hangs out over the water to leeward.

Then what? Good question. Before furling it, I'll climb back into the cockpit and winch the boom on centerline, then rig a preventer line to hold it rock solid. I need the boom to be firm as I wrestle the sailcloth into folds and lash it with gaskets. All hatches to be closed and locked, so I don't fall through them. Remember to keep knees bent, and stay low and in balance. If knocked down by a sudden motion of the boat, grab and hold on. If thrown into the sea we'll still be connected to the boat, but dragging in the water by the harness tether. Climb back aboard using the lines looped along the hull.

Now up, and do it. And back, we're done.

The wind is up a little, I think, but under a scrap of foresail alone we're in good control. Too much motion to read. I could use a dram of rum. The duplicitous olive oil bottle mocks me whenever I open the cabinet. It's wet outside, but dry here in ways good and bad.

1900 hours. Seas 8, wind 25-30, Course 090.

Call this Beaufort Scale Force 6, "Strong Breeze." At Sea: "Long waves begin to form. White foam crests are very frequent. Some airborne spray is present." On land: "Large branches in motion. Whistling heard in overhead wires. Umbrella use becomes difficult." I'm reading Chichester. As daylight fades in the portholes we're with him in his first transatlantic race, from Plymouth to New York, against the prevailing winds. He had expected two gales and has so far endured seven, one with winds of 100 miles an hour. That must be an estimate, because few wind instruments are calibrated above 60 knots. The self-steering gear he designed keeps breaking. He changes sails constantly, and whenever he puts it off he feels guilty. What a sturdy Englishman he is, square-faced in wire spectacles. He is covered with bruises and has cracked a rib. He makes mistakes sailors no longer make after learning from him. He's a strange man, a determined dreamer who has already won a bout with lung cancer. He is never sentimental, but thinks often of his wife. Wet and cold, he logs every sail change for the record. Before he took up yachting, Sir Francis flew a Gipsy Moth, the cloth-winged biplane of the 1930s. He set long-distance aviation records. In Japan, while a crowd watched, he flew into telegraph wires and crashed in the street, almost killing himself. He didn't succeed at everything he tried, but he tried everything. For being himself, and nobody else, he was knighted by his queen and became an example for the world.

Return Day 24, 0300 hours. Continuing on beam reach. Black night.

I can follow our progress easily without the sense of sight. The rigging hums, and sends resonance down the mast to the cabin. The wires of the steering gear grind and moan. The saloon smells of sweat and spilled kerosene, and the decks run water like a river bed. The tiny area of jib provides little steadying force, so the boat gyrates erratically. A halyard vibrates in the wind, high on the mast, at a frequency well off the end of any harmonica. The automatic bilge pump turns on and off, because the bilge water won't hold still. Too crazy to read. Too loud for music. But my bunk is dry. That's unusual in a small boat swept by seas.

If I could change one thing this night, it would be the bombs. Chichester named them that, if you recall. They go off without warning, and get under my skin. Usually we flog and slice through the waves. But maybe three times an hour a cresting wave and the side of the boat arrive in the same place together, and when that happens a thousand pounds of water explodes against the hull beside my head. It has the shock of a car accident. There's no warning at all, so I'm always caught off guard. Boom!

The boat was built for it. It's useful to believe in that. As William James says, you get more done.

1000 hours. Wild ocean. Chafing on topping lift, mainsail. Dinghy secure. Leakage minimal.

I put the wind now at a Near Gale, also called a Moderate Gale. That's Force 7, winds of 27 to 33 knots. "Sea heaps up some. Some foam from breaking waves is blown into streaks along wind direction. Moderate amounts of airborne spray." On land, "Whole trees are in motion. Effort is needed to walk against the wind." Force 8 has "well-marked streaks of foam," and on roadways, "cars veer." I don't think we're there.

But there's no need to put a number on it. The question is how *Thelonious* handles the sea and the wind. And the answer is, we're having a bit of a rough time with it. Our speed is down to three knots. The self-steering gear is working well but too many big waves now punch us with a closed fist. Therefore, I'm altering course 30 degrees downwind. A quick adjustment of the steering vane and off we go, gaining another knot. That's better, a little. Now we're headed for southern California instead of San Francisco. We have made 300 miles east that will pay off later.

It's waves that matter, and ours are only 10 or 12 feet high. They're steep, and they break over us as spray, not solid water that falls like a piano to carry away hatches and ports, lifeboats, and people. So, wet and loud but nothing broken. Are you good with that? Me too.

It's always the waves that I remember.

In a gale in the Gulf Stream many years ago they were 25 feet high, with the short wavelength typical when strong wind opposes a strong current. The ocean seemed to stand on a ladder and look down on us. The canyon sides of bright blue water were unnaturally steep, with clumps of sargasso weed hung like pictures on a wall. We were through the stream in one four-hour watch, during which the water temperature went from 70 to 85 degrees Fahrenheit, and on the other side, with the Island of Bermuda still 400 miles away, the wind died completely and we lay on a steaming, ironing-board sea.

On board Ted Turner's *Tenacious*, a 61-foot ocean racer with a crew of 19, the Fastnet Gale of 1979 caught us just after rounding the famous lighthouse off the coast of Ireland. The wind touched Force 11: "Exceptionally high waves. Very large patches of foam, driven before the wind, cover much of the sea surface." The seas were geologic in scale. Sometimes Tenacious sailed right off one, dropping ten feet to submerge in the trough. Sometimes we put our bow into them, lifting a wall of green water that ran two feet deep down the windward deck where we crew sat tethered, sea boots hanging over the side, to be washed together in a heap. It was cold, but jammed shoulder to shoulder we could feel the warm of each other's shoulders, an intimacy impossible elsewhere.

At night we just sat on the rail and took what came. But at dawn long mountains were revealed on either side of us, their peaks crumbling into surf that cascaded down the slopes, turning them white with foam as if an alpine winter landscape had been transplanted to the North Atlantic.

We were never in danger, never stopped racing, and when the results came in we had won the trophy. Elsewhere in the storm around us 18 people died, 77 yachts were rolled, five sunk, and hundreds of rescuers risked their lives in what was called the largest ocean rescue effort in peacetime. Every gale is different for every boat.

I don't know how long this wind and sea will last. It is true that if we hit a lost shipping container tonight we'll probably go down fast, and although I have rehearsed the abandon-ship drill things may not come out as planned. But that won't happen. And right now it is so loud, and there is so much to monitor, and we are hurtling so violently in exactly the direction of home, that my usual list of concerns has vanished. I just listen for the telltale shaking of a blown jib, for the sound of collision, for the self-steering gear to fail.

And it just did. My harness is on, I clip in and launch on deck. The vane is completely gone. I grab the wheel and bring us back on course, noticing the wind-rows of spume on the wild ocean, not quite the "well-marked" foam of Force 8, only "sea foam blown into streaks." Conditions are holding. And there is the missing vane, fluttering in the wake by its safety line. It just blew off its mount, and in five minutes with a wrench all is well again and we're back on course.

Hours pass without change. When darkness comes again I snatch a nap on the cabin floor. My calories are from a product called Instant Breakfast, a tasteless blend of lukewarm something or other that goes down grudgingly, but stays there. Our condition seems objectively uncomfortable and unpleasant, but it's not. We are just going along with what the North Pacific has planned. We cling to every moment like a starfish on a rock, waiting for the tide to recede.

I'm not in charge, and I know it. Most of the time we expect to have a say, and feel cheated if we're not: exploited, demeaned, enslaved. The news is full of people rising up to be acknowledged, commanding change, sure of their rights.

Here, there is no self-regard or claim to individual worth. Humility comes easy.

Return Day 24, 0900 hours. Wind moderating.

After 50 hours of it there was no question but that the seas were breaking less frequently. At noon I shook out a reef and deployed half of the jib. The sun appeared between clouds and the rain stopped completely. I made tea and toast with butter, which before I could eat it flew off the stove onto the wet, greasy floor, where I followed to devour the soggy bits. Eventually the wind declined to 20 knots and held there and I slept six hours, dreaming of nothing at all.

When light came again I noticed how bleached the oiled teak of the cockpit had become, and how clean the yacht, and how white our newly rain-laundered sails. I had missed the noon transmission yesterday at the height of the blow. Knowing the family would be concerned, I managed to get off a satellite email explaining that conditions had made communication inconvenient.

We had made good mileage, all of it in the right direction, and I was surprised to see that on the chart we were 400 miles off San Francisco and 800 miles from home. Almost there. It felt strange to think it. I had not in a long time considered that this might end, and that soon everything would change.

Do I feel alone? There's a fulmar, wheeling overhead. They mate on remote islands, but spend their lives out of sight on land.

Is a fulmar alone?

CHAPTER 44

COASTING

R ETURN DAY 27. 1100 hours. Course 105° for the Channel Islands. Wind from astern at 20. Air 60°F.
During the gale we went three days without charging the batteries, and this morning the diesel sputtered, faded and died. I have just finished changing the primary fuel filter, and now the engine runs fine again. It's confirmation that the agitation of heavy seas stirs up particles in the fuel tank.

The California coast is only 50 miles away. We're headed south along it, wing and wing and rolling a little. The sky is gray, as it was when we left these waters two months ago. I was excited when the AM band on the radio worked again, and for an hour listened carefully to traffic reports from San Luis Obispo, baseball scores, and to a doctor who has invented a cure for intestinal gas, which I had not realized was such an impediment to social progress, or that his treatment is usually covered by insurance. I have not seen land yet, but I've heard it.

Six ships have passed in the last 12 hours, all hurrying toward Vancouver or San Diego or Mexico. Why they should converge here I don't know. Maybe we're the ones converging. High overhead the first commercial airliners have appeared, streaming contrails and glinting. We sail through gray water littered with Velella, small radiant jellyfish related to the Portuguese man o' war. They're uniformly scattered as far as the eye can see, one every square yard. Thousands of them, maybe millions or billions, propelled by the wind, as we are. Wherever they're going, they're not alone.

1400 hours. Unidentified Bird.

While I was sitting in the cockpit eating the last can of tuna on a crumbly cracker, mayonnaise long gone and no pickles left, either, a bird circled the boat. I thought I was seeing things, because it was a land bird, not at all the sort of bird expected here offshore in misty fog. He circled the boat 10 times. No, make it 20. I could see how tired he was, how his flight dipped and swerved close to the sea, and how he approached and then veered away. After a long time he came straight at the stern rail 10 feet from me and landed in the sort of controlled crash naval aviators use to make sure they stick to the deck of the aircraft carrier.

"Hello," I said to the bird. My unpracticed voice sounded loud and harsh, not as welcoming as I had planned.

The rail tubing was wet and slippery with salt. He couldn't find a comfortable grip and flew off into the mist again. But in a moment he circled back for another landing, this time entirely out of fuel, to cling to the canvas of the weather cloths, ruffled like a tiny feather duster.

I should concentrate on San Miguel Island, 100 miles ahead, where we will make a left turn to leeward of the Channel Islands for our final course home. I've put a waypoint on the chart, and as we approach we can cut the corner. I should call Tracy and give her a revised estimate of arrival, but I'm putting it off. I don't want to give a time and then be late. So we roll dead downwind with a single bird on the railing. It's gray and cool, not like Hawai'i.

He, or she, is apparently exhausted. I can approach, but the bird shifts claw to claw in preparation for flight. His back is to me, which seems unwise in a creature who survives by alertness. Except for a seed-cracking beak, I can't find any feature remarkable enough to identify in the bird book. Sea birds are effortlessly athletic. Fulmars and tropicbirds soar with swiveling neck, always scanning. Shearwaters bank and swoop with a certainty of themselves I have never known in a person. Storm petrels dance in the wave troughs no matter how rough the sea. This bird is far from home, and I think he has given up going back.

I crumbled some pretzels and spread them on deck as food. The movement sent him flapping off again precariously low, and during two circuits of the boat he never rose above a few feet before alighting heavily again, this time on the foredeck. I put a saucer of fresh water near the crumbs.

Off Point Conception, which marks the eastward retreat of the coast at Santa Barbara, the wind came up to 25 knots as dusk approached. I reefed down the mainsail and reduced the genoa, but didn't go forward to contract the whisker pole. The wind from the stern blew the crumbs toward the bird, who huddled under the protection of the dinghy. Cool spray was everywhere, and the bird sat wet and wretched. I was glad to be carrying him. He was company, of a sort, the way a pet is, and like a pet my consciousness included his. His didn't seem to include mine. The fulmars had always communicated, but he did not. I put off going to the foredeck for my evening checks there. It seemed wrong to disturb him.

With 25 miles before the turning point I went below and slept, wedged in the port bunk, one foot against the table base, one hand on the table top, one leg keeping pressure on the forward bulkhead. I listened for the sound of children in the rigging, or fragments of a horn section in unisons of B-flat, and heard only the music of a sailboat making rapid passage, the groan of lines, the snap of Dacron. I thought of who I was, and it did not seem like much, but it seemed enough. It felt like the voyage was coming to an end. I had put off so long thinking about the future that I wasn't used to doing it, and the thought lay inert. Dozing while holding on is uncomfortable, and it is being tired, not a clock, that brings sleep. As usual I awoke every hour or two to survey the rig and the full moon, which through the marine layer was a dull silver ring.

When morning came I discovered that the bins containing our food were almost empty. Someone had swept the varnished floorboards clean of crumbs and soggy goo. The swinging stove was newly polished. The head smelled of cleanser and the kerosene cabin lamp was rehung and newly polished. The lenses of the hatches shined, their months of salt scrubbed away. In the warm icebox lay my last beer and a half-bottle of wine, next to a spotless sink with a new roll of paper towels above it.

Someone had prepared the boat for land. On my clothes bin, a new shirt and clean shorts lay waiting for someone to put them on. I nibbled a cookie, half-asleep as I was used to being so much of the time, day and night.

I could not remember cleaning the boat. But someone had, and I guessed it was me, and I guessed I knew why.

CHAPTER 45

ALONE TOGETHER

R ETURN DAY 27. *0611 hours. Abeam San Miguel Island. New course 065m.*

At first light the sea was gray and agitated, and we were on the wrong jibe in 25 knots of wind. San Miguel Island was 10 miles to windward, just visible through the mist, and to make our final turn meant changing the pole from starboard to port. It took a long time on the foredeck to safely disengage the pole, wrestle it in its storage hooks on the stanchions and jibe to the broad reach toward home. I looked under the dinghy for the bird. No trace of him remained. Even his crumbs were gone, swept away in the night by heavy seas. I like to think he saw the island before I did, and was home already.

In a few hours, in the lee of the Channel Islands, the sea moderated and we coursed along at six and a half knots. I kept staring at San Miguel as if it were a formation of clouds.

The only food remaining was the last choices, and dehydrated minestrone soup for breakfast was so unappetizing that I dumped it over the side. By afternoon there were sails in the distance, making for the summer anchorages of Anacapa and Santa Cruz. I called home to predict a morning arrival, tomorrow. I left my message on an answering machine, and was relieved not to talk to anyone. I don't know why.

We should do some chart work now, because our present course and speed suggest that we will cross the heavily traveled Santa Barbara shipping lanes at 10 tonight. On the angle at which we cross, we should be in them for 14 miles, or about three hours. Running lights will be important again, and alertness. I have just sounded the fuel tank, and we have 10 gallons of diesel remaining. That's nearly a hundred miles of motoring in case the wind dies near the mainland tonight.

1300 hours. South of San Miguel. Pleasant breeze.

The GPS died a few moments ago for the first time in the voyage, and just when we need it most. The screen at the binnacle was crisscrossed with unfathomable esoteric characters. The electronic charts of the GPS give our exact position among the buoys and boundaries of the ship channels. I was about to transfer our position to the paper chart when, automatically, I headed below to get the toolbox. I don't know how to fix a GPS, with its circuit boards and full-color screen. But I took apart what I could, cleaned the connectors with fresh water and a toothbrush, and upon reconnection the screen lit up as before. I could probably use a shower myself.

All afternoon we cruised past San Miguel, the air temperature rising. Hours without incident, hours the same as those far at sea, hours with the same quality of forever. Late in the afternoon I ate sardines and drank the last warm beer. In the evening there were broken crackers for dinner and the final glass of wine as the sun set and for the first time, the gray marine layer having abandoned the coast, I saw rise majestically over the bow a full harvest moon.

Wing and wing again we sailed straight toward the moon and the shipping lanes ahead.

2200 hours. Shipping lanes.

We coast silent towards home, 40 miles ahead. There are four ships simultaneously in sight, bright lamps of white, red or green all around us, the commerce of the coast, separated by maritime agreement in their transit between Mexico and Canada and every port between. The steering vane keeps us steady, and because our little ship is long since prepared for its dock there is nothing at all to do. So I watch the moon, drinking hot tea and eating the dust of the last cookies.

I put our arrival now at 5 a.m. If you prefer, we could heave to off Santa Monica and wait to go in at first light. But I know the entrance to Marina Del Rey well, and would scarcely hesitate to go out for an evening sail and return in the dark, when Santa Monica Bay is mysterious with soft-blinking navigation channel lights and the loom of cities. We shall have to go out some time together for a sociable evening sail. It will seem different after this. We will say much to each other just with a glance and a private smile.

0200 hours. Shipping lanes astern. Engine on.
About midnight the breeze died and I furled the jib and took down the mainsail for good. The self-steering vane, too, because I doubt we shall have any more wind. The electric wheel pilot can take it from here.

Tracy is planning a celebration on the dock at 11 o'clock this morning, with the people we know best and nine bottles of prosecco. She can see this enormous moon at home, she said. It is lighting up all of Southern California tonight, and the air is unusually clear. You could read a newspaper in the cockpit just now, although I don't have one. But there will be three in the driveway tomorrow, and I'll know I'm back.

There's time for a short nap, and I ought to take it to be fresh for the harbor entrance and meeting people again. It seems strange to set the iPhone alarm clock, doesn't it? We never bothered offshore, where there was no appointment to keep. The diesel fills the cabin with sound and the plates and silverware rattle in the drawers. Dawn will come soon enough, with all its questions. How are you? How was it? Long time, no see.

We were gone 48 days at sea and sailed 6,000 statute miles. I turned 71 on the tenth day out. It feels not old enough to understand and still too young to teach. We saw seabirds and pilot fish and all the kinds of winds. We were burned by the sun and had just enough pride to carry us through without offense. There were moments of doubt but more of joy in doing what we set out to. We lost track of time, but better find it again now. I'll put the iPhone alarm by my head, so as to wake up in no more than an hour.

What will we say, you and I, when they ask about being alone?

Everyone knows I'm scared of it. I need company and the comfort of conversation. I'm no good alone, and wasn't built for it.

We were alone together. For weeks we didn't see a ship, and the radio returned nothing but static. The TED Talks on the stereo might have been from ancient Egypt, so distant and otherworldly they were. The satphone allowed weekly communication, but its voices were ghosts. Now you know why I needed you here—so the endless loop of myself didn't feed back in one long shriek.

But if we were alone, when was it? Not on Day 2, when the Coast Guard boarded and young Lt. Dan Trainor stood unsteadily below, learning his trade. He stayed with me for hundreds of miles. Not when the halyard went up the mast and I faced having to climb it. All my sailing friends were there then, and our combined knowledge snagged it to bring it down. Not in the doldrums, where my brother joined me to wonder when the wind would return. Not during the near gale, or when the lost bird landed, because a bird had landed on a boat 40 years before, and I had caught it in my hand, and handed it to my father at the helm. And not now, in these few hours remaining before our course crosses its outbound track off Marina Del Rey, when I am most certainly not alone, on the edge of sleep.

In these long months on the North Pacific, when time so often stopped, *Thelonious* seemed more crowded than she ever is on an afternoon cruise with chatting friends and scrambling children. I was always in the presence of people, minds, and intimate ideas. At no moment was I left alone or abandoned to my own devices. There was always a voice, a presence, one companion or an army of them. It was not just my wife, whom I had neglected to kiss goodbye but whose hand I could always feel in mine. It wasn't just Tandy, Alexandra, Drake and Christian, my children, who were there every time I put on the safety harness or ducked the boom in a jibe, counseling care, reminding me that they were part of me and I of them. The boat was filled with acquaintances and even old antagonists. Nor was our company confined to the living, for at night Chichester was there, and Disko Troop of "Captains Courageous," who fished spoiled 15-year-old Harvey out of the north Atlantic and made a man of him, and whom I first met, myself, at the age of 15.

On our voyage Captain Troop shook hands with Starbuck, mate of the *Pequod* in "Moby Dick," and as I watched, with Herodotus too, and Charles Darwin, all of them listening to Xenophon tell about his famous march as Alexander the Great looked on. Why, I could hardly make my way through the cabin past those lively spirits, for I was not only myself but all of them and all of us, everyone I had ever read or ever met, and all together we crossed the ocean and now have returned. Don't you feel it?

Alone is impossible. To be, is to be us all. Even the dead live on, extending a hand to those not yet born.

Well, that's how it seems to me. Rest now, the alarm clock will go off in an hour, and then to harbor. It would not do to be lost at sea in these last crowded hours.

Return Day 28, 0400 hours. Malibu coast.

All the voices aboard are shouting warnings in my ears. Hundreds of them, urgent and concerned, mocking and scolding. I blink eyes open and sit up, panicked. When I thrust my head out of the hatch bright shore lights loom hugely close. I rub my eyes, disbelieving. The iPhone alarm clock continues to beep, almost inaudible under the clattering roar of the diesel. My god, I have slept right through it and almost run us dead aground in full moonlight on the cliffs of Malibu.

I spin the wheel to a new course, and watch the lights move down the port side until in front of the bow a tiny red light appears, blinking red every six seconds, the north breakwater of my home port. It's still dark as we enter through an obstacle course of racing shells working out in their pre-dawn practice routines, a harbor alive with shadows.

0537 hours. First light.

Glide into the slip. Dock lines cleated. Sails furled, finished with engine.

0700 hours. Home.

I can see Tracy running toward me down the dock in shorts, her red hair streaming.

Say, thanks for coming along.

Afterword

THE LEAK THAT SO plagued *Thelonious* for the first week, and thereafter disappeared as mysteriously as it had arrived, turned out to be a one-way valve in the bilge hose. The valve was there to prevent water in the 15-foot run of hose from returning to the bilge when the pump stopped. I took the valve apart at sea, and found it functioned perfectly. Yet the "leak" continued.

Several months after our return, with the issue still unresolved, I woke up one night with a fragment of the pump installation manual forefront in the mind. It noted that the electric pump was not self-priming. Dawn had finally come: the one-way valve not only prevented water draining back to the bilge, but also deprived the pump of its prime. Although it had run every hour, noisily, it hadn't been pumping anything at all.

With the one-way valve removed the pump passed every test and was still protected from backflow by its vented, anti-siphon loop. You may well wonder, as I still do, why this was not apparent at sea. The answer is that on *Thelonious* the bilge pump sits on the keel bolts, so there are always a few gallons of water in the bilge that the pump can't remove. That water sloshes continually in a seaway, making measurement impossible. A small hand pump to empty the bilge completely would have revealed that no problem existed at all.

The toilet issue had a similar explanation. The backflow of effluent defied explanation until I eventually realized that the simple Jabsco Y-valve was set wrong. Sewage was not going overboard, but pressurizing the holding tank instead. The trouble was that the valve could be interpreted as "closed" in either position. In none of the dozen manuals on board was there an explanation of how the Y-valve worked. It was located upsidedown in an inaccessible location, and I simply never figured it out. Once on land, a schematic of the mechanism made obvious what in a week of trying I had failed to deduce.

As for the engine, the worrisome shriek came from the failing water pump, not the transmission. My jury rig of latex and a capture jug held for the final thousand miles.

In every case, another person on board would have meant a dialogue and quick exposure of the faults in my solo logic. One limitation of sailing alone is the absence of fresh eyes unburdened by assumption. It's like failing to find the cream in the refrigerator after a repeated search. Then someone else opens the door, reaches in, and hands it to you with a condescending smile. "Oh. Thanks."

We need other people. Even observation is a dialog.

Although I came back from the voyage 10 years younger, some of *Thelonious'* gear aged a decade. My annual number of sailing hours is normally about 100, but the trip totaled more than 1,000 hours, half of it in strong winds day and night. Damage was minor, however. Everything on board, equipment and skipper, seemed to profit from heavy use. Perhaps the best lubricant for any friction, physical or emotional, is simply doing, and rest is overrated as a cure.

The stitching failure of the hard-working genoa jib was the result of periodic flogging. No sailor lets the sails shake and rattle, it is lubberly and annoying. But when a singlehander broaches at midnight or the boat is knocked down by a squall, it takes a while to suit up and respond, and that's just the way it is. When my sailmaker at home eventually looked over the damage he declared it of no account, and in a few hours put main and jib back to first-class condition. Modern sails, especially those reinforced by radial tapes, are remarkably tough.

The all-important winches of *Thelonious* lost their holding power occasionally offshore, and always at the wrong time. A winch pawl that fails to engage leaves the operator holding 200 pounds of force on a handle eager to turn into a chain saw. My winches were declared recently serviced by the previous owner. But they weren't. When I took them apart later, the internal gears were caked with dried grease. You might think that a year's careful preparation should have included disassembly and inspection of the winches. So do I.

Of inexcusable errors, my inability to climb the mast to solve such a common problem as a lost halyard tops the list. I have in my files a thick manila folder of all the mast-climbing systems known to yachtsmen, and there are half a dozen of them. But I spent my time studying instead of choosing, implementing, and practicing. Some tested means of climbing the mast is mandatory.

Several commentators have remarked how lucky it was that the pedestal broke so near to Kaua'i, so I could turn back immediately for repairs. And in fact, had the pedestal broken a few days out, I would have faced returning into the teeth of two hurricanes. But I probably would have just kept going north under a jury rig. I don't know just what rig that would be: perhaps a system of lines and supports to prop the pedestal up. Maybe a resort to the emergency steering tiller, which connects directly to the rudder post. Probably I could have rigged the self-steering vane to that. No doubt any jury rig would require frequent readjustment, and perhaps numerous redesigns. In a gale it would add to the test. It would complicate things psychologically, adding uncertainty to arrival time and the concerns of people at home. But I never felt lucky or unlucky about the time or place of the steering pedestal collapse. Luck is an emotion. Damage is a predictable circumstance.

Of all the gear on board the most untested was the skipper. And yet, I functioned as well as the blocks and line and sails. Nobody likes safety tethers, but I wore mine because I had promised I would. It wasn't fear of drowning, but fear of leaving a widow to explain her marriage to a nitwit whose boat has arrived in port without him. The web of responsibility proved a release from complexity. Even alone, I discovered, we live for others.

I am proud of my lack of bruises, which I put down to rehearsed movements. I taught myself where to put my feet and where to place my hands for all activities, so that even at night and while groggy I rarely had a misstep or a close call. I always closed and locked the companionway and other hatches when working on deck (to forestall fouls or falling through them); always wore deck shoes; always planned the steps of a task before starting it. Perhaps that was less necessary when I was 25, and could do a lot of chin-ups. Now athleticism is no longer such a reliable solution, and confidence becomes more a mental than a physical factor.

A year has passed now, and I understand better where *Thelonious* and I have been.

It is a place not unlike where all of us are now, this moment, every moment. If something breaks we must try to fix it. If a different course is required, we must take it. The past is finished, the future is unknown. Here is where we are. The world is in the moment.

Define Yourself

Steven S. Hodges, winner of the 2014 Singlehanded Transpac race, is a physicist. His perspective:

"*Alone is impossible. To be is to be us all. Even the dead live on, extending a hand to those not yet born.*"

—*Christian Williams in Alone Together*

In modern physics, quantum mechanical principles generally apply. These principles use a unique mathematics that describes entities in the physical world, and their dependence on each other. The math depends on imaginary numbers, such as the square root of -1 (termed i), to keep simultaneous track of the amplitude and phase (with respect to arbitrary reference levels) of the descriptive and dynamic elements. With apologies to Euler, physics is lubricated by many i's.

In the quantum mechanical world, each physical entity can be described using a function (of imaginary quantities) that is a weighted sum of the link between the entity being described, say *You*, and everything else, countless non-*You* entities, The_m:

$$You = \sum_{m=0}^{\infty} C_{my} The_m$$

The mth non-*You* entity in the world is linked to you with a dynamical strength factor C_{my}.

Of course it is also true that each of the many *The* entities depend on *You* with similar but different weightings:

$$\text{You} = \sum_{r=0}^{\infty} C_{rt} \text{You}_r$$

You and *The* are weighted composites of all there is and all that is possible. There are countless possibilities, including the special case of $You_r = The_m$. The coupling C represents the external world, often assumed to be objective. A change in the environment, represented by certain C values increasing, induces an entity to evolve in some way, so that other C values may diminish as newly important ones grow.

Note that in the above equations, the linking constant is not reciprocal, that is C_{pq} is not the same as C_{qp}. This reflects the seemingly obvious reality that the effect of one entity on another is not the same as the reverse. If the relationship with a long-dead author, *a*, affects *You*, then the link C_{ay} is finite, while the reciprocal link, C_{ya} is essentially 0. Contrariwise, soulmates might have relatively strong and reciprocal link strengths. Entities that interact, especially knowingly, will have relatively strong, temporally coherent links.

The influence of entities upon each other, represented by the link strength factor, C, rises and falls in time, sometimes erratically, quickly or slowly. Entities are close for a while and then drift apart, or one ceases to exist. But once a link exists it will tend to remain finite; the departed live on in our memories.

It comes to this: *You*, The_m and C_{my} are real entities represented by sums of imaginary coupled functions of time, all awash in the jostle and slosh of our oft-chaotic ocean of experience. Alone is indeed impossible.

-seh

Acknowledgements

FIRST, MY ADMIRATION FOR Tracy Olmstead Williams, who after 26 years of marriage remains a fascinating labyrinth and the most fearless person I know. My four children also supported this venture, each in their own way: Tandy Elizabeth, Alexandra Ruth, Drake Diana and Christian Cadwalader. Six grandchildren continue with hands on hips, rolling their eyes, which I take as a very positive comment on "Poppy."

This book was twice born. The first was a call from my old friend Bob Woodward in Nawiliwili Harbor, inquiring to know whether I had "the documents." When I confessed to a logbook of more than 100 pages he declared that research was sufficient, and to start typing. Reporters often make notes and do nothing with them, however, and the world is sometimes better for it. But a half-hour home movie I posted on YouTube unexpectedly drew half a million viewers and a thousand messages urging me to tell more about the experience of singlehanded sailing. So *Thelonious* and I set off again, this time through 1,200 pages of paper, of which 300 survived to tell the tale.

In addition to everyone I ever met, heard of or read, all of whom were aboard, I thank especially the crew of *Timeless*, Woodward's 45-foot ketch, in which we sailed, drank and waterboarded each other for thousands of miles: Carl Feldbaum, Paul Richard, Patrick Tyler and Tom Wilkinson. And my father, Manley Cadwalader Williams, and my brother Jeffrey, with whom I learned first about sails and sand and water, and often still consult in memory.

My great appreciation to Feldbaum, Tyler, Jacob Epstein, Jeffrey Lewis and Ignacio Gonzalez for careful reads and corrections of the manuscript, and to Skip Allan for generously sharing his story.

Thanks most of all to those who read this book. On your adventures, wherever they carry you, I hope to come along too, and share in your findings. We are all on our journey together.

About the author

Christian Williams was an editor and reporter for The Washington Post from 1972 to 1986. He later wrote and produced television dramas from "Hill Street Blues" to "Six Feet Under" before retiring in 2010. He has four children and lives in Pacific Palisades, CA, with his wife, Tracy Olmstead Williams.

A NOTE ABOUT THE BOOK DESIGN

This book is set in 11-point Sabon, an old-style serif typeface based on a design of Claude Garamond (1480-1561). Released in the 1960s, it filled the need for a type that would look the same whether set by hand or by Monotype or Linotype machines. In recent years Sabon has been used for the 1979 *Book of Common Prayer* of the Episcopal Church in the United States and as the logo of Stanford University.

The trade paperback format retains the size of a hardcover edition, permitting a larger text than mass market paperbacks and a quality binding. This book was manufactured using Print on Demand technology and the date of printing is recorded within. Print on Demand frees publishers and authors from the need to estimate sales and maintain warehouse inventories of titles. Although costs are higher than for large orders of offset printing, POD increasingly makes out-of-print books available again and supports small publishers and individual authors.

Book design by Perceptiv.

Photos by the author, unless credited.

Made in the USA
Middletown, DE
30 October 2018